IF IT'S Smoking IT'S Done

A Cookbook
-by-
Bart Boos

First Edition, I Guess?

Edited & Designed by J.R. Boos

Pre-Ramble

· ·

Sitting at the dinner table one evening, my lovely and caring daughter Kristine stated, "You know Dad, if you die, we don't have any of your recipes on hand. Maybe you should jot them down for us."

It was bad enough that my beloved children have been dividing my estate up since they were three years old. Now they want the only asset I possess that's of any real value!

Rather than be pestered about my mortality and the meager size of my estate, here are a number of recipes that I've stolen, begged for, plagiarized or simply invented with my own pea-sized, emotionally-charged little mind. Enjoy making them as much as I've enjoyed sharing them at my table.

To my children: It's all you'll receive. I spent all the money!

—Bart

Spruce Grove, Alberta (at the moment)
bartboos.ab@gmail.com

Table of Contents

Beef (cont.)

Poultry

Pork

Fish & Seafood

Miscellaneous

Sauces, Seasonings & Dips

Sauces, Seasonings & Dips (cont.)

Side Dishes & Starches

Desserts

Rambles & Recollections

Recipe Legend

 Certain recipes in this book will pre-require elements prepared from other recipes. These ingredients will be marked with the ship's wheel icon, like so.

An Introduction

-or-
Oh My God, He's In the Kitchen and He Has a Knife!

First Things First

We should celebrate the first being, that ancient man or woman who decided to improve upon the day's hunt with some extra ingredients. Maybe he or she added fragrant leaves or flowers to the meat. Perhaps some gathered tubers, berries or fruit were added to a clay vessel over a fire, creating the first prepared meal in history. No mirepoix, no enamel-coated cast iron cookware, not so much as a pepper grinder back then.

In this primitive milieu, countless brave souls risked their taste buds and even their lives to sample new flavours of flora and fauna. Their efforts set in motion a culinary evolution. Thank goodness for bipedalism, a large cranium, opposable thumbs—and a gag reflex.

As civilization moved forward and became more, um, civilized, we learned to record our activities, our feelings and our history. Some of the oldest stone tablets ever discovered were Akkadian and Sumerian recipes for bread and beer. Cookbooks, of sorts, came to exist in ancient Rome, China and Arabia, all transcribed by loving hands from the most ancient recipes.

In medieval times, the Germans, Valencians and Tudors, among others, were egotistical enough to think their cookery was something special, giving us collected recipes (and illustrations I'm using here because I don't have to pay for them) that survive to this day.

When Steve Guttenberg invented the printing press, the cookbook really took off, allowing chefs to collect centuries worth of scrap paper and oral tradition into an easily-reproduced form. Now here I am, collecting my own favourite recipes from nooks and crannies and the ancient manuscripts of my mind. Against the weight of history, you could call it fate.

Memories

My Mom and Dad are great cooks. While I was growing up, I watched them break all the cooking rules and create memorable disasters as they walked the fine line between creativity and food poisoning. Somehow all their children survived. We learned to be adventurous. We learned to ignore convention and search out novel morsels for our developing palates.

Sure, our gag reflexes came in handy at times, but hey, even Picasso ruined a few canvases. (Mind you, with Picasso, how could you tell?) My parents proved something important: what makes a chef great isn't just the food, but the ability to inspire and share the love—to get people excited about what they eat and how.

I've tried to carry on that tradition with pride. Food has played an important part in my life, not only as fuel but as comfort, pleasure, warmth, calm and joy. In addition to dining and cooking, a whole span of food-related rituals are important to me: perusing recipes, shopping, hunting and fishing, and of course sharing all those experiences. I scour the internet for recipes, beg servers in restaurants for them, and peruse cookbooks for them. I read about food, watch TV programs about food, talk about food. I even wrote a book about food. (This one.)

When it comes to food, I'm game for anything.

A swine-gutting station is de rigueur in the modern kitchen.

Well, almost anything. I have my dislikes, and they're reflected in this book also. Eggplant, green peppers, eggplant, organ meat of most kinds, bear meat, eggplant, some types of squash... but mostly eggplant. When I was young, Dad cooked eggplant in over-abundance and I hated it. Gagged on it. Cried over it. To this day I avoid it like a wet kiss from a drunken aunt, which is pretty much the same texture. So if you're an eggplant-lover, you won't find your favourite recipes in here! My apologies, you weird mutant.

Still, I have my parents to thank for my cooking interest and ability. Both my parents worked outside the house, so it was left to the kids to prepare dinner after school. Since I was the oldest, it fell to me to be the chief chef and bottle washer. Mom would take meat out of the freezer in the morning with instructions for me to turn the lifeless parcel into dinner.

After getting home from school, I would phone her at work and she would dictate instructions to me. Her cooking magic was transferred to me, and voilà! During this time of my childhood, my Mom's boss was a man named Mr. Jukes. At my wedding reception, Mr. Jukes told me that when he heard my Mom give me cooking instructions, his mouth would water. He joked that he learned to cook as well as I did just by eavesdropping on my instruc-tional sessions. The mark of a truly great teacher, Mom taught and inspired without even realizing it.

There were occasional disasters in the kitchen, instructions or none. But I came to enjoy them, since they allowed us all to go out to a great pizza restaurant instead of eating my charred mistakes.

This sacred place, on Kingsway in Vancouver, was called The Two Men from Verona, as I recall (it was, at least, similar to the title of the Shakespeare play). In this era, before the advent of two-for-one factory and chain restaurants, pizza was a rare treat. But I swear I never messed up a recipe on purpose just for pizza. At least not as far as anyone can prove.

Through difficult times later, when friends abandoned me and family shunned me, food remained my source of strength. Okay, alcohol played an important role too, but it was usually washed down with food. A love of food carried me through the recession of the '80s—as my oldest children will recall, I perfected an inexpensive yet delicious spaghetti and provided it nearly every day. Day after day. Day in and day out. According to the blood tests, my children are about 90% spaghetti to this day, which is as close to a paternity test as I dare attempt. And we have no regrets. When faced with the choice of hunger or pasta, always, always, *always* choose pasta.

I have made my mistakes. Besides eggplant, there have been contenders for the title of "Worst Meal" as I've traveled continents over the last forty-odd years. Long ago, I had a sauerbraten dinner that, even now, throws my swallower into hard reverse so fast it almost breaks my neck. A disaster of Biblical proportions and *X-Files* explanations. That's a story for later. The point is: as long as you don't die, there can even be joy in the worst food... even it's just in the retelling.

With food so central to joy in my life, and given my sloth-like exercise regime over the years, it was amazing that my waist size didn't grow larger than my IQ until I hit 40. After noticing my physique had gone from Greek hero to Greek gyro, I took charge of the problem: I bought bigger clothes. It was either that or give up my loving relationship with food, and the latter simply isn't going to happen. A good Hong Kong tailor can work miracles, no matter how many years you've spent drinking gallons of hollandaise sauce and watching other people exercise.

I've passed on the joy of food to my children and their friends, whom I call my children too. Although I warn them, the day will come where the love of food may catch up with them and they'll end up looking like their dad. My advice is: Start exercising now so you can keep indulging later!

The only thing I enjoy more than food is cooking for others and watching them enjoy it. Okay, there might be one thing I enjoy more than that—but that's for my second book. Having friends over to entertain and feed is one of life's enjoyable pastimes. We can sit and visit, laugh and enjoy life in each other's company. It's what separates us from the animals. Well, that, and not licking ourselves in front of others. (Try as I might, I simply don't have the flexibility.)

Since I can't sing, dance, play musical instruments or offer other types of God-given talents, cooking has allowed me to entertain friends and family and provide us all with pleasure and satisfaction. I figure this is a heck of an accomplishment, when you consider that years ago, I didn't know the difference between a mirepoix and a ménage à trois. Since those early days, I've enjoyed thousands of mirepoix and not a single ménage à trois. But I don't regret that choice… much.

Not that cooking is an impediment to one's love life. If anything, it's the opposite. It always amazes me that a lot of guys can dismantle and rebuild complicated things like cars, or bikes, or nuclear reactors, or even IKEA furniture, but still insist they can't cook. Pity these lost souls as they stagger home to their inflatable dates after striking out again at closing time. To change their fates, all it would've taken was a quick read of a cookbook before going out on the town. When talking with the lovely brunette perched drunk at the bar, you can drop a line like, "How

'bout I cook you a great breakfast quiche tomorrow morning?" When she responds, "What the fuck is a quiche?" you'll know the magic is working.

On that note, food convinced Susan to marry me. I'm sure she fell in love with my signature Crab & Black Bean dish before she fell in love with me. This was one of the first dinners I prepared for her at Heartbreak Hotel, my apartment at the time. Long story short, there have been many, many more dinners prepared and shared between us since.

In love and life, I can't recommend cooking enough as a way to connect with people. Countless memories have been created with friends over the brunches, luncheons and dinners I've made for them—laughs, warm embraces and heartfelt emotions, whether at home, or at the campground, or at a vacation rental. With every visit there's a memory that I treasure. Some I treasure by remembering the time I spent with them, and others I treasure as I remember them finally leaving. You know who you are.

I'm heartened to know that long after I'm gone, my children will talk about the meals, the times past and the Old Man—fondly, I hope. They might also remember the boats, RVs, vacations and occasional lean times (mostly a result of boats and RVs, oops) between all the fun stuff. And I think it'll be my cooking that binds those memories together, as well as their memories of me.

After all, my children are all food aficionados, if not straight-up snobs. When they dine out, a restaurant chef faces a challenge in satisfying their palates, as the kids mentally compare the restaurant's creations to their memories of my cooking. Oftentimes the restaurant comes up short, and my kids love to tell me I'm still the winner. I must say, I enjoy being held in such high regard, even if it's only in comparison to cold McNuggets and warm Bud Lite. I take my compliments where I can get them, thank you very much.

In fact, I know my kids could even dine at Rob Feenie's or Emeril's or Wolfgang Puck's, and my rendition of their favourite dish might still win out. Not to say I can beat the best alive at the cooking game (although…), but my kids are comparing the restaurant's dishes to their own treasured memories. Even the top chef in the world can't compete with that.

Food is a glue that keeps families together. By sharing dinner in the evenings and making it a part of your lifestyle, it will nurture your children's souls and outlooks. And when kids are at the table eating with the family, they're not out performing Stupid Child Tricks with the bad elements of society. They'll have to wait until they're adults to do that, just like we did.

In closing off this section I'll just say this: Cook, dine together and love each other. Often. Daily is best!

Practice, excel and eat well!

A Wide World of Food

Being raised in Vancouver was an endless world culinary tour. Seafood varieties that would make Poseidon green with envy. Japanese food. Chinese food. Indian food. Italian! Vietnamese! German and on and on and on! Many of my neighbours were recent immigrants to Canada, and as a result I tasted prosciutto and other European origin dry cured meats early on, as well as foreign vegetables from the market gardens in Richmond. I sampled homemade red wine to excess and enjoyed Portuguese sausage from a friend's house. The memory of it all still makes my mouth water.

Thanks to my exposure during my upbringing, I carry a love of Asian food with me to this day. As you might discover while reading along a little further, Asian cuisine is always my top pick when trying to decide what I want to make at home or order in a restaurant. I've been told, given my love of the food, that I should have been born in Asia—but Vancouver is pretty close. It was glorious to be a food freak in Vancouver. And it's even better now than it was then.

I'll rave about Japanese food to anyone who'll listen, and right now, that's you. Food in Japan is five-star, prepared and served in spectacular fashion by people so polite and caring that it's unnerving for a rude and obnoxious person like me. And the sheer variety! Sometimes the novelty proved a challenge for my friends and I, but I'd go back

to Japan in a heartbeat, both for the food (especially the curry!) and the most pleasant group of people I've ever had the pleasure to meet or mingle with. There were a couple meals that stalled us in our tracks. I'll detail those elsewhere. Suffice it to say, there are some laugh-til-I-die memories...

Food is central to enjoying a vacation. In its absence, a vacation can be a dreary time indeed. Liquor, sun, sand, surf, and bikini beauties only go so far! The opportunity to sample new foods is one of the greatest things about travel (as Anthony Bourdain taught the world before his early passing).

Between Canada and the USA, or even between the provinces and regions of Canada, there are major differences in cuisine. Every place has unique advantages. In Quebec you can enjoy poutine, tourtière and French pastries, Sortilège maple liqueur, unusual preparations of duck and even horse, a wide variety of Jewish and Lebanese and other Middle Eastern food, and so much more that we can't really find here in BC.

Tops for me in my North American travels are West Coast fusion, Deep South American barbeque, and Vancouver Chinatown Asian restaurants, with San Francisco and Edmonton Chinese food coming up close behind. Alberta beef, PEI mussels, BC tree fruit, Idaho huckleberries, California and BC wines with Oregon and Washington making a strong showing—all favourites. The joy of culinary travel! Come to think of it, I can't really come up with an area unrelated to a good food experience. Except grits in Nashville, or grits in Atlanta, or grits anywhere else. Grits: just say no.

I'm surprised when I learn that dishes I hold dear turn out to be unpopular with others. For example, take fries and gravy. It's a standard in many restaurants in Canada, and turned into a true feast by way of poutine, one of Canada's most famous comfort foods. But if you ask for gravy with your fries in most places in the USA, the server will stare at you as if you have two heads and one of them is screaming racial slurs. (Down there they call that bipartisanship.)

Still, it's worth asking for, because the USA does a great gravy, even at KFC. Yes, I do love KFC gravy.

However, I don't eat either fries or gravy except once or twice a year, for fear of the massive coronary they might unleash. A greasy meal like that will fly right through me, but the guilt takes weeks to digest.

One year, Susan and I were travelling through the Midwest on vacation, and we stopped at a KFC for lunch. We ordered French fries and then asked for gravy. The teller did a classic double take, pausing, then entering the additional item into the electronic register, then paused again, thinking about our order no doubt, and stared at us. She took our money, surrendered the change and headed into the kitchen.

There she said in a loud, incredulous voice to a cook in the kitchen, "You won't believe what just happened! Some guy ordered fries and asked for gravy!"

"Gravy?!" boomed the voice from the back.

In a loud voice, dripping with her heavy accent, the teller opined, "I ain't never been asked for gravy for fries before!"

"Unbelievable!" gasped the voice from the back.

In a voice loud enough to be heard next door, the teller pondered, "Must be from Minnesota!"

She returned with the small Styrofoam container of gravy, placing it in front of me like it was radioactive. Then she turned and walked away, shaking her head.

Susan and I left laughing, convinced that while our teller may not have understood gravy and fries, she most likely ate grits, so her taste in food was questionable. I'm sure if she'd had poutine described to her, it would have bowled her over completely. We must pity the American ignorance of fries and gravy, to say nothing of the fresh cheese curds (squeakers) that create a poutine masterpiece.

Grandma Boos

Grandma Boos was such an important influence on me, both as a person and a cook, that she gets her own section here. It's the least I can do for someone whose memory I treasure deeply, and whose recipes form the backbone of this book!.

Grandma Boos was a great old broad. If you called her that, she'd thank you for the compliment. For much of her life, she chained-smoked and drank beer and rye whiskey like a trooper. Upon her retirement she gave up these pastimes, which probably allowed her to outlive a husband, boyfriends, some of her siblings and most of her friends. She even outlived her least-favourite Prime Minister, Pierre Trudeau—a life goal for her, given that she and Trudeau were born on the same day in the same year. While I didn't loathe Trudeau to the same extent she did, I did attend Grandma's little celebration party in 2000 when he finally kicked off.

I loved to push her buttons, and Grandma had more buttons than a NASA computer. Politics, unions, the family members she disliked, among many other things. I fondly remember the time Mike Harcourt and his New Democratic Party (NDP) were elected in British Columbia, defeating Grandma's beloved Social Credit Party (SoCreds) in November of 1991.

After casting our ballots in Prince George, Susan and I spent the evening enroute to Edmonton before settling in at the Fantasyland Hotel in West Edmonton Mall. A Roman-themed room, as I recall—great kitsch is so easy to remember.

As we prepared for bed, we tuned the TV to the election results. The SoCreds' brutal loss to the NDP came as no surprise to anyone who'd followed the election. When the talking heads finished describing the destruction, I turned the TV off and reached for the telephone. The fun was a mere eleven button-presses away.

It wasn't unusual for me to call Grandma in the middle of the night—or even later, depending on my rum consumption. No matter the hour, she was always willing to talk and mentor, if not scold and berate. That night when I reached her, it was after midnight in Kelowna where she lived.

When she answered the phone I simply asked, "So, what do you think of the election results?" Well, that's all it took. She launched into a tirade about the intelligence of the BC electorate and went on to describe Mike Harcourt in terms of both male and female genitalia, epithets invoking bodily functions, sexual activities, descriptive accounts of orifices and of activities involving said orifices. Grandma had firm opinions on the pedestrian nature of the NDP, and some intriguing theories about the new Premier's paternal heritage by way of Satan.

Then she really got wound up. The call lasted over an hour. Even by her standards, it was impressive. She might have continued ranting for the rest of Harcourt's political reign if I hadn't finally managed to say goodbye, and she undoubtedly did continue ranting to whomever would listen in my absence. I sure miss those rants. I really do.

Along with her husband (my grandfather) and later her youngest son Dale, Grandma owned and managed a trucking company called Falher Transport in a time when most women were relegated to duties in the home. Trucking was, and still largely is, a man's world, so Grandma was a pioneer during her 1960s heyday. Falher Transport was a small Albertan operation, but it had a celebrated history and was populated by colourful characters, each with a million stories to tell.

Many of the stories involved Grandma in some way or other. She was a complex, dichotomous person. On one hand, she was a rabid right-wing proponent of work-or-starve ethics. On the other, she would act as the mother hen, or even a mother grizzly if one of her "boys" was in trouble.

Occasionally, an employee would find himself in financial arrears, usually lifestyle-related, and a legal type would show up to Grandma's warehouse to serve papers garnisheeing his wages. For Grandma, it would set off an emotional explosion and a legendary baring of fangs. How the mother grizzly could roar!

Once, as was common, a bailiff showed up to the warehouse with garnishee papers and asked the staff for directions to Grandma's office. The warehouse men obliged him, lit their smokes as they watched the bailiff make his approach, and waited for the inevitable. When it came, the staff could hear it through the walls: yelling, screaming,

pushing, shoving and punching, perhaps a little scratching. Whatever the papers had said, Grandma had found it particularly noxious.

After a couple minutes of sustained barrage, the bailiff came running out of the office with Grandma in close pursuit. As he hightailed it past the workers he yelled, "This woman's fucking crazy!"

As the bailiff jumped off the loading dock and fled across the lot like his hair was on fire, a warehouse boy shouted back, "You bet she is! And fast, too!"

With the bailiff vanquished and receding into the horizon, Grandma stomped back towards her office. As she passed her men, she looked at them and yelled, "You could have given me a hand, you assholes!"

"Help you?" one replied. "Fuck that! We thought we'd have to help *him!*"

At that point she swore at them and went back to her synoptic ledger. In all ways, it was just another day at Falher Transport's Edmonton operations.

Grandma could be fierce, but she was a great cook, and generous to the very limit of her ability. She fed the company's various staff members, salesmen, bankers, truckers, delivery drivers, scallywags and ne'er-do-wells showed up to the lunch table in her Edmonton warehouse. Each day at lunch hour, Grandma served up a hearty homemade meal: soups, stews, chili, pierogi, cabbage rolls and casseroles, all hot and nutritious and free of charge.

Some of her diners, being "colourful" types, depended on the nourishment that Grandma offered, as their off-work lives were fueled by booze and tobacco. Others trekked from afar to the warehouse simply for the good taste and the laughs, both of which were served aplenty. Grandma's lunchtime ritual went on for many years, and became synonymous with Falher Transport. Long after the company itself ceased to exist, the memories of Grandma, her fiery temper and her generous feasts remain.

She, like me, was able to connect to people through the love of food and cooking. When I was very young, Sundays at Grandma's house were times to play cribbage, eat, drink and be merry, at least until a fight started and everyone got sent home. It wasn't always Grandma doing the cooking; in those early days of my cooking career, I often had free rein in her kitchen to attempt her classic recipes and others.

Afterward, Grandma would enter to observe the results of my work and ask, "What the hell happened here? The Normandy invasion?" (Some things never change, it seems. I'm a rather untidy chef to this day, according to some accounts—including those of my children, who have cursed my name to the dark gods while doing the dishes in my wake.)

At times during my own trucking years, I boarded at Grandma's place in Kelowna, sleeping in her guest room two days a week. Frequently I'd bring back specialty ingredients from my trips to Vancouver and try to whip up new and interesting meals for both of us. She was pleased to be on the receiving end of the feasts after so many years of giving.

On one occasion, I brought back a few pounds of mussels, clams and a couple of Dungeness crabs. When I got to Grandma's place quite late, I placed the crab container on the counter and covered it with a wet cloth before I went to bed. An hour or so later, Grandma ran into my bedroom yelling, "Whatever you brought here is clicking!" Groggily I insisted nothing was wrong. Indeed, some food ingredients are supposed to click. I fell back asleep. But another hour later, Grandma was back in my bedroom demanding I take care of a problem.

"I don't know what the hell is going on," she yelled, half-panicked. "But those clicking things are moving and one of the little fuckers tried to bite me!" It seemed Grandma's curiosity had gotten the better of her and she'd ended up being attacked by the irate Dungeness under the cloth. She had narrowly escaped its claws, and now refused to go back into the kitchen until the threat was contained.

Of course, I got up and played crab-wrangler. The next day, to soothe Grandma's lingering misgivings, I cooked up a delightful Bouilla-baisse with that very Dungeness. Grandma had

a smile on her face for days. Like most of us, she would rather eat a crab than wrestle one. And you know what they say: revenge is delicious.

I could write an entire book on Grandma Boos, and one day I just might. But for now I'll stick to passing down the recipes she gave me—the recipes that turned a trucking company's lunch hour into a feast, and bound together employees and strangers alike as tight as family.

Grandma's submissions to the book include her pierogi, Baked Beans, Pierogi Dough, Noodles and Cabbage Rolls. I've made all of them many times, with the Baked Beans as a particular favourite. Grandma had a way of making ingredients stretch; she could go into a kitchen with barren shelves and come out an hour later carrying enough food to feed the fleet. Through it all she remained nonplussed. The kitchen's most difficult tasks looked as easy to her as making a pot of tea.

When she passed away in her eighties, Grandma had accomplished much of what she wanted to do in life. We had become closer friends, and I loved her like no other. I think of her every day. I love to talk about her with anyone who'll listen, and always end up laughing when I do.

Many years after her passing, I still miss her cooking and her parties. Most of all, I miss her.

She was a unique, wonderful, great old broad.

On Recipes

Growing up, I learned to reverse-engineer a recipe by dissecting the dish in front of me and tasting one molecule at a time. Often I'd find a similar recipe in a cookbook and alter it until I reached a semblance of what was served to me by my parents or my favourite restaurants.

I've kept at it. Since those days I've collected, invented, perfected or blatantly stolen recipes for years and years. I've been putting off compiling them for just as long.

But now, with kids having staged their jailbreaks, it's clear I need to get my techniques into a book to save me from having to answer hundreds of their emails asking me how I made such-and-such all those years ago. So all my scraps of paper with chicken-scratch Bartcode writing, stains and grease smears are now collated here for posterity.

I'll try to give credit where credit is due, but many of these recipes were scribbled down from old books, newspaper articles, recipe blogs and the like, mostly lost to time or altered beyond recognition. Anyway, I make no claims to originality. The recipes contained herein are just family favourites, cooked with regularity by Susan (the local baking expert) or myself.

Not to say this was easy to write. On the contrary. I've traditionally tossed my favourite meals together from memory and flavoured them to taste—until now, those ingredients have never been measured with spoons or cups. To put them to paper has demanded that I finally decide on precise quantities, which amounted to reinventing my whole process at times.

Note that I'm not talking about baking here. Baking does have specific rules, and for good reason. Baking is a controlled chemical reaction that requires precise measurements and timing. Since I'm not good at following laboratory-style rules with precision, my wife Susan takes on the household baking along with our meth cooking, and does both extremely well.

In the end, I think I did the recipes justice. You can be the judge of that. Most of them will survive adding a little more of one ingredient or a little less of another to truly make it your own. Go long. Go short. A culinary experiment gone wild may not offer an edible result, but it can be fun to make, and your dog will probably eat it if you won't. An experiment gone right might create unforgettable memories and end up in the family cookbook for generations to come. If all else fails, you can call me for advice and redirection, and maybe some sharp rebukes depending on how late at night it is.

In the meantime, walk with me and enjoy. Among these recipes I've included vignettes and stories that the impatient cud-chewers online typically skip, but you won't, will you? Will you?! The stories will expand on the recipe's meaning, or celebrate the personalities of the person that I stole it from, or provide some other anecdote you can pilfer as your own when enjoying the meal with company.

And remember that if I could do it all, so can you. You don't need to be a Roads Caller to cook. If you can read this without moving your lips, you're already starting off in a better position than I was.

Grandma Boos feeding the hungry boys at Falher Transport.

Entering the Kitchen
-or-
Advice I Should Have Taken

Discovery

An adventure is an experience that can transport you to another realm, and cooking is an adventure second only to eating. That's the whole premise of this book. Cooking doesn't have to be a chore or duty, and you don't have to be a graduate of the Culinary Institute of America or be a Michelin chef to become a competent and qualified cook in your own home. An adventure simply means challenge—and fun.

I myself cook comfort foods, served family-style, and likewise, my recipes are intended for an average family kitchen. That means mine and yours. Chef's training also instructs on the business side of cooking, but as a home cook, you don't need to be an expert at that either. To assist my retirement path, I've considered running my kitchen as a for-profit monopoly and charging a 500% markup for the meals I create, but my wife and children insist they'll stage a communist revolution if I try. Sigh. Some of us just aren't cut out for the restaurant biz.

Besides, professional chefs have a discipline, drive, ambition, creativity or energy that most of us don't. Certainly I don't, and nor do I own one of those silly hats. If I could do life over again, I maybe would attend a school, if only to learn high-level culinary techniques firsthand. For now, though, I'm content to learn by trial and error, since I have an eager table willing to try just about anything I toss their way.

In lieu of professional training, cooking shows became my school. There are things books can't teach—tons of tricks, methods of using whisks and knives and kitchen gadgets to save time and heartache. Fancy words like "mirepoix" and "mise-en-place" that I had to learn through grueling experiment. In my younger years I learned from Jacques Pepin, Julia Child, Graeme Kerr and others on public television, and learned so much from them in those dark days before Internet recipes were easily accessible.

Mind you, Graeme Kerr sometimes cooked up things more suited to a biohazard bin than a dinner plate. Calf's brain! He ate that! Not even on my drunkest bet would I have dared. (Well, maybe on a bet. How much cash are you carrying?)

I've never stopped learning and discovering new things even now. I'm a fan of the Food Network to this day. Watching others cook has improved my game, and it'll improve yours too. If you were absolutely dying to know how I cooked a thing, you could even come over and watch me cook. I mean, I'm not quite as pretty as Rachel Ray... but almost. Almost.

Safety

Cooking can be dangerous, even fatal. Here I won't get too complicated or too wordy—well, maybe a little wordy, considering—but it's all to assist you in creating dishes your Mom would be proud to see you prepare. My goal is to help keep you safe from burns, explosions, food poisoning, and worst of all, disappointing your mother.

Let's start with the stove. A stove gets hot in many different areas including, but not limited to, the parts that glow red when you crank the dial. First, examine your stove and read the manual to learn what all the hot parts could possibly be, and then don't touch them.

Radiant heat isn't the only thing that makes a stove dangerous. If your stove is fueled by wood, natural gas or propane, you need to pay extra attention. If you don't know what fuels your stove, either do your research or leave the cooking to others. Or, hey, just blow up your house. You might have your reasons. I don't know what your insurance situation is like.

Never stir hot water or oil with your bare hands. Use a spoon, or at least a hand that's not yours.

A stove is just one tool in the kitchen that might kill you. Good news: there are more! Blenders, pressure cookers, even dishwashers can ruin your whole day if you're not careful. Even the dullest knife can have you regretting your life's mistakes from a hospital bed. If this scares you, please pass the book to your spouse or other legal guardian and get Domino's on speed-dial. Yes, Domino's. Because you deserve to suffer for your cowardice.

Aside from safety, though, there aren't many rules. Try anything once, don't spit in the bouillabaisse, don't fry bacon without a shirt on, and if it tastes good, eat it. Common sense should be your guide. Beyond that, feel free to be adventurous, and experiment.

Diplomacy

When cooking for guests, it's important to know their favourite meals for dinner (or breakfast, if things get out of hand) as well as their limitations. Trying to serve pork to a vegan doesn't yield warm memories, and nor does forgetting that Uncle Zippo goes into full-body shutdown if he walks into the same room as a peanut.

Plus, some foods aren't fatal but simply divisive: mushrooms, zucchini, eggplant (*eggplant!*), liver and organs, pineapple pizza, fermented foods like sauerkraut, and so on. It's always best to check with your guests before-hand so there are no hiccups on the path to glory and no sudden EpiPen emergencies around the table. If a guest seems to dislike everything, invite them to bring their own damn meal. It's cost-effective, and if you play your cards right, you get to keep the leftovers.

Knives (and Other Ways to Hurt Yourself)

To do it well (cooking, that is) you need a few tools. They don't have to be expensive, although if I'm honest, you get what you pay for, or often less. First and foremost is a selection of quality knives.

If you have a good set of knives, try not to have kids. If you do have kids, make sure they know how to treat both knives and dishwashers. An unnamed daughter once put my brand-new, very expensive chef's knife in the dishwasher, where it fell onto the heating element and melted into abstract art within thirty-five minutes.

Wash your good knives by hand. Always! Edges will stay sharp, wooden handles won't split, and you won't have to sell your children to Zwilling J.A. Henckels to pay off your knife debts.

I have a selection of paring knives and use them all, especially when my kids are doing the dishes. The sound of their lamentation, as they look upon the dirty dishes, is as savory as any meal I could make. "Aw, look at the mess, it'll take me all night to clean this shit up!"

I get all goose-bumpy when this high-pitched, nasally whine rises and the creaky vibrato adds to the harmony of sorrow. It's like a good country song. So I use lots of utensils. Paring knives are just a start; I recommend three to five in your arsenal.

A big sturdy butcher knife is a must. A butcher knife can tackle the toughest cut of meat and strike fear into the hearts of nosy neighbours or door-to-door salespeople, especially when you wield one whilst naked wearing only a backless apron and rubber boots and singing "Don't Be Afraid of the Dark" when you open the door. This will grant you more time to cook for your friends and neighbours, provided that you have any left.

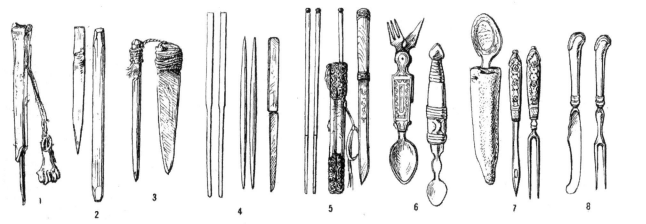

A chef's knife is valuable for carving roasts and precision cutting. As my friend in Hazelton and I can attest, it's especially useful when I'm in a hurry to fillet a salmon before the Department of Fish and Wildlife busts through the door. A chef's knife should be slender and flexible and have a smooth taper to it.

My favourite knife isn't really a knife at all, but a meat cleaver. Mine is a low-budget affair that I purchased in Vancouver's Chinatown many years ago. It's a genuine copy of the famous cleaver that Hop Sing wielded to chase Hoss Cartwright around in *Bonanza* all those years ago. When I'm using it I feel invincible. Bullet-proof and confident. Your human "police" can't stop me!

When faced with warm bread or overripe tomatoes, or if all the other knives are dirty and you feel too lazy to wash them, you'll need a bread knife. A serrated bread knife is the only one of these to have.

Try not to take chances with equipment. Like you, I've watched the TV infomercials and witnessed the magical knives the late-night carnies flog to the public. You know the ones—the knives that cut through a knife, then through a piece of paper, then through another knife.

Those look amazing, you might think. You might even race to the phone and place your order right away so you can get the free bonus navel lint remover if you call right fucking now! However, when you finally receive your set of magic blades

for $29.95 plus shipping and handling, you'll try to cut green tomatoes and end up with tomato soup.

Having been suckered by this dollar-store-quality trash, you'll promise never to buy anything like that again—except for those fabulous faux pearls, or that lovely Capodimonte figurine, or that cool Cold Steel sword that can cut through all your other knives.

You've been there. We all have. That's why I insist you buy high-quality knives at a reputable store like Hendrix Restaurant Equipment Supply, The Bay, or someplace with "Gourmet" in the name. As a rule, stick with a top brand like Henckels, Wüsthof or MAC. You'll save a lot of money and heartache and won't be tempted to return your crappy knives to a lying salesman using the pointy end first.

Stainless steel knives are best for home use, unless you want to master carbon steel or ceramic, both more expensive and maintenance-heavy materials with different requirements that I'm too lazy to write about here. I don't use these because you can't use sharpeners or steels on them, but more on that below.

When purchasing a knife, make sure it has one-piece blade and tang construction. Tang isn't just a shitty drink for astronauts—it's the rear part of the blade that extends into the handle. In a good knife, the tang will extend all the way to the back, and you'll see several bolts through the handle, holding the knife together. A cheap knife may only offer a short tang stuck partway into a plastic handle, and may result in your knife breaking or falling apart at the worst possible moment. What's the moral here? As every chlamydia-riddled veteran discovered the hard way: never settle for cheap tang.

To keep your knives at their best, you need a good sharpener and a steel. Now, you might think these are one and the same. Wrong! First, a sharpener or whetstone grinds your knife edge into a jagged line of microscopic teeth, and then a steel lines those teeth into a fine razor edge. Ideally you'll own both, and use the steel after the sharpener.

If you have good eye-hand dexterity, a whetstone or ceramic rod is the cheapest option. That said, I've never been proficient with a whetstone. (My buddy Trevor is, and I envy him. He can put an edge on a knife you can shave a hairy boar or wife with.)

I often skip the whetstone entirely and use a pull-through carbide sharpener. If you're going to buy one of those, stick with a trusted brand and don't cheap out. A Henckels pull-through is a safe, affordable bet to sharpen knives, cleavers, garden shears, scissors—even a whole guillotine if you've got a revolution on the calendar.

Me, I swear by the Chef's Choice 1520 electric knife sharpener. I received this beauty for Christmas after leaving my family many hints, clues, glowing arrows, proclamations and finally sad, begging entreaties. It's by far the best electric knife sharpener I've ever used. Combined with a simple tuning on a steel prior to use, your blade will practically become a lightsaber. You could dice up a moose carcass or play Fruit Ninja in real life all day long.

When using a steel, lay the blade of the knife at a shallow angle to the steel and draw across. Use

"Who has the best knife?" is a question that has been the subject of much historical debate.

caution! And if you're in Alberta, also use safety glasses, gloves and steel-toed boots. If you're not careful, you could lose something you might want to use on a later date, or on a date later.

After you've rounded up all your fancy knives, don't store them loose in a kitchen drawer. Rattling around with your other junk, they'll grow duller than an NDP cabinet minister. I recommend a knife block, or a knife magnet secured to the wall. A wooden knife block is my favourite—just remember to store your knives sharp-side-up. It not only looks nice, but you need to be speedy sometimes, and a good offense is the best defense.

A few important points on knife use to save you from a trip to the emergency ward or prosthetic finger store:

Grab the knife by the handle (the really thick part at one end) using your dominant hand—you know, the hand you write, wipe, or… you get the idea. Wrap your fingers around the handle and fit the grip comfortably in your hand. Now, at this juncture, the pointy part should be facing away from you. If not, you've grabbed the wrong end, and it may be too late to help you.

Here comes the very important part, and I'm typing very slowly here for those of you who received schooling in Ontario: With the pointy part facing away from you, the sharpest part of the knife, sometimes called the edge, should be facing down, not up. If you have everything lined up, when you pull the knife across a piece of meat or a vegetable, it should render a cut across the face of the item—not across the wall, or your hand, or anywhere else.

If you're still getting sub-optimal results here, please do not use knives anymore, unless you truly enjoy meeting new friends in the healthcare and physiotherapy industries. Don't be the person those snobs in the hospital refer to as, "What the Fuck Did You Do to Yourself?" If you plan to plunge headlong into advanced knifing without preparation or practice, please at least take a video for the next Darwin Awards compilation on YouTube. You may be hopeless but you can still serve as a warning to others.

As we've discussed, quality equipmant can be pricy. But fear not, because there's always a foolproof way to acquire expensive things you can't afford: Stealing!

My mother-in-law Doreen knows that I covet a certain lovely bone-handled knife of hers. Listen, I love Doreen like my own mom, but in her family, people live a very long time. Too long for impatient people like me. Meaning that sometimes a good heist becomes necessary to expedite the inheritance process. Susan, get your purse, we're going to Mom's for a visit!

If you plan to steal knives, then, like Arsene Lupin, you must do it with skill, daring and panache. When you visit your intended purloinee, bring a partner or spouse who carries a large purse or bag. Not only can your partner carry the goods, but if you get caught, they can take the fall for it. (Also make sure you can run faster than this person.)

And always have a good excuse ready. A good excuse is, "My wife suffers from unmedicated kleptomania and we're both very sorry." A bad excuse is, "I'm morally flexible and I thought you were dumber."

Of course, it's usually safer just wait it out and try to finagle yourself into the will. This brings me to my last point regarding knife theft. The most important thing is to exercise caution during your heist, because you're at a tactical disadvantage: your mother-in-law is armed with a knife, and you aren't. And she never liked you much to begin with.

Summary:

✕ *You should have a selection of paring knives, a butcher knife, a chef's knife, a cleaver, a steel, a knife sharpener and a proper storage thingamajig.*

✕ *Choose stainless steel construction.*

✕ *Look for a one-piece blade and tang.*

✕ *Choose knives with balanced feels and comfortable handles.*

✕ *Don't let Lorena Bobbitt spend the night. I only got to make this mistake once.*

✕ *Always use a sharpener and tune up a knife on a steel before using.*

✕ *Keep knives sharp to reduce risk of injury.*

✕ *NDP cabinet ministers are dullards.*

✕ *Buy the best you can afford, or better.*

✕ *Chef's Choice knife sharpeners are terrific.*

✕ *Don't buy knives from the TV. In fact, don't buy anything from TV. Don't even buy a TV.*

✕ *Mother-in-law will lock her kitchen drawers after reading this.*

7   8   9   10   11   12   13

Pots and Pans *(and Other Vessels to Burn Dinner)*

In some areas things in life, size does matter. It's certainly true of pots and pans, where you'll need a variety from the largest to smallest. Stainless steel, non-stick, copper-bottomed, cast iron, glass-topped, round, big, small... you can never have enough, until your intervention officer or the host of Hoarders says so.

If my finances and the square footage in my kitchen allowed it, I'd have the world's largest collection of pots and pans. I'd admire them and show them off and roll around in big piles of them like Scrooge McDuck. However, as most of us are broke flatter than a cow pie in a rainstorm, we must do with what our finances allow.

The best judgment of quality I can think of is the weight of the pot: the heavier, the better. That means stainless steel, cast iron, or ceramic-coated cast iron. Thicker metal warps less, holds heat longer and can help you flash-fry meat without boiling it in its own juices.

As a rule, stay away from aluminum. Aluminum is a fool's metal. It distributes heat poorly and can warp at high temperatures, leading to 'hot spots' on the bottom of your pan. And it's not magnetic, meaning it won't work at all on a fancy induction stove. (Upgrading to an induction stove and finding that all your old bachelor-pad pans don't work is one of life's milestone heartbreaks.)

Plus there's the poison thing. I'm not one to be scared of headlines, but there's growing evidence that ingesting too much aluminum can have ill effects on your health—such as giving you the ability to hide

your own Easter eggs. Sure, sometimes it'd be nice to forget how old I am, but I feel like I have enough holes in my brain already. So I never use aluminum cookware except for one exception: Non-stick pans. These are are often made of aluminum, but because the non-stick coating prevents the metal from touching the food, it can safely be used at low heat.

> *Never put a non-stick pan on high heat. If you think aluminum is unhealthy, just imagine what all those vaporized DuPont mystery chemicals can do to you.*

Another indication of quality is the rims of the lids. When you look to purchase a set of pots and pans, check the lips and lids to see if they have sharp edges (this also works when inspecting a potential love interest). If you could conceivably conduct an emergency bris ceremony with the lid, don't buy the pot. I've done myself serious injuries with cheap pots and their cheap lids, so trust me on this one. The lids should fit snug on the pot or pan and not resemble rotary saw blades in any way.

You'll want pans that can be transferred from stovetop to oven and back. While you're in the market for cookware, don't just trust the words "oven-safe." Look for pans with all-metal handles specifically. Anything less will eventually melt, shatter, combust or otherwise disappoint you. Best practice is to ban plastic from any heat-related enterprise, or, even better, from your kitchen entirely.

The pots for which I truly pine have multiple layers of metal, usually steel and copper. Several brands offer thick, layered construction: All-Clad (for the rich folk), Paderno or Lagostina (for the middle-class folk), even IKEA or Costco's Kirkland brand (for us po' folk) are great performers with very good heat distribution. The better the pot distributes heat, the less likely you'll ruin your Kraft Dinner.

Not necessarily in order of importance, the basics are:

- ✗ 1½-quart pot.

- ✗ 2-quart pot for sauces and stuff. 2 are handy.

- ✗ 3-quart pot. Again, 2 of these are handy.

- ✗ Steamer baskets to fit your 3-quart pots.

- ✗ 6-quart pot.

- ✗ 6-quart or 8-quart heavy iron pot for baking and stovetop use. Also known as a Dutch oven.

- ✗ No, not that kind of Dutch oven.

- ✗ 8-quart, 2-part (pot + strainer) pasta pot.

- ✗ 12-quart stock pot.

- ✗ A wok, flat-bottomed (for electric stoves) or round-bottomed (for gas ranges.) You can also purchase woks as a separate cooking implement with its own heating element.

A selection of frying pans is a must as well:

- ✗ 12" frying pan with deep sides.

- ✗ 10" frying pan with deep sides.

- ✗ 8" frying pan with deep sides.

- ✗ 10" non-stick crêpe pan (essential for great desserts).

- ✗ 10"—12" shallow-sided griddle pan (non-stick is great).

A good set of pots and pans needn't break the bank. If you like those high-end culinary shops where some snobbish Poindexter looks derisively down his nose at your sweatpants, then be my guest. I've found that The Bay and Costco offer great pricing for quality kitchen needs, usually without any attitude. My advice is to wait for a sale, either way.

The best place to purchase kitchen hardware is a restaurant supply house, as their wholesale prices can't be beat. My Mom and sister are as cheap as Scotsmen on the dole, and they've discovered one excellent way to get bargains from wholesalers: by lying.

The key is this. Go to the restaurant supply house closest to you and tell the staff you're opening a new restaurant in a few weeks. With some finesse, you can score cutlery, dishes, pots and pans and almost anything else for wholesale prices. You can pay in cash, since your new restaurant hasn't opened accounts anywhere yet. Never mind the quizzical glances of the salesperson as he or she wonders what kind of restaurant only requires five place settings. It must be very exclusive.

Now, I'm only relating my mother and sister's experience in creative shopping because I'm a terrible liar when facing a fresh-faced sales clerk. If you have the same disability, just go shopping with my family and let them do the talking. But be warned, any money you save will soon be spent on Merlot or vodka gimlets or single-malt Scotch. Hang out with my sister long enough, and let her get drunk enough, and you'll learn that police pepper spray can really add some spice to your afternoon caesar. And when Mom wades into the fray to save her baby, things really get going. Sure, it's embarrassing to see a city cop lying prostrate and crying uncle, but have you ever met a cop that didn't deserve it?

Now, unfortunately, when it comes to major household purchases, you may have to consider your spouse. Left to my own devices, I'd buy every kitchen implement known to mankind, including, and especially, implements for preparing dishes that I only cook every tenth anniversary or so. But Susan doesn't share my fascination for novelty gadgets that take up counter space and drain the joint bank account. In fact, she's spent many a night plotting to punish me for my financial follies. I've become adept at breathing through a feather pillow held firmly over my face by a pissed-off woman who promises that, as soon as I stop moving, she'll feed my body through the Binford 4000 Meatgrinder & Sausage Stuffer that I bought off eBay. And here I thought she liked my sausage! Women, go figure.

It seems, "Fine, I'll rent a storage locker, just don't hurt me!" is the only pillow-talk I can muster up nowadays. Anyway, I've wandered off track. What have we learned so far?

- ✗ *Never use aluminum, unless it's coated in non-stick stuff. And keep those on low heat.*

- ✗ *Heavy bottoms are good. The heavier the better. Freddie Mercury was never wrong.*

- ✗ *Look for heavy-gauge construction of iron, steel, copper or combinations thereof.*

- ✗ *If you have an induction stove, only conductive metal like steel will work.*

- ✗ *Make sure all pots and pans come with tight-fitting lids. Avoid sharp edges (it's a sign of cheap construction).*

- ✗ *Susan does not share Bart's passion for kitchen gadgets.*

- ✗ *Pans should have bare metal handles for oven use. Avoid plastic.*

- ✗ *Bart is currently rolling around nude in a pile of pots and pans. He'll wash them later. Maybe.*

- ✗ *Wholesalers are a great place to shop, if you're a good liar.*

- ✗ *Bart's sister should not drink Scotch in the afternoon.*

- ✗ *That was the parole condition, anyway.*

In summation, (a big word for closing), good quality won't break the bank. The difference between cheap crappy pots and good ones is small financially, but enormous in the long term. Good-quality pots and pans are heirlooms will outlast 100% of the relationships they were purchased to celebrate.

Indeed, some relationships may end as a result of a husband being bashed in the head with a heavy steel pot as his punishment for purchasing the damn thing in the first place. But I wouldn't know anything about that. There's a lot I've forgotten since the concussion.

Trinkets, Baubles and Preciouses

I didn't set out in life to acquire enough kitchen gadgets to shame Ron Popeil; it just happened that way. I'm drawn to shiny, sparkly metal things in the manner of a magpie or ferret. And over time I've discovered that you get what you pay for. For instance, I used to buy cheap garlic presses, but after I did the math, I figure I've spent enough money over the years that I could've hired Gallagher to smash the cloves with a sledgehammer instead. (That's at least twenty dollars.)

So don't be taken in by price alone. Look over quality and construction. If a gadget looks, feels or smells cheaply built, it probably is. Go with hardy stainless steel and fewer parts whenever you can. After finally buying a good-quality garlic press, I can now safely crush enough garlic to finally destroy my nemesis, Italian Dracula.

Now let's talk Tupperware. I love Tupperware, yes, the brand-name, not the generic word for similar containers. It's perhaps the most convenient and cost-effective item in the gadget arsenal. Tupperware as a wedding gift stands a good chance of outlasting the marriage, the persons in the marriage, or the concept of marriage as we know it. Plus, Tupperware parties can be real barn-burners if you make enough margaritas along with the sausage rolls.

I've purchased many storage containers over the years, but none match up with the Tup. Don't bother with knockoffs. Impostors shrink quicker than a ding-dong in an icy lake, and become equally useless. Poor-quality containers have constantly shrunk, warped, melted, discoloured, split, or otherwise broken my heart. My brand-name Tupperware, on the other hand, has stood up to torture and manhandling better than anyone on *Game of Thrones*.

The acid test is when you attend a party somewhere and use your container to bring the horvey-dorveys. At the end of the party, when it's time to go home, it's always the Tupperware container that mysteriously goes missing, while impostors are returned to you disdainfully. In an unrelated anecdote, many of my Tupperware items are indeed of unknown provenance. The lesson here is: possession is nine-tenths of the law, and the other tenth is plausible deniability. They're mine now!

Another good place to get gadgets is from a Pampered Chef distributor. It's not cheap, but like a good Iranian single-malt Scotch, you get what you pay for. Again this requires a party in your home, but an evening acquiring good-quality gadgets is time well spent.

Usually Susan sits in for me at these events; I merely browse the catalogue and check off any trinket I need. Sadly, it's been my experience that other party attendees rarely share my passion for margaritas, sausage rolls and embarrassment.

As far as other gadgets go, I have too many to remember, but a few essential ones are:

- ✗ *Variety of metal whisks.*
- ✗ *Deep frying and candy thermometer.*
- ✗ *Meat thermometer.*
- ✗ *Susan hates me buying gadgets.*
- ✗ *Metal skewers (small, medium and large).*
- ✗ *Mortar and pestle.*

- ✗ *I am heading to The Bay kitchen department to buy more gadgets.*
- ✗ *Citrus peel zester.*
- ✗ *Meat tenderizing hammer.*
- ✗ *Cheese graters. Several of these.*
- ✗ *Susan is very angry about my new gadgets.*
- ✗ *Slotted spoons (Asian markets are best to find good ones).*
- ✗ *Measuring cups (stainless steel).*
- ✗ *Measuring spoons (stainless steel).*
- ✗ *Hardwood muddler for making mojitos (essential).*
- ✗ *Wooden spoons.*
- ✗ *Trivets.*
- ✗ *Peelers.*
- ✗ *Susan is throwing all my gadgets out the door.*
- ✗ *More spoons. Many types.*
- ✗ *Clay baking trays (Pampered Chef).*
- ✗ *Rolling pins.*
- ✗ *I'm screaming and blubbering on the lawn, holding my gadgets.*
- ✗ *Lemon/lime squeezer. Get a thick, heavy stainless steel one.*
- ✗ *On that note, it seems I'll be doing a lot of manual squeezing from now on.*

Cookbooks (or, Things That Hurt When Thrown)

Dogs are okay, but cookbooks are my real best friend. I covet cookbooks. I collect them. I relish them. I treasure them. For me, they're as much fun to read as fine fiction. As I read, I can almost taste and smell a fresh new dish cooking. Cookbooks have allowed me endless hours of travelling the world, dining on dishes that I may never get to taste in their lands of origin.

My mother-in-law Doreen has been prolific in the cookbook-giving department; one of my very favourite recipes comes from a book she gave to me. I've received some great ones from Susan, and have purchased many myself in far-flung, exotic locations like Chapters. Even Safeway yielded a bonanza once, when they threw a bunch in a discount bin and my timing was perfect. Some cookbooks I've taken without the permission of the owner, museum curator, auction house or estate trustee. One cannot overstate the value of reading the obituary pages to cost-effectively improve your cookbook collection.

Cookbooks should be primary items in your cupboard, right next to sloe gin and shot glasses. They should be from all different styles, countries, authors and chefs. They should look as well-worn as a good pair of shoes. I have my favourites, but I also make sure to appreciate the orphaned ones, the neglected ones, the ones that sit forlorn on the shelf. Like pets and children, books need attention on occasion, and their spines need to be exercised. However, unlike pets and children, they are useful.

Not all cookbooks are exclusively devoted to recipes. Many include vital techniques and advice. Some are full of history and food folklore. Some have info on specific cultural or regional cuisines. And some cookbooks are full of rambling, like this one!

Here are some favourites:

The Joy of Cooking
by Irma S. Rombauer and Marion Rombauer Becker

I was given my first copy of The Joy of Cooking by a family friend in 1981, and it changed my outlook on cooking forever. For decades it's been my go-to source of techniques, recipes, etiquette and more. Some of my most-requested dishes come from The Joy of Cooking, including dessert crêpes, hollandaise sauce, cream puffs, éclairs and other things your doctor will tell you not to eat, because doctors are joyless nerds.

The Joy of Cooking has been a constant teacher, inspiration, and source of creativity. The breezy writing makes difficult tasks easy, explaining every step so well that even I could follow them. This book was a major confidence and experience-booster for me, and I'm sure it will be for you too. It's been my central cookbook for most of my adult life. Buy it today!

Encyclopedia of Canadian Cuisine
by Jehane Benoit

Mme Benoit provided me another source of bravery to tackle difficult tasks in the kitchen. My copy was printed in 1963, and was a gift I gave myself (I ransacked my grandmother's apartment while she was out for a walk). Mme Benoit was a charming presence on Canadian TV early on in my youth. She was, and remains, a fantastic teacher.

La Varenne Pratique
by Anne Willan

This book is subtitled The Complete Illustrated Cooking Course, and complete it is, with beautiful photos. This is the book I still turn to if I need information on almost any food-related topic, no matter how obscure. Before we had the Internet, we had Anne Willan—and at the time of this writing, we're lucky we still do.

Company's Coming
by Jean Pare

I have reams of Company's Coming books and they're all treasures. Many were acquired through odd back-channels: magazine promos, direct mail, grocery store kiosks, trench-coated men in dark alleyways. These distinctive coil-bound books cover every cooking subject you can think of, from aperitifs to desserts, abalone to zucchini, alcohol to hangovers. Mme Pare is a welcome guest in my home, and has been for years. I don't know where she hides, but she cleans up after herself and is not a bother.

✕ Canadian Living Compilation Books

Canadian Living has been a fixture in my house for a long time and my mother-in-law's house for longer. They make for pleasurable reading, akin to a good Lawrence Sanders novel, and have provided me with recipes for some of my top comfort foods. The Canadian Living Italian sausage and spinach lasagna has no rival on the planet, and is so delicious that the day after I eat it, I have to tell a priest. Not because I feel guilty— just to brag a little, really.

✕ Harrowsmith Cookbook Compilations

Harrowsmith, like Canadian Living, is a domestic magazine which compiles recipes and techniques from readers. These comfort food recipes are rarely fancy, but they're time-tested and delicious. They'll feed your soul and your family so that both of them will stop squawking at you for awhile.

Other cookbooks I'd recommend to anyone:

✕ Charcuterie
by Michael Ruhlman and Brian Polcyn

✕ The Bread Bible
by Rose Levy Berabaum

✕ Hot Sour Salty Sweet
by Jeffrey Alford and Naomi Dugid

✕ The Complete Book of Spices
by Jill Norman

✕ Kitchen Secrets
by Readers Digest's Anonymous Boomers

Yes, *Reader's Digest*! As you might have surmised, I'm not a snob about a recipe's origins. As a suburban dad I've become a convert to domestic magazines such as *Better Homes and Gardens*, *Cooks Country* and *Canadian Living*, all of which I recommend for time-tested crowdpleasers. They aren't just filler to line the lobby at your dentist's office after all.

Herbs & Spices (Even if You're White)

To cook well, you need herbs and spices. It's that simple. In my pantry there sit myriad herbs and spices, all resting together in perfect harmony before I cruelly force them to sing for my amusement. I have just about every conceivable herb available in the western markets and a few that aren't. You should too.

Since our growing season is short above the 49th parallel and our "fresh-cut" herbs at the markets can be anything but, I often rely on dried herbs. While some food snobs insist that this is sacrilege, dried herbs are excellent for people who don't live within ten thousand miles of a sumac bush. Some dried herbs have unique flavours that their fresh counterparts don't, because curing or roasting can change a spice's flavours heavily, as with garlic and peppers.

That's not to say all herbs are good when dried. When dried, leafy herbs like parsley, basil and mint are very reduced in flavour compared to their fresh form. In that case, it's worth checking out your local fancy moneybags organic market. Pro tip: There aren't many security guards in the produce aisle, because who would shoplift basil of all things, right? If they only knew...

Regardless, well-stored dried herbs will keep their flavours for months. To ensure this, store them in airtight containers, away from heat and moisture. I've been using the same set of Tupperware spice containers for two decades, and you know how much I love Tupperware!

For fragrant herbs and spices like star anise, cloves, cinnamon, curries, and pepper varieties, I'll use glass spice jars or Mason jars, which keep the smells in the spice cabinet from mingling.

One good idea, though I've never put it into practice, is to write your date-of-purchase on the jars and discard old herbs after their 6-month anniversary. I'm just suggesting it because I know you don't do it either and now we must share the guilt.

Older herbs won't go bad, but they lose their potency over time, and you'll have to use more and more herb to get the same effect. You cannabis connoisseurs know what I'm talking about.

Basic dried herbs and spices are easy to find at the supermarket, and a good Asian market will fill in your pantry gaps with masalas and peppers of all kinds, in addition to more exotic herbs like Thai basil, kafir lime leaves, Sichuan peppercorns and lemongrass. There you'll also find spice-based pastes and hot sauces like sriracha, sambal oelek, gochujang and so much more.

If you want to be fancy, organic herbs do pack a bigger flavour punch, but you'll also have to sell your first-born child to Whole Foods to get them. For instance, I used to have a son, but now I have organic oregano. Good trade!

Here are the basics of a solid pantry. Note that all spices listed are the dried versions. Most are available in convenient powdered form, though I recommend grinding your own spices whenever possible.

You may find yourself stepping out and sampling more and varied spices as you go along. Be brave. Be adventurous. Buy spices and herbs you've never heard of and look up recipes that require them. Sample the leaves of fresh herbs just to try 'em out. Hell, grow your own! Whatever you learn, it will improve your cooking and your character.

God knows *something* has to.

Spice List

- Basil
- Oregano
- Parsley
- Curry powder
- Chili powder
- Cayenne pepper
- White pepper
- Black peppercorns
- Sage
- Thyme
- Garam masala
- Coriander
- Fennel
- Cloves
- Cinnamon
- Onion powder or granulated onion
- Garlic powder or granulated garlic
- Bay leaves
- Mustard seed
- Kosher salt

Recipes and Memories

Once I got started in earnest (the verb, not the guy) on writing my cooking meander, I asked my family for ten of their favourite dishes I've cooked for them. I was surprised by what they sent me—I suppose I should've talked to them as they grew up—and it just goes to show that the smallest things can mean so much.

Kristine and Jordan were eloquent in their listings. The younger ones were forthright in telling me what they liked and what they didn't, and for me to stop making things they don't like. Susan's was an expansive list, given she likes almost everything I cook. The lists gave me a place to start on the book.

Kelsey loves shrimp grapanay (au gratin). Kaitlyn loves red Thai curry chicken. Kristine loves borscht. Susan loves exploding chicken. Jordan loves teriyaki chicken. But *all* the lists included Dungeness crab with black bean sauce, making it the number-one overall recipe of my family. This is a bitch for me, as I have to refinance my mortgage every time I budget for crab night. But it's all I can do now that we've eaten the family fortune and the kids' college funds. Just kidding! They never had college funds.

Thus Spake Kristine

"When you asked for ten, I thought, 'Is that all?' There are a couple extras…"

Spring Rolls
The best you can find anywhere. Cleaning the grease splatters on the stove is worth it!

Salad Rolls with Peanut Sauce
Healthy and delicious. If I could live on one thing, this would be it. The homemade peanut sauce it the best I have ever tried.

Beef Stroganoff
Calorie-free of course. Nothing tastes quite as good a rich and creamy Stroganoff over egg noodles.

Stir-Fry
When Dad makes it, you'd think the army was coming for dinner, but no, it's just so good that you eat and eat and eat… and then you eat some more, and then comes the complaining that it hurts to move.

Wild Rice Stuffing
This is the only stuffing I will eat. Puts bread to shame.

Eggs Benedict
A Boxing Day favourite. The blender Hollandaise sauce is second to none.

Hot and Sour Soup
This soup is 10 times better than anything you can find in a restaurant, and believe me, I have tried!

Crab with Black Bean Sauce
A favourite since childhood. I can still see the dining room draped with old sheets to stop the splatters from staining the carpet… and the walls… and the chairs…

Chinese-Style BBQ Pork
The food colouring makes it visually appealing. The most delicious way to cook pork.

Grandma Boos's Baked Beans
Great Grandma's recipe passed down to Dad. You'll never eat canned beans again.

Borscht
Despite the fact I don't like cabbage or beets, this is my all-time favourite soup. Topped with sour cream, it's the best thing on a cold day. Cans well too!

Country Chicken and Gravy
A fat-free favourite also known as "Exploding Chicken". This dinner will stand out in my mind forever. Must be served with mashed potatoes.

Portrait of the author when he was young and virile.

Appetizers

-or-

What to Eat Before You Eat

I love appetizers. In fact, I could live on appetizers, except for the unfortunate fact that any appetizer worth making is normally loaded with fat and salt—the main two food groups other than sugar and alcohol.

Certain events scream out for specific appetizers. Televised sports, or any other testosterone-fueled Sunday afternoon events, demand finger food artfully paired to beverages. I'm a big fan of pairing NASCAR races with hot wings or dry garlic pork ribs and nachos. Crashes, screaming, fortunes won or lost, tantrums, fighting, betrayals—and that's just my house before I turn on the TV. You can't blame me for wanting a little escapism.

Chicken wings are among the worst foods you can ingest, health-wise, but hey, this is a cookbook, not a doctorin' book. As long as you're tempting fate, be sure to add pico de gallo and guacamole to the cheese-drenched nachos accompanying your Last Supper. Cars will crash, the Lions will choke, the Canucks will fold like a cheap suit, and your heart will get some great exercise without you leaving the chair.

Want to walk on the wilder side with appetizers? The Spanish have a special dining style for appies, called tapas, just for this purpose. Tapas restaurants offer loads of small dishes best shared among friends and washed down with wine. It's wonderfully civilized, depending on how much wine you drink.

I've included some of my favourites appetizer recipes here. Some I claim as my I own, some I don't, but I love 'em all equally. You will too.

Crab-Stuffed Mushrooms

SERVES: *5* | METHOD: *BAKE* | APPROX. TIME: *30 MINUTES* | DIFFICULTY: *EASY*

The most appetizing combination: sea bugs and fungus. You can substitute regular bread crumbs for panko crumbs here, but panko has a flaky, light texture that's hard to beat. While you scarf this delectable treat, pity the mushroom-hating mutants like my children Kaitlyn and Jordan. They don't know what they're missing.

Ingredients

- 24 large mushrooms, stems removed
- 12 mushroom stems, minced finely
- 1 tablespoon olive oil
- 3 cloves garlic, minced or pressed
- 2 large shallots (or ½ medium onion), minced finely
- 4 oz. cream cheese
- ¼ cup mayonnaise
- 2 cans crab meat
- ¼ cup Parmesan cheese
- 1 tablespoon Dijon mustard
- 1 splash good-quality sherry (you get to decide how big a splash is)
- ¼ cup melted butter
- ¼ cup panko bread crumbs
- 1 teaspoon Creole seasoning
- 1 teaspoon Worcester sauce
- 1 teaspoon Tabasco sauce

Preparation

1. Preheat oven to 400°.

2. Remove stems from mushrooms. Mince ½ stems finely and set aside. Scrape out black gills from inside each cap, being careful not to rip it.

3. Brush melted butter on outside of mushroom caps and place upside-down into shallow baking dish, like little bowls.

Directions

4. Oil hot non-stick skillet with 1 tablespoon olive oil. Add minced mushroom stems, garlic and shallots. Sauté about 4 minutes, splash sherry into mix, and cook down until alcohol is rendered out.

5. You'll probably have sherry left over after this. If you don't know what to do with it, you need more help than this book can provide.

6. Remove mix from heat and let cool for about 5 minutes, then add cream cheese, mayonnaise, mustard, Worcester, Tabasco and Creole spice to warm pan.

Crab-Stuffed Mushrooms
(CONTINUED)

Jordan says mushrooms are only fit to be eaten by the slithering beasts of the Earth. That's me!

7   Stir until cream cheese is melted and all ingredients are blended. Now add crab meat and gently toss until all is fully mixed again.

8   Add one heaping tablespoon of crab mixture into each mushroom cap. Fill all caps evenly.

9   Realize you're not actually done. Use up remaining filling by piling it onto the caps until they bulge and structural integrity is threatened.

10 Sprinkle stuffed caps with panko crumbs.

11 Bake at 400° for 10 minutes. To brown, switch the oven to broil during the last 5 minutes of cooking, and keep an eye on it so it doesn't burn!

12 Serve hot to anyone who likes mushrooms. That's you!

Crispy Pork Ribs with Spicy Salt

SERVES: *4* | METHOD: **DEEP FRY** | APPROX. TIME: *1½ HOURS* | DIFFICULTY: **BE CAREFUL**

These are so good, even vegetarians will break down the door to snarf some. Veggie folk are sneaky, on account of years disguising tofu as hot dogs and burgers, and they know ancient forest magic that becomes most powerful on nights of the solstice. They can usually be placated with bowls of almond milk and garlic Tofurky on your doorstep. But bar the door just in case.

Special Equipment

- Deep fryer

Ribs and Marinade

- 2 lbs pork ribs, cubed and trimmed
- 4 cloves garlic, pressed
- ¼ cup dry sherry
- ¼ cup soy sauce
- 2 tablespoons light brown sugar
- 2 tablespoons fish sauce
- 2 tablespoons chili sauce (Sriracha)
- 1 tablespoon sesame oil

Coating

- ¼ cup cornstarch
- ¼ cup flour
- ¼ cup water
- ½ teaspoon salt
- ½ teaspoon ground pepper
- 2 egg whites, beaten (for egg wash)

Spice Mix

- 1 tablespoon five-spice powder
- 1 tablespoon salt
- 2 teaspoons peppercorn (ground or crushed)
- 2 teaspoons garlic powder

Preparation

1   Mix all marinade ingredients together with ribs. Marinate in fridge for 4 hours until fully chilled.

Directions

2   Place ribs with their marinade into pot and add enough water to cover. Bring to boil, then turn down heat and simmer for 1 hour.

3   Now's the time to preheat deep fryer to 375° (or stovetop oil pot to medium high).

4   Remove simmered ribs from heat, drain well, spread out on platter and cool in fridge for 15 minutes.

Crispy Pork Ribs with Spicy Salt
(CONTINUED)

5   Add all coating ingredients together in large bowl. Mix thoroughly until you have a wet dip-type batter. Remove ribs from fridge and douse in batter until coated evenly.

6   Place ribs in small batches into hot fryer. Fry for 4—5 minutes, stirring ribs to prevent sticking and clumping. When cooked, remove from oil and drain on paper towel. Repeat process 'til all ribs are done.

7   To make the spice mix, heat all ingredients in frying pan on low heat for approximately 2 minutes, stirring constantly until you can smell spices roasting. Remove and serve with ribs, or sprinkle on just before serving.

The author, returning home with almost enough pork to feed Kaitlyn.

Fried Chicken Wings

SERVES: 4 | *METHOD:* **DEEP FRY** | *APPROX. TIME:* **30 MINUTES** | *DIFFICULTY:* **BE CAREFUL**

If Jordan and Kaitlyn are in attendance at this feast, I recommend taking a loan out at the bank to order a truckload of wings, sauce ingredients and body armour. You can use any remaining money at the bookie's kiosk, placing bets on who'll be left standing. For my children, eating wings is a full-contact bloodsport and no prisoners shall be taken. Please remember to keep your hands outside the octagon.

Special Equipment

✕ *Deep fryer*

Ingredients

✕ *3 lbs. chicken wings*

✕ *¼ cup corn starch*

✕ *¼ cup water*

✕ *1 tablespoon salt*

✕ *2 teaspoons garlic powder*

✕ *2 teaspoons onion powder*

✕ *1 teaspoon ground black pepper*

Optional Additions

✲ *Honey garlic sauce for wings*

✲ *Hot sauce for wings*

Preparation

1. Wash chicken wings. Split wings by removing wingtips and cutting remaining meat at the joints, making 2 pieces of each.

Directions

2. Place chicken wings in large bowl with all other ingredients. Mix well, ensuring chicken is coated evenly. Coating should be wet but not dripping. If too dry, add water incrementally

3. Let sit for 10 minutes for flavour to soak in.

4. Preheat deep fryer to 375° (or stovetop oil pot to medium high).

5. Place coated chicken wings into fryer (singly or in batches, depending on your fryer), stirring so they don't stick together. Fry 10 minutes or until 180° internal temperature is reached and skin is golden brown.

6. Remove from oil and plate 'em up. Serve coated with your favourite sauce, or a tasteful sprinkle of salt and fresh-ground pepper.

✕ *If your wings are ready too soon for dinner, keep them hot and crispy a short time by placing them on a baking tray in the oven at 400° until ready to serve. But don't wait too long!*

Honey Garlic Sauce for Wings

SERVES: YOU | METHOD: SAUTÉ | APPROX. TIME: 15 MINUTES | DIFFICULTY: EASY

Directions

1. Place butter in small pan over medium heat and sauté garlic for 2-3 minutes, until it's softened but not yet brown. Add soy sauce and honey and mix well, bring to a boil, then immediately lower heat to minimum.

2. Allow to stand at a near-simmer for 10 minutes, then remove from heat.

3. In large mixing bowl, pour sauce over fresh, hot crispy wings and toss to coat evenly. Serve immediately.

Ingredients

- 2 tablespoons butter
- 6 cloves garlic, pressed
- 1 cup honey
- 3 tablespoons dark soy sauce

Hot Sauce for Wings

SERVES: YOU | METHOD: BOIL | APPROX. TIME: 10 MINUTES | DIFFICULTY: LAUGHABLE

Ingredients

- 1 cup Frank's RedHot
- ½ cup sriracha hot sauce

Directions

1. Mix both sauces. Heat hot sauce in saucepan and stir over medium heat until hot. Yes, that's all!

2. Place hot crispy wings in a large metal mixing bowl, then apply heated sauce and toss until wings are coated evenly. Serve immediately.

- *The tartness of Frank's mixes well with the sweeter sriracha for a nice East-meets-West combo.*

Two-Day Agony Hot Wings

-or-
Do They Make Solarcaine Suppositories?

I love Frank's RedHot. As the advertisement states, I do indeed put that shit on everything. Frank's has great heat and flavour, without the vinegar taste of similar sauces like Tabasco. I could drink Frank's by the gallon, and if you knew me during my "I dare you to do this" days, you've probably seen me try.

Years ago in Prince George, Susan and I often gathered on weekends with our dear friends Shelly and Trevor to eat, drink and play cards. Often we'd craft homemade wings as part of the ritual, and our favourites were hot wings. The hotter the better—or so we liked to tell ourselves.

In the Central Interior in those days, before the Internet, the best way to learn new things was intuition. Lacking such a trait, one day I pranced home from a specialty food market with a pack of six plump Scotch bonnet peppers.

At the time, these things were fairly rare. Knowing nothing about them other than "they're hot," I felt sure they'd be just the thing to add a new kick to my homemade hot wings. After all, I'd grown up in Vancouver and I was fairly experienced with hot foods. This was just a short step forward, right?

Without any instructions on how to use the peppers—or more importantly, how not to—I decided to do as I did with any sun-dried tomato or jalapeno. I put all 6 peppers into a saucepan with a cup of Frank's RedHot and simmered until they were soft, then pureed the pulp in a blender.

Now, some geniuses out there tell me I should've sampled the sauce before I slathered it on the wings. But I knew I had something special on my hands, and I didn't want to spoil my tastebuds prior to the flavour journey of Trevor and I.

I will admit that my watering eyes were a bad omen.

I set about coating the cooked wings in the normal way and Trevor and I set in for the morsels of goodness. Or so I thought. It turns out that Scotch Bonnet peppers are hot. Very, very hot. Especially in liquid form. The word 'heat' doesn't quite describe it. The phrase I'm looking for... what's "White light from the Ark of the Covenant" in Hebrew?

According to the Scoville scale that measures such things, a Scotch bonnet pepper is 50 to 100 times hotter than an average jalapeno. Do some rough math with me: without realizing it, I had infused the heat of 300 (or more!) jalapenos into one cup of Frank's RedHot.

"My numb is tongue," I tried to say, but said tongue could no longer hear my brain. We were both sweating, our faces turning the same colour as the hot sauce. Each second became a new exponent of heat, the way nuclear fission begins. We lost the ability to use our mouths for anything except yelps of pain, and then our limbs went numb and our eyes lost focus.

We tried to cool the raging inferno with cold rum. You know what happens when you pour alcohol over a fire.

By the end of the evening, we had lost all control of our faculties, had no feeling in our extremities, and far, far too much feeling in our guts. After our long-forgotten cards fell out of our limp and sweating hands, Susan sent me to bed to recover. There I moaned out my fever like a typhoid patient until the next morning, when I was struck by a sudden, extremely urgent need to visit the bathroom.

Then the second day of agony began.

By telling you this story, I now realize I've just given you the recipe for Two-Day Agony Hot Wings. There is no way to use this information wisely. So don't try.

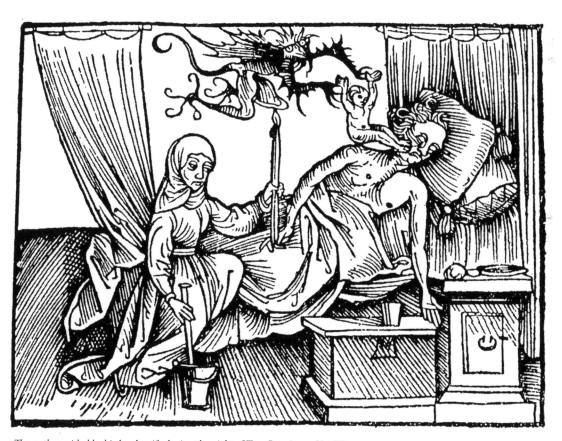

The author, aided by his lovely wife during the night of Two-Day Agony Hot Wings.

Steak Bites

*SERVES: **2*** | *METHOD: **GRILL*** | *APPROX. TIME: **20 MINUTES*** | *DIFFICULTY: **EASY***

Lazy Bastard (me) hasn't had an original thought in his brain. If I haven't ripped off an idea from someone or some magazine, then I don't have an idea, or even an inking really, and like most foods I serve, I ripped off the recipe from someone else. In this case it was stolen from my father. No doubt dear old Dad stole it from someone in turn, just as my children have stolen it from me. This is our legacy.

If you don't have Tramezzini bread, you can substitute any baguette or sourdough. Just slice thin, cut the crusts off and you're ready to go. (Don't use Wonderbread or any shit like that. It's too sweet.)

Ingredients

- 1–2 barbequed steaks (12 oz. total)
- ½ cup mayonnaise
- 1 tablespoon horseradish (not the creamed version)
- Salt and pepper to taste
- Dijon mustard (garnish)
- Capers (garnish)

Preparation

1 Grill steak medium-rare according to instructions in this book. Barbeque is best, but stovetop will do. When cool, slice into cubes about 1½" square.

Directions

2 Toast bread on both sides. Slice into 12 equal-sized pieces, about 1½" square.

3 Mix mayo and horseradish with pinch of salt and fresh-ground pepper. Spread generous amount of mix on squares of bread.

4 Place steak slices atop mayo spread on bread.

5 Garnish with capers and dollop of Dijon mustard on top.

Prosciutto-Wrapped Asparagus

SERVES: 2–3 | *METHOD: BOIL* | *APPROX. TIME: 1 HOUR* | *DIFFICULTY: TRIVIAL*

Lorelei made these one time, and I immediately copied her and began to call the recipe my own. I've been serving them to friends and family ever since. They travel well, so they're great for a potluck dinner.

I love these little hummers. In fact, I can't think of anyone I've served them to who didn't like them. Well, there was that itinerant vegan once—I was taken in by her sign, Will Yodel For Food. And you know how much I love a good yodel. These days, I rely on Susan to do all the local yodeling, although chocolate works better as a bribe. She does a great knock-off of my Slim Whitman favourites. You know it's a party when all the dogs in the neighbourhood start to howl along.

Ingredients

- ✗ 1 lb. fresh crisp medium-thick asparagus spears (about 16)
- ✗ 16 slices lean prosciutto, thin-sliced but not shaved
- ✗ ½ cup soft spreadable cheese of your choice (we use Laughing Cow)
- ✗ Fresh ground pepper

Preparation

1 Wash and drain asparagus and trim woody portion of spear off the bottom. I trim them all equally for presentation.

2 Prepare large bowl of ice water to cool cooked asparagus later.

Directions

3 Boil 3 quarts of water over high heat in large pot. Plunge trimmed asparagus into boiling water for 30–40 seconds, blanching them. Don't cook longer than 40 seconds!

4 Drain asparagus well, then place into ice water to chill. Once chilled, remove from water and pat dry with kitchen towel.

5 Place 1 slice of prosciutto flat. Spread 1 teaspoon of cheese evenly over prosciutto. Lay cooled dry asparagus spear on bias (diagonally) with bottom of spear over th prosciutto. Roll prosciutto until asparagus is fully wrapped. Place on platter.

6 Chill for at least 1 hour. Serve chilled.

Fried Green Tomatoes

SERVES: *4* | METHOD: *DEEP FRY* | APPROX. TIME: *1 HOUR* | DIFFICULTY: *BE ALERT*

Until 9 years ago I don't recall eating fried green tomatoes at any prior point in my life, and then I traveled to Tulsa, Oklahoma on business. Oh my. As a local guided me around down-town Tulsa, we stopped for lunch at an unassuming joint I wouldn't have have entered unassisted, but which was apparently a local favourite. Its specialty was fried catfish and other deep-fried goodness, including fried green tomatoes. Well, they were utterly spell-binding, especially with the catfish. I promised myself I'd have to try them again one day.

After much gentle prodding and less gentle haranguing I cobbled together a number of raised garden beds for my wife to exercise her green thumb, and one of her exercises was tomato plants, one of which was a beefsteak plant, and by late August the tomatoes were huge but green. So we picked them to ripen indoors to beat the frost, and as we were packing them I remembered my deep fried culinary adventure in Tulsa, and fried green tomatoes were being demanded by my memory, hence, the recipe below was the result.

Ingredients

- 2 lbs. large green tomatoes (about 4)
- 1 teaspoon salt
- 2 cups all-purpose flour
- 1 tablespoon salt
- 1 tablespoon pepper
- 1 tablespoon garlic powder
- 1 teaspoon cayenne pepper
- 1 cup masa harina (corn flour)
- 2 eggs, beaten until you get a confession
- ¼ cup water

Remoulade

- 1 cup mayonnaise
- 2 tablespoons chili sauce
- 1 tablespoon Creole seasoning
- 1 tablespoon horseradish
- 1 Tbsp fresh lemon juice
- 1 Tbsp hot sauce (I like Cholula)
- 1 tsp capers, minced fine (optional)
- 1 clove garlic, minced fine or pressed
- Salt and pepper to taste

Fried Green Tomatoes

(CONTINUED)

Preparation

1   Pre heat oil to 350° in large pot or deep skillet. Oil should be at least 3" deep.

2   Combine all remoulade ingredients, whisk well, and chill in covered bowl for now.

Directions

3   Cut tomatoes crosswise into ¼" slices. Spread slices on, wire rack, then sprinkle both sides with salt. Wait 15 minutes, then pat both sides dry with paper towel.

4   Mix wheat flour, salt, pepper, garlic powder and cayenne in shallow bowl or pie plate.

5   In medium bowl, blend eggs and water together. Set aside.

6   Dredge tomato slices in flour mixture until well-coated. Place coated slices back on wire rack and refrigerate 15 minutes.

7   Add masa harina to flour mixture you used previously. Mix well.

8   Once the coated tomato slices have rested in the fridge, dip the tomatoes in the egg mixture, and then dredge each slice in the flour-masa mixture.

9   Place tomatoes them back on rack and allow to sit for at least 20 minutes in fridge. This ensures the coating stays stuck to tomatoes while frying.

10   Add the tomatoes to the hot oil and fry in batches of 3-4 slices, do not crowd them!

11   Fry until golden, about 1-2 minutes, then flip (the tomatoes, not you) and fry for a minute or two longer until they're golden brown and crisp.

✕   *Tomatoes, like many deep-fried foods, will float to the top of the oil when fully cooked.*

12   Drain cooked slices on a paper towel for few seconds, then place onto serving plate to serve.

13   Garnish with minced chives or shallots, or serve them naked (the tomatoes, not you) to eager diners along with remoulade.

Bacon-Wrapped Scallops

SERVES: **2–3** | *METHOD:* **BAKE** | *APPROX. TIME:* **20 MINUTES** | *DIFFICULTY:* **EASY**

This is a simple recipe, but many people ask why their attempts end up chewy, rather than tender like mine. The very hot oven is the secret. At 450° or above, the bacon will crisp fast and the scallops will remain soft and tender. If cooked at a lower temperature, the scallop will be a hockey puck by the time the bacon crisps. You can use a deep fryer to get similar and slightly faster results, but somehow deep-fried bacon seems just excessive. If you insist, deep-fry your scallops for 2 minutes at 375°.

Keep your statins close at hand, and try not to deep-fry those too, you glutton.

Ingredients

- ✕ *16 large scallops*
- ✕ *16 slices bacon*
- ✕ *½ fresh lemon, squeezed*
- ✕ *Seafood cocktail sauce, store-bought or homemade (I like Club Brand Hot)*

Directions

1 Preheat oven to 450°.

2 Clean scallops by removing side-muscle (a little nib of a thing which gets tough when cooked). Once scallops are clean and rinsed, place in strainer and refrigerate 1 hour to cool and dry a bit.

3 Once scallops have drained, roll each scallop in bacon slice on an angle, like a spiral, and secure with toothpick.

4 Place scallops on parchment-lined cookie tray a few inches apart from each other (they don't like to be crowded, agoraphobia I think), then place tray into 450° oven.

5 Roast for 10 minutes or until bacon is crispy.

6 Once bacon has achieved your preferred level of doneness, remove from oven and plate up. Sprinkle fresh lemon juice over scallops. Serve with dollop of seafood sauce.

Vietnamese Crispy Spring Rolls

SERVES: **2–3** | *METHOD:* **DEEP FRY** | *APPROX. TIME:* **1 HOUR** | *DIFFICULTY:* **WATCH OUT**

Special Equipment

✕ *Deep fryer*

Ingredients

✕ *2 oz. rice vermicelli, soaked, drained and chopped*

✕ *½ oz. dried wood ears, soaked until soft and minced finely*

✕ *1 oz. (6) dried Chinese mushrooms, soaked until soft and minced finely*

✕ *8 oz. minced pork*

✕ *4 oz. real crab meat*

✕ *1 large carrot, grated*

✕ *1 medium onion, minced finely*

✕ *2 tablespoons nuoc mam (Vietnamese fish sauce)*

✕ *½ teaspoon ground black pepper*

✕ *1 egg, lightly beaten*

✕ *12—14 sheets banh trang (rice paper wrappers)*

Additions

✳ *Spring roll dipping sauce*

Directions

1 Put all ingredients except rice paper in a large mixing bowl and hand-mix until fully blended. Divide mixture into 14 equal portions.

2 In bowl of warm water, place sheet of rice paper and soak until just pliable. Remove from water and lay flat on clean work surface.

3 Place portion of mixture on bottom of softened rice paper, and work with your fingers to make it into a cigar shape. Begin rolling mixture into rice paper and roll over once.

4 At this point, stop rolling. Fold rice paper sides over to seal package ends, then finish rolling up tight. You should end up with a roll about the size and shape of a cigar, egg roll, or other phallic symbol of your dreams.

5 Repeat Steps 2—4 until you run out of ingredients and rice paper.

6 Line baking sheet with plastic wrap and space all rolls evenly. Place sheet in fridge uncovered for 2—4 hours. This allows rolls' paper skin to dry and mixture to blend flavours. When skins are dried this way, they won't stick together in the fryer. Remove rolls from fridge when done.

7 Gently lower each roll into oil to deep-fry at 350° until light brown and crisp, about 3 minutes (cook in batches as fryer capacity allows). Remove from oil. Drain on paper towels to cool.

8 Serve with spring roll dipping sauce. Just when you thought you were done mixing stuff!

Vietnamese Salad Rolls

SERVES: **6** | *METHOD:* **BOILED** | *APPROX. TIME:* **45 MINUTES** | *DIFFICULTY:* **REPETITIVE**

Of everything I've made over the years, these salad rolls are the most requested, along with the matching recipe for peanut sauce. They have been served to many dozens of guests at home and on vacation. Many of the children's friends will comment on these tasty things and beg me to make them over and over again.

I've taught many people to make them over the years, and I enjoy being the recipient of hugs and kisses for my instructional abilities. Kaitlyn's friends Riley and Hillary were among the most ardent fans of my cooking, and I was humbled by their praise. Really! Me, humble! Can you believe it?

Special Equipment

✕ *24 rice paper sheets (8", round or square)*

Ingredients

✕ *1 head iceberg lettuce, finely shredded*

✕ *2 pounds braised pork, pulled and shredded*

✕ *24 large shrimp, cleaned and deveined*

✕ *8 oz. rice vermicelli noodles*

Related Recipes

⚙ *Bart's Asian braised pork*

⚙ *Vietnamese peanut sauce*

Directions

1   Boil vermicelli noodles per package instructions, then rinse in cold water and drain in colander to wait.

2   Soak rice rounds in warm water to soften for a few seconds (don't let them get soggy, remove just as the paper starts to wilt) then remove to a clean flat surface.

3   Place 3 tablespoons noodles, 3 tablespoons lettuce, 2 tablespoons pork and 3 shrimp on softened rounds at front edge, laying a strip about 4 inches wide. Roll filling halfway, then tuck open ends over towards centre and finish rolling up. At this point your roll should look like a translucent burrito.

4   Place finished rolls on serving tray and cover each layer with plastic wrap, as these yummy things will stick together on the plate, as clingy as your most annoying ex.

5   Once all salad rolls are finished and placed on a serving tray, refrigerate for 1—2 hours prior to serving.

6   Serve with warm peanut sauce or plum sauce or just devour naked (the roll, not you, unless you're into that).

Lettuce Eat Already!

-or-
How to Make Veggies Unhealthy

Dressing for the Occasion

Some of my favourite foods are hot savory soups and crisp salads. While I admit to using commercial salad dressings like good ol' Kraft, as well as strange bottles from farmers' markets and boutique shops, nothing beats a homemade salad with fresh dressing.

Salads offer a bewildering variety. As we've traveled this great continent and stopped into the culinary hidey-holes, I've made it a tradition to try the house salad. Sometimes, enraptured by some flavour I've never tried before, I beg the server for the recipe of the house dressing. Often I'm told, "It's a secret!" Thus I leave the restaurant sullen, disappointed, feeling as empty as their tip jar.

As you might know from talking to me for three minutes, I'm a big fan of vacationing in Idaho. Every time Susan and I end up there, we make sure to stop in at our favourite steakhouse (whose location I won't disclose, lest you all mob the place and increase my wait time for a table). For ages, every time we've visited, we've ordered the house salad, which comes tossed with a huckleberry vinaigrette that's unlike anything else on this planet. For years we kept a tradition: We'd order the house salad, I would beg for the recipe, and I would be told by the server, "It's a secret!"

I don't recommend applying the "no means yes" philosophy to any other aspects of your life. But in pursuit of recipes, there are no rules, no laws, no Geneva Conventions. When food hangs in the balance, you can't let yourself be dissuaded. In the summer of 2009, I returned to the steakhouse

fully prepared. I cleaned my least moth-eaten suit. I Brylcreemed all seven of my remaining hairs. I dusted off my crushed-est velvet lapel shirt. Then I schmoozed up to the server with flattery. Charm and smarm. A little flirting, just enough to let him know what he was missing. I buttered him up real good, all but literally. Finally, mustering up my silkiest voice, I whispered in his ear, "How do you make that huckleberry vinaigrette?"

And still the bastard told me, "It's a secret."

That's when I sighed and hauled out my final negotiation tactic: a gas-can and a lighter. After I described to him in detail how steaks aren't the only meat that can be cooked medium-rare, the server was suddenly much more cooperative. Fawning, even. And that's how the restaurant's secret became mine. It was that easy. Just call me Mr. Too Damn Smooth.

We learned, however, that the "house dressing" wasn't house-made at all. The steakhouse actually used a commercial variety made by Litehouse Foods, purchased in bulk from a Yoke's Fresh Market in nearby Sandpoint. Thus informed, we released our hostages and off we drove.

At Yoke's we gathered a few forklift pallets worth of salad dressing to smuggle home. Since that day, we've been serving huckleberry vinaigrette to our friends and telling them it's our homemade secret recipe. Of course they all beg me to reveal my recipe, and of course I tell them all to get bent. Hey, it was me who did all the legwork and risked arrest in Idaho, not them. Make your own arson threats, you lazy bums!

On another occasion, Susan and I stopped into a seafood restaurant in lovely Edmonton. The house salad turned out to be a wonderful butter lettuce arrangement with apple and almonds, served with a creamy mandarin orange dressing. It was Heaven on a plate—I'd never had anything like it before. We yummed it up so quickly the tablecloth got sucked up in the vortex.

The server rushed over to rescue the linens and ask us to leave, as our disgusting display was ruining the appetites of the other diners. I told him I'd leave peacefully on one condition: if he gave me the recipe for the house dressing. He promised he'd ask the chef and scurried back to the kitchen. Imagine my surprise when he came back with, not a SWAT team, but rather a scrap of paper with the recipe on it, courtesy of the chef!

Frankly, I was in shock at my luck. Perhaps the chef knew me by reputation, or by my brief segment on *COPS*. At any rate, before the restaurant staff realized the priceless treasure they'd given up, I grabbed the paper from the server, stashed it upon my person in a place only a TSA cavity search could find, and made a break for it.

Susan followed, mumbling apologies and excuses for my actions (and after over thirty years of marriage to me, she knows a few). In our wake, we left behind a huge tip to thank the staff for their kindness. Well, Susan left a huge tip, as I was already far away—far, far away, cackling to myself like a lunatic as I disappeared into the woods with my prize.

I enjoy that recipe to this day. If any Edmonton seafood restaurant staff are reading this, I do apologize for my actions on that day, but I still wouldn't have done anything differently. Yes, I still have your tablecloth. No, I'm not giving that back either.

Another dressing I love was given to me by my niece Nicole. The warm honey-mustard dressing atop a spinach salad makes my heart sing praises. Even spinach-haters Kaitlyn and Kelsey have become devoted converts. Armed with such sorcery, I feel like I should start a religion. Let's talk about Xenu...

Keeping It Cleanish

Salads are simple in concept, but can be time-consuming in preparation. Best to begin by washing every item that has a skin, starting with yourself. You could even say that washing is the most critical part of salad making.

Think about it. Have you ever been to a grocery store and witnessed a feral child slobbering over the pepper shelf like it was a ball pit at Chuck E. Cheese's? Or some drip-nosed pervert fondling the lettuce? Or the old woman coughing like a tuberculosis patient, spewing lung juice all over the pears and apples before wheezing off into the dairy section? Have you considered where the old pervert Farmer Jeb was sticking that cucumber before it went on the produce truck? Well, you should, although not in any detail. The point is, wash your produce! Every damn time!

Leafy greens are hard to wash, I know. To save yourself some grief and/or Ebola, you can always buy the bagged or plastic-boxed salad with the words "triple-washed" on it. But even then, it's worth a rinse or two. You never know which disgruntled supermarket employee is misting the parsley shelf with something other than water.

Larger creepy-crawly things can hide in your Romaine too. During the washing, I suggest you submerge your leaves in ice-cold water. You might just see some multi-legged critter clamour up to save itself from drowning. Sucks to be a bug! But it'll suck worse for you when you're chowing down on a Caesar salad, notice something crunchy that doesn't taste like a crouton, and see half a Madagascar cockroach dying on your fork.

Now, we all know that tossing a salad and, er, tossing the salad are entirely different activities, but the same rule applies to both: wash before you toss. I detail this further in my second book, where we move from the kitchen to the Shed of Sin. Until then, wash like your good health depends on it. Because it does!

Spinach Salad & Warm Honey Dijon Dressing

SERVES: 4 | *METHOD: SAUTÉ* | *APPROX. TIME: 20 MINUTES* | *DIFFICULTY: EASY*

Everyone in my family loves this salad, except for confirmed mushroom-haters Kaitlyn and Jordan. Because Jordan lives on his own, I can no longer force-feed mushrooms to him, but he sends this advice back from an undisclosed location: You can substitute julienned carrots for a similar crunchy texture.

Ingredients

- 1 small shallot, minced finely
- 1 clove garlic
- 2 tablespoons Balsamic vinegar
- 2 tablespoons Dijon mustard (must be Dijon, don't substitute with yellow variety)
- 2 tablespoons honey
- 4—6 tablespoon olive oil, to taste
- 300 grams fresh spinach
- ¼ cup pecans, lightly toasted
- ¼ cup bacon (6 slices), freshly fried and crumbled by hand, gently, carefully, compassionately...
- 8 small white button mushrooms, sliced

Directions

1. In saucepan, add 1 tablespoon of olive oil, add garlic and shallots. Sauté over low heat for 2 minutes, but don't allow to brown!

2. Add vinegar, mustard and honey and whisk until shallots and garlic are softened to taste.

3. Remove pan from heat and drizzle olive oil in, whisking until oil and liquids are emulsified. Taste occasionally until desired flavour is reached (I normally use about ¼ cup olive oil).

4. On salad plates, assemble spinach, sprinkle pecans and bacon bits overtop, and add sliced mushrooms. Keep prepared salad in fridge until ready to serve.

5. Once hunger overwhelms you, remove plated salad from fridge, drizzle warm dressing overtop (a gentle reheat may be necessary if you wait long enough), and serve.

Caesar Salad

SERVES: 4 | *METHOD: RAW ASSEMBLY* | *APPROX. TIME: 20 MINUTES* | *DIFFICULTY: EASY*

A fresh Caesar Salad that pays homage to the inventor, Caesar Cardini, is a great thing, and rare. 99% of restaurants have no idea how to do it, including many fancy places.

This recipe is very garlicky, as caesar salads should be, but you can mellow it by roasting the garlic in the oven before using it in the recipe. First, trim a head of garlic by cutting the top ¼ off. Drizzle a little oil over the cut top and wrap the head in foil. Place in preheated 350° oven for 20 minutes, then remove from oven and let cool. Peel skin off garlic and use as normal.

Ingredients

- 1 large head romaine lettuce
- ½—¾ cup virgin olive oil
- 2 cloves garlic, peeled
- 2 anchovy fillets, crushed to paste
  OR
  2 tablespoons anchovy paste
- 1 tablespoon capers
- 1 teaspoon Worcestershire sauce
- 1 teaspoon Dijon mustard
- 2 tablespoons fresh-squeezed lemon juice
  OR
  1—2 tablespoons red wine vinegar
- ¼ teaspoon fresh-ground black pepper
- 2 yolks from coddled eggs (see instructions)
- ½ teaspoon Tabasco sauce
- 4 tablespoons Parmesan cheese, fresh-grated
- ½ cup fresh-made croutons
- Salt to taste (optional)

Directions

1. Clean lettuce and shred into bite-sized pieces.

2. Coddle eggs as described on next page.

3. Crush garlic cloves and capers into a paste. Add anchovies, Worcestershire sauce, Dijon mustard, egg yolks, lemon juice and pepper in order, smushing it all into a fine goo.

4. Whisk in oil and mix well until it reaches a consistency you like. Mix should be runny, not clumpy. Add half your Parmesan (2 tablespoons) and whisk again until combined.

5. Place lettuce in a large salad bowl. Drizzle dressing over leaves and toss well to coat. Top with croutons and remaining Parmesan.

6. Serve chilled.

Caesar Salad
(CONTINUED)

How to Coddle Your Eggs

Don't. They have to learn that life is unfair. Ha! Bazinga! Okay... "coddling" in this case means cooking the eggs with water just below the boiling point. (Poached eggs are a form of coddled eggs, but we're not going that far.)

1. Let eggs sit on counter until they warm up to room temperature.

2. Once eggs have warmed to room temperature, heat up a pot of water.

3. Place eggs (uncracked) into pot of simmering water, as if you were making hard-boiled eggs.

4. Simmer for 2 minutes, then drain.

5. Cool eggs in ice water bath for 10 minutes, then crack.

If you did it right, the yolks will be soft and the whites will be white but runny. This is one of the only times in your life you'll do this to your eggs on purpose, because damn, that doesn't look appetizing at all, does it?

Notes

This is my Mom's favourite salad recipe and she gave it to me, with some tweaking to my liking. And now I give it to you. Thanks, Mom! Thanks, me!

Our friend Joann will travel vast distances for my Caesar salad. She has a preternatural sense for knowing when I'm preparing it, and once she catches a whiff of that fresh garlic, no obstacles will stand in her way.

Joann has even followed us on our remote vacations to Idaho, *Cape Fear*-style, just to satisfy her ravenous cravings for Caesar salad. Now Joann, you can make your own damn salad and stop trying to pinpoint the location of my backwoods bunker in Idaho. I've still got a warrant out here, remember?

Kaitlyn and Kelsey would drink this dressing out of shot glasses if I let them. I don't let them, of course, because that's completely uncivilized. (I make them use the brandy snifters.)

Bread Reckoning
-or-
Blowing Your Carb Load

Susan makes great bread, just like her dear old Ma. I'm not much of a bread baker, but I am a world-class bread eater, as my waistline will attest. Bread is a necessity for homemade soups, chili, stews and all manner of things.

As I'm not the baker in the family, I won't go on too long, so let's get right to the recipes. The sooner it's baked, the sooner we can eat!

Susan baking dutifully while I do the hardest job of all: supervising.

Basic Bread & Buns

SERVES: 4—5 | *METHOD: BAKE* | *APPROX. TIME: 1½ HOURS* | *DIFFICULTY: EASY-ISH*

Ingredients

- ✕ 1 cup milk
- ✕ 4 tablespoons margarine or butter
- ✕ 1¼ cup cold water
- ✕ ¼ cup sugar
- ✕ 2 teaspoons salt
- ✕ 2 tablespoons baker's yeast
- ✕ 2 eggs, well beaten
- ✕ 6—7 cups of flour

Preparation

1 Scald milk by heating to a near-boil on stovetop pan, then reducing heat to cool.

Directions

2 Melt margarine or butter in warm milk in large mixing bowl. Add water, sugar, salt and stir liquid well. Now add yeast. Wait until yeast activates and starts to bubble, 15 minutes or so.

3 In separate bowl, beat eggs until emulsified and add to main mix along with flour. Knead until you have smooth, solid dough. Add flour as consistency requires (it varies a little depending on all kinds of factors).

4 Let dough rise until doubled in size. Now create buns by rolling dough into rounds about 2" across.

5 Place on baking sheet, well separated, and cover with damp cloth. Let rise again for ½ hour, until dough is doubled in size again.

6 Bake buns at 400° for 30 minutes or until top of bun has nice golden-brown crust.

Bran Muffins

SERVES: 4–5 | *METHOD: **BAKE*** | *APPROX. TIME: **1 HOUR*** | *DIFFICULTY: **EASY***

These healthy-ish, delectable morsels will become a family favourite, and your doctor will breathe a sigh of relief that you're finally including some fibre in your diet. To you and your colon: Enjoy!

Ingredients

- 4 cups bran cereal (such as All-Bran)
- 1 teaspoon salt
- 1 qt. (4 cups) buttermilk
- 2 cups water
- 5 cups flour
- 2 cups wheat bran
- 5 teaspoons baking soda
- 2 cups white sugar
- 1 cup brown sugar (packed)
- 1 cup canola or corn oil
- 4 eggs

Optional

- Fruit or berries (fresh or frozen)

Directions

1. Boil 2 cups water. To boiling water add bran cereal, salt and buttermilk. Stir well, cool to lukewarm and set aside.

2. In another bowl, mix together flour, wheat bran and baking soda. Set aside.

3. Put away your electric mixer 'cause you're doing this by hand. In third, really big bowl, mix white sugar, brown sugar and vegetable oil. Then add eggs, one at a time. Add liquid buttermilk mix to big bowl and stir well.

4. Now add flour-bran mixture, and mix just enough to moisten flour. Don't over-mix! I mean it!

5. Preheat oven to 375°.

6. Grease muffin tins, then pour enough batter to fill each muffin cup ⅔ full.

7. If desired, add 2 tablespoons fresh or frozen blueberries, raspberries, blackberries, cranberries, etc. just before baking. No more than that, as too much fruit will make the muffins too moist to bake.

8. Bake 20—25 minutes for small muffins, or 30—35 for larger ones.

9. Store muffin mix in the fridge for up to 1 week. Take out only the amount you wish to make each day. don't stir again before putting in muffin tins.

Naan (Indian Flatbread)

SERVES: 4—5 | *METHOD: BAKE* | *APPROX. TIME: 1½ HOURS* | *DIFFICULTY: EASY*

Special Equipment

- Clay baking sheet

Ingredients

- 1 cup whole milk
- 2 teaspoons sugar
- 2 tablespoons active dry yeast
- 4 cups all-purpose flour
- ¼ cup additional flour for dusting
- ½ teaspoon salt
- 1 teaspoon baking powder
- 2 tablespoons vegetable oil
- ⅔ cup plain yogurt
- 1 large egg, beaten lightly

Preparation

1   Scald milk on stovetop, then let cool fully. Add sugar and yeast, stirring well to dissolve. Let stand until mixture is slightly frothy (about 15 minutes).

Directions

2   Add flour, salt, baking powder, oil, yogurt, and egg to mixing bowl. Use hands to work and knead. Gradually add milk mix. Knead until you have soft, smooth dough (5—7 minutes).

3   Transfer dough to greased bowl, cover with damp cloth and let stand in a warm place until doubled in size (about 1 hour).

4   Preheat clay baking sheetin oven to 450°. Or use cast-iron pan on stove, greased with butter.

5   Punch down dough and divide into 12 equal-sized balls. Roll one ball lightly in flour, and shape with rolling pin into a circle 7—8" wide. Dust with flour to prevent dough from sticking to surfaces.

6   Place dough on preheated baking sheet or pan and cook until dough surface bubbles lightly and the underside is lightly browned in spots (about 2 minutes). Flip naan and cook another 2 minutes.

7   Remove naan from cooking surface. Place on serving dish, brush with melted (preferably clarified) butter and cover with aluminum foil to keep warm. Bake remaining dough the same way and serve warm with curry, chutney or just by its delicious self.

Scruffies (Rugelach)

SERVES: **4** | *METHOD:* **BAKE** | *APPROX. TIME:* **45 MINUTES** | *DIFFICULTY:* **EASY-ISH**

This recipe is beloved of Grandma Doreen and of all who've met her. A cross between a cinnamon bun and a croissant, I've always known these as scruffies, although technically they are (I discovered late in life) a type of rugelach, a traditional Jewish pastry. They're light in texture and bite-sized, the perfect snack to eat thirty of in a single sitting without realizing it until you try to stand up again.

Dough

- 1 tablespoon yeast
- 2 teaspoons sugar
- 3 cups flour
- 2 tablespoons sugar
- ½ teaspoon salt
- 1 cup margarine (Parkay is best)
- ½ cup milk
- 2 eggs, beaten

Sprinkles

- 1 cup sugar
- 2 tablespoons cinnamon

Preparation

1   In large bowl, mix flour, sugar, salt and margarine. Add milk, beaten eggs and yeast mixture, then mix well into sticky dough. Cover bowl and leave overnight in fridge.

Directions

2   Scald milk on stovetop, then let cool fully. Add sugar and yeast, stirring well to dissolve. Let stand until mixture is slightly frothy (about 15 minutes).

3   Mix your sugar and cinnamon in bowl. This will be your sprinkle mix.

4   Now divide dough into 4 equal pieces. Roll one piece of dough into a pie shape (round). Sprinkle ¼ sugar-cinnamon mixture over dough.

5   Preheat oven to 350°.

6   Cut dough into 16 wedges (triangles) and roll up, starting at wide edge. You should end up with a small, oblong, dolma-shaped roll with a triangle flap in centre. Repeat 'til you run out of dough, spacing wedges evenly on greased baking sheet.

7   Bake 10—15 minutes until golden brown, then serve. Goes great with tea or coffee. Will keep for a few days, but I promise they won't last that long.

Yorkshire Pudding

SERVES: 4 | *METHOD: BAKE* | *APPROX. TIME: 1 HOUR* | *DIFFICULTY: TRICKY*

This recipe is a perfect marriage of, flour, eggs and milk. A wonder of nature. I've tried to locate its origins on the Internet, but it seems lost to time, so by maritime rules of salvage, it now belongs to me. You may thank me with a PayPal transaction.

Special Equipment

- ✕ *Electric hand blender*
- ✕ *Sieve*
- ✕ *12-cup muffin tin*

Ingredients

- ✕ *4 large eggs*
- ✕ *Equal quantity milk to eggs*
- ✕ *Equal quantity all-purpose flour to eggs*
- ✕ *1 teaspoon salt*
- ✕ *3 tablespoons canola oil*

Preparation

1. Ensure you have equal volumes of eggs, flour and milk. First, crack eggs into measuring cup and note amount, then use measuring cup to demark same quantities of milk and flour.

2. Pour eggs and milk into large mixing bowl. Add salt. Blend thoroughly with electric hand blender, then let stand for 10 minutes.

3. Gradually add flour into milk-egg mixture and blend at high speed for 3 minutes to ensure batter is smooth and lump-free. Pass liquid mixture through sieve to remove any remaining lumps.

4. Let batter rest for 2 hours at room temperature.

5. Preheat oven to 450°.

Directions

6. Using 12-cup muffin tin, place 1 teaspoon oil in each muffin cup. Canola oil is best for this because of its high smoking point. Place oiled tin in oven for 5 minutes to preheat. While tin heats, whisk 2 tablespoons of ice-cold water into your pudding batter to shock the mixture.

CONTINUED NEXT PAGE

Yorkshire Pudding
(CONTINUED)

7   Remove hot tin from oven and quickly fill each muffin cup halfway. You should see batter bubbling on sides of each cup—that means it's very hot, which it should be!

8   Place muffin tin in 450° oven. If you use a convection oven, place rack at dead center of oven, equally distant from top, bottom and sides. If using conventional oven, place rack in top-third (otherwise your Yorkshires may burn, since heat comes from bottom of oven).

9   Bake Yorkshires for 10 minutes at 450°. Then turn down heat to 400° and bake 20 minutes more. Turn oven off and let puffs of goodness sit for 10 minutes more to firm up, giving you that dark crispy exterior and ensuring the centres don't collapse. Don't open oven door at any time until the full 30—40 minutes have elapsed! If you want to monitor your Yorkies, use the oven window—that's what it's for!

✕   *You'll need to run a test batch or two to get your timing down pat, since every oven is different and so are other variables like the type of flour you use and even your altitude. Once you've perfected your method, Yorkshires are easy and quick to make, and taste like a million bucks, especially with prime rib roast!*

Cleanup Tip: Tell your children or other slaves never to wash muffin tins with soapy water. Treat all tins as you'd treat a good cast-iron skillet: simply wipe them out with a clean cloth and a little hot water. Re-oil, heat in a hot oven for 10 minutes, then cool and store.

Notes

I recommend you make a double or triple batch of these, as I do whenever I prepare roast beef. In times past, I'd cook 24—36 puddings, and they were never enough. Once the high-speed Yorkshire pudding eating contest was finished at the dinner table, the kids would continue to Hoover them up as they did the dinner dishes, creating an unholy din that neighbours could hear from a block away.

It was an unsettling sound—something like a truck full of Jello being torn apart in a wind tunnel—but after a short time all our neighbours moved away and the noise complaints ceased.

Foolish me, I would always hope there'd be enough for lunch the next day to make a cold roast beef sandwich. What was I thinking?

Chicken Soup for the Glutton's Soul
-or-
The Other Kind of Liquid Breakfast

Soups are a canvas that I paint on frequently, and are a source of satisfaction for my soul. While I have some favourites, many times a soup is an extension of how I'm feeling at the time. Soup is a failsafe dinner when served with fresh rolls or bread from Susan's oven, and for me it's something hard to screw up, and that's worth something to me.

The building blocks for a great soup are laid down when you make the broth. No soup can be called great if the broth is insipid or devoid of pizzazz, so care and attention must be taken at the broth stage. Once perfected, you can do almost anything to the broth and end up with a fine soup. It also helps if you have a Susan close at hand to fashion up some great dinner rolls to frame your work of soupy art.

Broth is the foreplay of soup, if you will. It (broth-making, that is) needs to be taken slowly and gracefully. You'll disappoint yourself and your soup-mates if you rush through the beginning stages toward the visceral satisfaction part too quickly. Guy thing! So slow down, use a slow hand and a slow burner, and you'll be rewarded for your patience.

First, you need a pot full of bones from some unfortunate critter. Beef, chicken, pork or almost any beast is fine. Regardless of how you acquire your bones (I don't recommend the SPCA, not after last time), you'll need to place them on a shallow roasting pan and roast in a 350° oven for 1—1½ hours, until golden brown. Roasting the bones gives a richer and deeper flavour to the finished broth, so it's a vital step.

Now you may be asking yourself, "How many bones do I use?" A good measure is the bones from 1 roasting chicken or 2 frying chickens, or 2—3 pounds or more of beef, veal or pork bones. This will make enough for about 2 quarts of finished broth. The bones from a 20-pound turkey will yield enough for 4 quarts of broth.

In all, don't be stingy, because over-boning is better than under-boning. You always regret the boning you didn't do more than the boning you did.

When your bones are roasted, remove from the oven and place into a large dutch oven or stock pot along with your best friend in culinary seasoning, the mirepoix. Classic mirepoix contains two parts onion, one part carrot and one part celery, all minced finely. (I also include several minced cloves of fresh garlic as a staple, but this isn't part of proper mirepoix.)

Cover the roasted bones with water, enough to completely submerge them. That's at least 4 quarts for a small batch, or 8 quarts for a large turkey batch. Add the mirepoix (2 cups for small batch, 4 cups for big batch), a couple bay leaves and a little salt to taste. Don't add pepper at this point. Pepper can impart a bitter taste to the broth and should only be added prior to serving the finished soup, if at all.

Now you can crank the heat to high. Just as the broth reaches the boiling point, turn the heat down to a very low simmer. As it simmers, skim off the foam and oil that floats to the surface. This will keep the broth clear, removing any grit or bitter taste boiling off the bones.

Gary and Martha Soup, the inventors of soup.

Simmer for 2—4 hours. Once finished, remove from heat and let cool for at least one hour, or long enough to avoid tragic burns, then train it through a fine mesh sieve or even a cheesecloth to make it just perfectly clear. Is clear for you?

If you cook the broth too long or keep it at a rolling boil, the bones will give off a natural thick-ener and make the broth heavy and cloudy. This is okay or even preferable for some soups, but I prefer to keep my broth light and clear. I do, however, simmer turkey broth overnight, as most turkey dinners finish late at my house, and wine consumption impairs my broth-straining skills.

In addition to the mirepoix you can toss in some garlic, red or green peppers, and other aromatic vegetables if you like. All the solids will be removed later, so it's just pure flavour. However, avoid adding strongly-flavoured vegetables like cauliflower, broccoli, asparagus or the biggest broth-killer of all: brussel sprouts. They may be delicious in a final soup, but in a broth? Never!

When your broth is cool and well-strained through a fine sieve or mesh, it's complete. Now you can begin your soup odyssey or freeze the broth to use at a later date. I usually freeze the broth in freezer bags in 2-quart measures, but other solutions such as Tupperware also work.

But broth isn't just for soup. It can also also be a base for stew, chili, various sauces, gravy, and as flavouring for other dishes like mashed potatoes. You may find yourself returning to your stockpile (stock, get it?) fairly often.

There are times I'm bereft of broth, with barren and bone-less freezers. On these occasions I'll use a commercial broth such as Campbell's or Western Family, always the "No Sodium Added" kind in a Tetra-Pak. It's more versatile than the MSG and salt-laden powder stocks, and actually tastes better than some homemade broths I've had.

On that note, avoid the salty powders when making your broth. There's a time and place for it, but not in a homemade soup. Your heart and palate will thank you.

In my repertoire of favourite soups, I have a few I replicate faithfully:

- ✕ *Borscht*

- ✕ *Chicken Corn Chowder*

- ✕ *Split Pea with Ham*

- ✕ *Clam Chowder*

- ✕ *Beef and Barley*

- ✕ *Hot and Sour*

- ✕ *Minestrone (Susan's recipe)*

Other soups, be they chicken or beef-based, are often an excuse to clean out the fridge of leftovers, especially veggies nearing their expiration dates in the crisper. A good broth can make a tasty soup of anything! Pasta noodles, salsa sauce, sausage bits, leftover chicken or turkey: all make excellent sacrifices to the soup gods.

Once you've made it a few times and have arrived at a consistent end result, you can branch out and be daring. Your soups might vary from in consistency from, well, soupy, to thick and stew-like. My Saturday lunch time offering is seldom the same from week to week, but it's always tasty and always welcome, especially on the bitter, cold winter days that Edmonton offers us most of the goddamn year.

I hate winter. Did you know that? If you don't, it's a subject I will return to. Again and again, until you *understand*.

To recap...

- ✕ *Good soup starts with good broth.*

- ✕ *A good broth starts with roasted bones and a mirepoix.*

- ✕ *Great broth is slowly simmered and strained to make it clear.*

- ✕ *Vegetables would rather end up in a soup than a Garburator. I asked them.*

- ✕ *Soup is best served hot.*

- ✕ *To me soup has a trinity of meat, veggies and a starch (pasta, potatoes, etc.)*

- ✕ *Susan's buns are great with soup.*

- ✕ *I will not make a joke about that because she's staring at me and holding a rolling pin.*

- ✕ *Chicken soup can cure depression and cancer. Don't quote me on it, but it's true.*

- ✕ *Soup is meant to be shared.*

- ✕ *My kids love soup, especially Dad's soup. I practically raised them on soup.*

- ✕ *Cold soup is yucky.*

- ✕ *Most chowders are best-tasting as leftovers on the second day.*

- ✕ *Soup must be served hot. Did I mention that before?*

- ✕ *My buns are very soft and tender after being smacked with a rolling pin.*

Hot & Sour Soup

SERVES: 4 | METHOD: BOIL | APPROX. TIME: 45 MINUTES | DIFFICULTY: EASY

With the promise of hot and sour soup, I could get my daughter Kristine to do almost anything. Cleaning her room. Doing laundry. Vacuuming. With the promise of adding a little extra shrimp to the broth, she could even be talked into cutting the lawn. And we didn't have a lawnmower!

Ingredients

- 8 dried shiitake mushrooms
- 2 large pieces of wood ear (black fungus)
- 1 oz. (¼ package) bean thread noodles (mung bean threads, not rice noodles!)
- 8 oz. firm tofu
- 8 oz. Chinese-style barbeque pork (or substitute other meat as needed)
- 4 teaspoons cornstarch
- 6 cups chicken stock
- ½ cup bamboo shoots, julienned
- ½ cup small shrimp
- ¼ cup vinegar
- 2 tablespoons dark soy sauce
- 1 tablespoon sugar
- ½ teaspoon white pepper
- 2 eggs
- 1—2 tablespoons sesame oil
- 1—2 tablespoons chili-garlic paste
- 2 green onions, finely sliced

Preparation

1   Julienne 8 oz. of cooked meat. I recommend Chinese-style barbeque pork, a recipe that's included in this book.

2   In small bowl, cover mushrooms and wood ear with 2 cups hot water. Let stand for 20 minutes or until softened. Drain, reserving liquid.

Directions

3   Discard mushroom stems and finely slice caps. Julienne wood ear finely. Set aside.

4   In bowl of hot water, soak noodles for 5 minutes. Drain, place on cutting board and chop into 1" lengths. Cut tofu into small cubes.

5   In large pot, bring chicken stock to gentle boil. Add pork, fungus with soaking water, noodles, tofu, bamboo, vinegar, soy sauce, sugar and pepper. Return to gentle boil, then simmer for 5 minutes.

6   In small bowl, whisk cornstarch with 3 tablespoons cold water. Add to soup slowly and simmer for 2 minutes. Remove from heat.

7   In small bowl, whisk eggs with 1 tablespoon water, then slowly drizzle into soup, stirring slowly with spoon. Stir in shrimp, sesame oil, chili-garlic paste and onion.

8   Let stand 2 minutes before serving.

New England Clam Chowder (White)

SERVES: 6 | *METHOD: BOIL* | *APPROX. TIME: 1 HOUR* | *DIFFICULTY: MEDIUM*

Ingredients

✕ 6 slices lean bacon, minced

✕ 1 large onion, minced

✕ 2 stalks celery, diced

✕ 2 large carrots, diced

✕ 3 large potatoes, diced

✕ 3 tablespoons all-purpose flour

✕ 1 cup water

✕ 2 tablespoons dry fine sherry

✕ ½ teaspoon thyme

✕ ½ teaspoon oregano

✕ ¼ teaspoon white pepper

✕ 3 cans baby yellow clams (30 oz. total)

✕ 1 bay leaf

✕ 2 cups milk

✕ 1 cup cream

Optional

✕ 3 sprigs fresh parsley, chopped

✕ 1 tablespoon nuoc mam
(Vietnamese fish sauce)

Directions

1   Open cans of clams, drain and separate. Save juice for later.

2   Cook bacon in a large saucepan over medium heat. Drain excess fat. Add onion, carrots and celery to bacon. Sauté 5 minutes or until onion is soft. Add flour and cook for 2 more minutes.

3   Stir in potato, water, sherry, clam juice, thyme, pepper and bay leaf. Add optional Asian fish sauce to taste, in place of salt. Bring to a boil. Cover, reduce heat, and simmer 15 minutes or until potato is tender, stirring occasionally.

4   Add milk and cream to mixture bring to almost boiling, but do not boil, or you'll curdle it and ruin everything! Reduce heat and gently simmer for 5 minutes, add clams and simmer for 5 minutes longer. Again, don't boil the soup! Stir frequently. Remove bay leaf and feed it to neighbour's annoying cat.

5   Serve hot and garnish with chopped parsley, if desired, just before serving.

✕ *Pro Serving Tip: If you have too much money on hand, give me some. Then buy some sourdough bread rounds, cut the top off to form a lid, then hollow out the round by removing the light and soft bread. Ladle soup into the hollowed-out bread bowl. Now that's presentation!*

Borscht

SERVES: **4** | *METHOD:* **BOIL** | *APPROX. TIME:* **2 HOURS** | *DIFFICULTY:* **EASY**

This is one of my all time favourite soups and I love to make it in large batches—very, very large batches. Borscht freezes well in bags and defrosts just as delicious as the first day.

You can add just about any vegetable to borscht. My preference is for the ingredients below, but there are no hard and fast rules. Borscht is an Eastern European peasant soup, intended to feed hungry farmers with the cabbage and beets that were plentiful on the steppes. Traditional borscht is meatless, but as it happens, I'm a carnivorous type of peasant, and if you're reading this, you probably are too. Go with beef!

Ingredients

- 8 cups beef broth
- 1 tablespoon olive oil
- 1 lb. boneless beef shank meat, cubed 1" × 1"
- 1 large onion, minced
- 6 large beets, peeled and grated
- 6 large carrots, peeled and grated
- 4 cups cabbage, grated
- 2 large tomatoes, skinned and chopped
- 1 head garlic, pressed
- 2 cups fresh young spinach leaves, chopped
- 2 tablespoons parsley
- 1—2 teaspoons dill
- ½ teaspoon tarragon
- Salt and pepper to taste

The Secret

- White sugar, ½ teaspoon at a time, to reach desired sweetness

Directions

1   Wash beets but don't trim them; leave leaf stubs and root attached to prevent bleeding. Use your hands to evenly coat washed beets in oil.

2   Place oiled beets in roasting pan, cover, and roast at 375° for 30—45 minutes. Once cooled, peel off skins and shred or grate the beets.

3   Heat oil in large 8-quart soup pot on medium-high heat. Add beef and fry until browned, then add onions and garlic. Sauté until onions are soft.

4   Add beef stock and other ingredients and bring to a low boil, then reduce to a simmer. Add dill 1 teaspoon at a time, tasting after each to prevent overpowering.

5   Skim off gathering detritus as soup simmers. Cook 1—2 hours or until vegetables are soft, meat is tender and flavour is well balanced (adding sugar if necessary).

6   Serve topped with dollop of sour cream.

Chinese Chicken Corn Drop Soup

SERVES: 4 | *METHOD: BOIL* | *APPROX. TIME: 1 HOUR* | *DIFFICULTY: MEDIUM*

. . . .

Jordan and Kristine suggest this is one of their all time favourites. I've been making this for 25 years and I never tire of it. Served with a fresh bun or two, it's a full meal deal.

You can substitute chicken with genuine crab meat if you're feeling like a Rockefeller. Crab takes this to another realm of taste sensation and elevates you to God-like status in the eyes of your children. So do it! Rob the Federal Reserve and buy a pound of fresh Dungeness. I dare you.

As far as experimentation, I like mine on the sweet side, so I often add a touch more sugar than the recipe calls for. Obviously, you won't hurt my feelings if you don't follow the recipe exactly. I'll simply stop talking to you and badmouth you behind your back forever. You're welcome!

Ingredients

- 8 cups chicken broth
- 2—14 oz cans creamed corn
- 1 cup cooked chopped chicken, diced
  OR
  1 cup genuine crab meat, shelled
- 2 tablespoons cornstarch
- 4 tablespoons water
- 2 eggs, lightly beaten with 2 tablespoons water
- 1 teaspoon sesame oil, or to taste
- 1—2 teaspoons sugar
- ½ teaspoon white pepper
- 1 pinch cayenne pepper
- Salt to taste

Directions

1   Dissolve cornstarch in water and stir into thin slurry. Set aside.

2   Bring chicken broth to boil in large soup pot over medium heat. Stir in creamed corn and return to boil.

3   Add sugar, white pepper, cayenne pepper and chicken. Cook for about 2 minutes until boiling again.

4   Pour cornstarch liquid into hot soup, stirring constantly. When soup has thickened, remove pot from heat.

5   Slowly pour beaten eggs into soup in a steady stream. Stir swiftly to form thin shreds of cooked egg. If using crab in place of chicken, this is where you add crab.

6   Ladle into bowls and place a few drops of sesame oil in each bowl. Serve immediately.

Ham & Split Pea Soup

SERVES: 8 | *METHOD: BOIL* | *APPROX. TIME: 3 HOURS* | *DIFFICULTY: EASY*

I use yellow peas because Susan has a thing about green pea soup (I think she watched The Exorcist one too many times). Same great taste, fewer demonic flashbacks. Hey, it's all about her, after all. Isn't it?

And now back to me: the barley is my own personal favourite addition. Once you try it, you'll never make pea soup without it again, no matter what your wife or her flashbacks have to say about it.

Stock

- ✕ *1 leftover ham bone, with most (but not all) meat removed*
- ✕ *3 bay leaves*
- ✕ *3 stalks celery*
- ✕ *2 carrots, chopped*
- ✕ *1 large onion, chopped*

Soup Fixings

- ✕ *2 cups ham, cubed into bite-size pieces*
- ✕ *1 cup dried split yellow peas, cleaned*
- ✕ *2 cups grated carrots (about 3 large carrots)*
- ✕ *¼ cup pearl barley*
- ✕ *1 tablespoon olive oil*
- ✕ *1 large onion, minced*
- ✕ *2 stalks celery, minced*
- ✕ *2 cloves garlic, pressed*
- ✕ *½ teaspoon ground white pepper*

Directions

1. In large soup pot, place ham bone and other stock ingredients. Cover with 12 cups water. Bring to boil, then lower heat to simmer for 2 hours.

2. Once stock is ready, remove from heat and strain through kitchen sieve. Top up ham stock with chicken stock (if needed) to make 8 cups.

3. In soup pot, place oil, onion, celery and garlic. Sauté until onions are translucent. Add stock and all other ingredients except pepper and ham. Bring to boil, then reduce heat to simmer.

4. Simmer soup for 1—2 hours, or until peas break down and soup becomes creamy. Add ham and pepper now, then simmer for 10 minutes longer. Serve hot.

Beef Barley Soup

SERVES: 4 | *METHOD: BOIL* | *APPROX. TIME: 1 HOUR* | *DIFFICULTY: EASY*

I love beef barley soup. I've kept the knowledge of its making on hand for decades now, especially after one incident in my trucking days, when I stopped during a long drive down from the Yukon into one Husky truck stop in Dawson Creek. The truck stop shall remain nameless. In fact, I don't think it had a name. I sat down and was initially overjoyed to see that the house special was beef barley soup. The waitress came over rather grudgingly, not sharing my excitement in the least. This was my first hint that a Bad Food Experience (BFE) was on its way, but am I good at taking hints?

When the soup arrived, I dug in with gusto, and immediately my swallower went into overdrive reverse. The causes of my gustatory upheaval? Broth devoid of substance, smell, flavour or even temperature. Cubes of grey SPAM-like matter posing as beef. And worst of all: no barley in the beef barley soup.

When I left the diner, I told the waitress that the shittiest soup on Earth, in combination with her bovine features, had put me in danger of never eating again. Of course this was a lie—I immediately went to the KFC down the road and cried out my rage into a pile of tasty sodium slop. Colonel Sanders might not make for a Michelin-starred restaurant, but at least he doesn't cook with SPAM.

Ingredients

- 8 cups beef stock or broth
- 1 tablespoon olive oil
- 1 large carrot, chopped
- 1 large celery stalk, chopped
- 1 large onion, chopped
- 2 cloves garlic, pressed
- 2 cups cooked beef, cut into 1" cubes
- ½ teaspoon basil
- 1 teaspoon parsley
- 1 tablespoon tomato paste
- ¾ cup pot barley
- Salt and pepper to taste

Directions

1 Heat olive oil in 4-quart soup pot over medium heat. Add carrot, onion, garlic and celery. Sauté until vegetables are soft.

2 Add remaining ingredients and bring to boil. Reduce heat to simmer and cover. Simmer for at least an hour, or until barley is soft and trebled in size.

3 Serve hot.

Minestrone Soup

SERVES: **8** | *METHOD:* **BOIL** | *APPROX. TIME:* **45 MINUTES** | *DIFFICULTY:* **EASY**

When Susan makes soup, this is her go-to. She lifted it from a cookbook long ago—I was never able to find the exact source ever again. But we've sworn by this minestrone for years. Especially when the temperature outside is 40 below, which it always is in this frosty hell we've chosen for ourselves.

Ingredients

- 2 tablespoons olive oil
- ½ lb. Italian Sausage
- 1 large onion, minced
- 2 cloves garlic, pressed
- ½ cup celery, minced
- ½ cup carrots, minced
- ½ cup red bell pepper, minced
- 2 tablespoons parsley
- ½ teaspoon basil
- ¼ teaspoon thyme
- 1 can chopped tomatoes (19 oz.)
- 6 cups chicken stock
- 2 cups shredded cabbage
- 1 can kidney beans (red or white)
- ½ cup pasta of choice
- ½ cup Parmesan cheese, grated

Directions

1   Heat oil in heavy-bottomed soup pot. Add onions, Italian sausage, garlic, celery, carrots and red pepper. Sauté until onions are translucent.

2   Add parsley, basil and thyme. Once spices are incorporated, add tomatoes, chicken stock and cabbage. Bring to a boil, reduce heat, cover and simmer for 10 minutes.

3   Now add beans and pasta. Bring back to boil, then reduce to simmer for 30 minutes.

4   Serve hot with sprinkle of Parmesan cheese.

Lobster Bisque

SERVES: 6 | *METHOD: BOIL* | *APPROX. TIME: 1½ HOURS* | *DIFFICULTY: MEDIUM*

This is so yummy I can't describe it—just make some and taste for yourself. You may want to splash a little more sherry once it's been thickened and simmer for 5 minutes longer. More sherry makes everything better. Including the writing of this book!

Ingredients

- 2 whole lobsters
  OR
  2 lbs. whole shrimp, peeled and deveined
- 2 tablespoons olive oil
- ¼ cup tomato paste
- 1 onion, sliced
- 1 large celery stalk, sliced
- 1 small carrot, sliced
- 1 garlic head, cut in half crosswise
- 1 tomato, sliced
- 2 tablespoons chopped fresh tarragon
- 2 tablespoons chopped fresh thyme
- 2 bay leaves
- 8 whole black peppercorns
- ½ cup brandy
- ½ cup dry sherry
- 8 cups fish stock
  OR
  8 cups bottled clam juice
  OR
  8 cups lobster base
- ½ cup whipping cream
- ¼ cup butter
- 4 tablespoons all purpose flour

Directions

1. Peel, devein and chop shrimp into bite-sized pieces if necessary. If using lobster, cook as you like and separate meat from shells.

2. Heat olive oil in heavy large pot over high heat. Add lobster or shrimp shells, tomato paste and sauté until shells just begin to brown, about 8 minutes.

3. Add onion, veggies and herbs. Add brandy and sherry, then simmer until liquid has reduced by half, about 2—4 minutes.

4. Add seafood stock of your choice. Simmer 1 hour over low heat, then remove from heat and let cool to room temperature.

5. Strain soup through sieve or cheesecloth over large bowl, pressing firmly on solids to drain completely. Top up with water or fish stock (if needed) to make 8 cups. Add cream to soup stock and set aside.

6. In 4-quart pot, melt butter and add flour. Whisk over medium heat until it begins turning light brown.

7. Add stock and cream mixture, stirring constantly. Bring mixture to near boil. Turn down heat and let simmer gently for 5 minutes.

8. Add meat to serving bowls in portions and ladle soup overtop. Serve!

Pho

SERVES: *8* | METHOD: *BOIL* | APPROX. TIME: *ETERNITY* | DIFFICULTY: *MEDIUM*

Pho is a staple in my kitchen. All the kids love it, as does Susan. They would willingly forego burgers, pizza, fried chicken and most any other fast food for a meal of pho, and I never tried to sway them—except when I was having KFC cravings, in which case I always won that debate handily.

In any civilized society, and even Whitehorse, there are Vietnamese restaurants serving pho, so finding a good one shouldn't be difficult. Once you try a restaurant version, you'll want to learn the culinary secret. This recipe is, if not the most authentic you can get, a very tasty place to start.

But don't blame me if you end up so addicted that the cops catch you licking the windows of a Vietnamese restaurant after closing hours. I already had enough grief bailing my son out of jail.

Soup Broth

✕ *3 pounds beef soup bones*

✕ *1 onion*

✕ *4 celery stalks*

✕ *2 carrots, chopped*

✕ *1 tablespoon peppercorns*

✕ *1 tablespoon salt*

✕ *10 cups water*

Broth Directions

1. Spread bones and veggies evenly in baking sheet and place in preheated 400° oven for 1 hour, or until bones turn deep brown.

2. Place roasted vegetables and bones into water with peppercorns and salt. Bring to near-boil on high, then reduce to a simmer for 2 hours. Don't allow to boil!

3. Skim gunk and foam from surface as it rises.

4. After the 2 hours, cool broth, remove solids and strain liquid through cheesecloth. You should end up with about 8 cups of broth. Place in fridge until chilled, then remove solidified fat from surface. You should end up with a beautiful, clear, delicious-smelling broth.

✕ *In the interests of saving time, you may use a store-bought, no-sodium stock such as Western Family or Campbell's. It's not as good, but it's good enough.*

Pho

Soup Base

- 10 whole cloves
- 8 star anise
- 20 coriander seeds
- 1 tablespoon sugar
- 2 tablespoons nuoc mam (Vietnamese fish sauce)

Ingredient Options

- 1 fistful thin rice vermicelli (wheat noodles are a no-go here!)
- ½ cup bean sprouts, rinsed
- ¼ cup green onions, chopped
- 3 sprigs Thai basil, fresh
- 1 stick lemongrass, sliced
- 5 thin slices raw beef, shaved (the soup's heat will cook them)
- ¼ cup cilantro, chopped

Garnish & Dip Options

- Hoisin sauce
- Sriracha hot sauce
- Lemongrass chili paste

Soup Directions

1. Heat heavy frying pan on high until very hot. Remove empty pan from heat and add whole cloves, anise and coriander. Shake pan until spice oils are released and you can smell them vividly.

2. Place spices into square of double-folded cotton cheesecloth (do not use synthetic materials here.) Close cloth by bringing four corners together, then twist and tie with twine to keep closed. You've now made a spice sachet. Easy!

3. Place spice sachet into broth along with your sugar and fish sauce. Simmer broth on low for 1 hour and adjust salt and sweet to taste.

4. Soak one package of thin rice noodles in very hot water for 4 minutes until tender. Drain hot water. If not using immediately, run cooked noodles under cold water to prevent sticking.

5. Place drained noodles into soup bowl. Pour pho over noodles and top with ingredients of your choice.

- *Everything is optional except the noodles, but I recommend you have at least one kind of meat and a green vegetable for a balanced meal. Experiment with this dish and find the combination you like best.*

- *The three garnish options can be utilized separately, combined, or ignored. All of them make great dipping sauce for your noodles or add pizzazz as a light drizzle on top of the soup.*

My Steak's Still Mooing
-or-
Everything About Beef that Isn't Bull

....

How to Butcher Your Bank Account

I like just about every kind of protein on the hoof, fin or feather, but this section is for beef, so I'll stick to that. Care must be exercised when you choose the cuts of beef, so as I may have mentioned elsewhere, your neighbourhood butcher is your best friend here.

I don't use a wide array of cuts, but then, I'm a fussy bastard. I prefer dry-aged beef, if I can get it. In today's world of cheap and ready-made, beef aging has suffered from cost-cutting, so dry-aging has almost gone the way of the dodo bird. Most butchers get their beef pre-cut into smaller pieces called boxed beef, which is sealed in plastic bags to age. This is called wet-cured beef, and it's the cheap, common way to do things.

Dry-aging or dry-curing runs up to 21 days, which concentrates the flavour of the beef. The carcass loses moisture weight as it hangs in the cooler and requires additional trimming, so the butcher needs to charge more by weight. It's money well spent, if you can find anyone who actually sells dry-aged beef.

If you can find the mythical butcher who offers dry-aged beef (preferably grass-fed and natu-rally-raised without hormones or antibiotics), you're truly blessed. Scout all your organic stores, farmer's markets, local butcher shops and upscale grocery stores. Don't bother with a supermarket chain, as the likelihood of finding dry-aged beef there is all but negligible.

If you've made the attempt and still can't find dry-aged beef, don't panic! Boxed beef cuts are perfectly serviceable, but they'll take a little more time and attention. I like to dry-age my supermarket roasts and steaks for a couple days in the fridge before cooking.

How? Simply remove the beef from the package and place over paper towel on a plate. Dry the beef with paper towel, drape a clean dry tea towel over the beef, and refrigerate. Every day, replace the paper towel liner and tea towel with fresh ones. The point is, you must keep the beef as dry as possible to avoid spoilage.

In this manner, you can age a cut for 3 days or even up to 5 depending on your fridge. While this extra aging may seem unnecessary, you'll improve and intensify the flavour of your beef and really wow your guests when it's time to serve.

When cooking a steak or a roast there are just a few tips I can offer. The biggest tip for beef: bigger is better. (I've been told this before, usually accom-panied by a derisive giggle and a sigh, but that's my cross to bear.) A larger cut of beef contains more natural flavour, which will concentrate better with the aging process I've described without going dry.

For roast beef, whether whole or sliced, I prefer rib cuts over the cheaper round or sirloin tip cuts. The latter are great in shepherd's pie, or as slow-cooked roast for a beef dip, but for a sliced roast beef dinner, I use only prime or standing rib roast, AAA and dry-aged. It's worth the money and the time spent searching.

If I'm grilling a steak without a liquid marinade, I prefer tenderloin, t-bone or Delmonico cuts (especially ribeye). For 24-hour marinated steak, sirloin, chuck or blade steaks, trimmed of as much fat as possible, are all excellent and slightly cheaper. For any steak recipe to turn out well, always select steaks with a minimum thickness of 1½".

As a rule, I cook all steaks and roasts to medium-rare, unless there's a boor or certain President of the USA in the crowd who demands a tasteless, burnt meat effigy instead. For civilized palates, medium-rare is perfection—a tasty and juicy treat.

The only way to ensure this perfection is by using a thermometer. I use an instant-read for steaks and a probe-type for roasts. You should have both; they'll save you countless hours of heartache. I cook the steaks or roasts to an internal 130°, then remove from the heat and let rest. I let roasts rest for a ½-hour minimum, so the inner and outer temperatures balance to a medium-rare 140°—145°.

Be careful in the kitchen to ensure that your steak is the only thing bleeding on the counter. Don't cook after drinking a dozen beers, or a couple bottles of wine, or three-quarters of a bottle of Jameson. Save the liquor binge until after cooking, like I do... sometimes.

So in recapping this section:

✕ *Dry-aged beef is best.*

✕ *Pay attention and don't take shortcuts.*

✕ *Beef is expensive even when it's cheap.*

✕ *Cook roasts and steaks to medium-rare only.*

✕ *Invest a good thermometer or two.*

✕ *A good butcher is good to find and support.*

✕ *Cows don't share my passion for beef.*

✕ *Kelsey likes beef... somewhat.*

Roast Beef

There's no mystery to cooking great roast beef, just a little black magic. The only way a roast beef can go horribly wrong is if you weren't paying attention. I've messed up a few in my time—my attention span is worse than a... I forgot what I was talking about.

Good roast beef begins with a good cut. I prefer prime rib, especially cut from the small end—the loin end. Make sure the chine bone (backbone) is removed. You probably won't have to ask for this because a good butcher removes it before you buy it. I like at least a minimum of 4 ribs, but 6 is better. The bigger the roast, the better it cooks and tastes and, of course, the more of it you have to eat.

Remove your dry-aged roast (I told you how to dry-age already) from the fridge, replace the paper towel and tea towel again, and let sit for a couple hours until it reaches room temperature.

Preheat oven to 450°. As the oven heats, season the beef with a dry rub of salt, pepper, garlic powder, onion powder, mustard powder, and tarragon or rosemary.

Place beef in roasting pan with the arc facing up, so the roast stands on the rib bones like little feet. Surround your lonely roast with minced onion, carrots, garlic and celery (this will give you great gravy drippings for later). Now insert an oven-proof thermometer into the roast and set the alarm for 130°. Insert the probe only from the top, and only into the middle of the roast, not all the way through.

Cook at 450° for 15 minutes, then turn down heat to 225°. To cook evenly with constant heat, avoid opening the oven door at any point until the temperature has fallen to 225°.

When the meat's inner temperature reaches 130°, remove the roast from the oven. Remove the temperature probe, then place the roast on a platter and cover it with aluminum foil. Let stand for a minimum of 30 minutes or longer. As the roast rests, the inner temperature will continue to rise another 10° and finish at a nice medium-rare 140°. Perfection!

Slice and serve with mashed potatoes seasoned with truffle oil and of course Yorkshire pudding. See my recipe elsewhere in the book.

If your timing is off and your roast is ready too early, don't worry. Just let it rest about ½ hour, then return to the oven at 160° to hold it briefly. Just don't leave it too long—the difference between 140° and 160° is the difference between tasty medium-rare and a grey, overcooked meat brick.

The time needed to cook varies with the accuracy of the oven and the room temperature of the roast. As a rule, cooking a 4-rib roast (6 pounds or so) will take about 2½ hours. A larger one will take longer. A rule of thumb is to cook for about 15 minutes per pound, but don't bet your dinner on it.

Steaks

By now you know how how to select the right steak and dry-age it in preparation. Now it's time to cook up.

Place steaks on a tray for 1 hour prior to barbequing. Let internal temperature rise to a minimum of 50°, although 60° (the lower end of room temperature) is better.

Once steaks are dried and warmed, season with your favourite dry rub. You can't go wrong with simple salt and pepper, but dry rub is an entire art unto itself and worth digging deep into.

Preheat your barbeque using a high flame. Place the steaks on the grill and let them cook undisturbed for 3 minutes (use a timer!). At the 3-minute mark, turn the steaks over and grill another 3 minutes. You can baste with barbeque sauce at this point.

Don't turn steaks over more than once, and don't cut the meat open or poke with a fork to check its colour or doneness. If the steak was cold, or if it's thinner or thicker than ideal, cooking time will vary. If you're not a steak expert, use an instant thermometer to get the right results, like a civilized person!

Tri-Tip Steak

My favourite cut of steak is tri-tip, known also as bottom sirloin or triangle steak. It's hard to find in Canada, but worth looking for. When I barbeque tri-tip, I remove as much of the fat as I can, then sprinkle a liberal amount of Montreal steak spice and let sit at room temperature for 1 hour before cooking.

Cooked to medium-rare at most, tri-tip is a wonderful, juicy and flavourful cut as you can find. If your palate insists upon well-done, near-cremated steak, then disregard this advice, don't bother with tri-tip at all, and go back to eating the raccoon you ran over.

Just before serving, slice tri-tip thinly across the grain and place on a serving tray with steep sides to prevent the liquid from this juicy steak from ruining your carpet.

Experienced cooks can gauge a fairly accurate temperature by pressing gently on the flank with the back of a fork to check its firmness. However, this takes years of practice and trained Jedi powers. You know what? No. You are too old to begin the training. Just use a thermometer.

At the 6-minute point, check the temperature. Once it reaches 130°, remove steaks from the grill and place on a platter. Cover with foil and let rest for 5—10 minutes before serving. Cooling will allow a steak's juices to 'lock in' or solidify and prevent bleeding when it's sliced.

Once it's ready, plate the steak and brush with a little bit of melted butter to finish it off. This little trick is one of the biggest reasons the steak you serve at home, even if properly grilled, never tastes the same as the ones at the steakhouse. Expert steak chefs will layer their butter finish with a secret house seasoning and barbeque sauce as well.

Follow my instructions and you'll be rewarded with a legendary steak, worthy of serving to your closest friends. Or to me! Yes. Please feed me

Korean Barbeque Beef (Galbi)

SERVES: 4 | *METHOD: SAUTÉ* | *APPROX. TIME: 24 HOURS* | *DIFFICULTY: EASY*

In galbi (kalbi), the traditional cut of beef to use is thin sliced short ribs, alternately called kalbi cut, Maui cut or Korean cut. They're expensive cuts, doubly so when you realize you can't eat the bone. I spied these cuts one day as I was traipsing through Costco. Intrigued, I took them home and then wondered what I could do with them.

This was the delicious result, probably my favourite barbeque recipe. Even the non-beef-eater in the house likes them and that's saying a lot. Galbi is best if the meat's marinated at least overnight, up to 24 hours, and drained very well before grilling.

Special Equipment

- Food processor
- Barbeque

Ingredients

- 3 lbs. beef short rib, sliced no thicker than ¼"
- 1 cup brown sugar, firmly packed
- 1 cup soy sauce
- ½ cup water
- ¼ cup mirin
- 1 medium onion, peeled
- 1 medium apple, peeled and core removed
- 1 kiwi fruit, peeled (for meat tenderizing)
  OR
  1 teaspoon baking soda
- 4 cloves fresh garlic
- ¼ cup sesame oil
- ½ teaspoon black pepper

Directions

1. Place onion, garlic, apple, and kiwi (if using) into a food processor and pulse until a fine mince or puree is reached.

2. Pour into large steel bowl. Add remaining ingredients and stir well to incorporate.

3. Add sliced beef to marinade.Cover and refrigerate for 12—24 hours.

4. Remove beef from marinade and let drain well

5. Place marinated beef onto a hot grill and cook until medium-rare and nicely browned, about 1—2 minutes per side.

6. Remove from grill and serve hot.

7. If serving as an appetizer, slice thinly and serve with lettuce leaves for a lettuce wrap. See my lettuce wrap recipe for more ideas..

Beef Goulash

SERVES: **4–5** | *METHOD:* **SAUTÉ & BAKE** | *APPROX. TIME:* **2 HOURS** | *DIFFICULTY:* **MEDIUM**

Ingredients

- 2 pounds stewing beef
- 4 tablespoons olive oil
- 2 tablespoons butter
- 1 teaspoon salt
- 1 teaspoon ground pepper
- 1 large onion, chopped finely
- 2—3 cloves garlic, chopped finely
- 1 red pepper, chopped finely
- 2 tablespoons flour
- 4 tablespoons paprika
- 2 bay leaves
- 1 tablespoon marjoram
- 2 teaspoons sugar
- 1 quart beef broth
- 2 tablespoons tomato paste
- Salt and pepper to taste

Best Served With

 Spaetzle

Directions

Chicken can be substituted for beef for a change of pace.

1   Preheat oven to 300°.

2   Preheat heavy-bottom braising or sauté pan over medium-high heat. Mix flour, salt and pepper together. Dredge meat in mix, remove and shake off excess.

3   Add oil to pan, then meat. Brown on all sides (you may want to do this in batches). Once brown, remove meat and keep warm.

4   Add butter, onion, red pepper and garlic to pan. Cook about 2 minutes, then add flour and cook slowly for 3–4 minutes.

5   Add remaining ingredients, starting with paprika and finishing with beef stock. Stir until smooth, then add browned beef. Bring it to boil, then remove from stovetop.

6   Place pan in 300° oven, covered, for about 1½ hours, or until tender. Stir goulash occasionally so it doesn't stick or burn. Skim off oil that rises to the top while cooking and discard.

7   Serve with egg noodles or better yet, spaetzle!

Tourtière

SERVES: 8 | *METHOD: BAKE* | *APPROX. TIME: 2½ HOURS* | *DIFFICULTY: MEDIUM*

Ingredients

- 3 medium potatoes, cubed (about 2 cups)
- 1 pound lean ground pork
- 1 pound lean ground beef or veal
- 1 large onion, minced
- 3 stalks celery, minced (about ¾ cup)
- 2 large carrots, minced
- 3 cups chicken stock
- 3 tablespoons fine dry sherry (more is okay too!)
- 4 cloves garlic, minced
- ¾ teaspoon salt
- ½ teaspoon each:
  - Black pepper
  - Savory
  - Sage
  - Thyme
- ¼ teaspoon each:
  - Nutmeg
  - Cloves
  - Cinnamon
- 3 bay leaves
- 1 egg yolk, beaten with 2 tablespoons water
- Pastry for 1 deep-dish pie

Directions

1. Boil potatoes until tender, about 10—12 minutes. Drain and mash, adding optional butter or flavours to your taste. Set aside.

2. In deep non-stick skillet, sauté pork and beef over medium-high heat for 10—12 minutes until browned. Add celery, onions, carrots and garlic. Sauté for 5 minutes.

3. Add chicken stock, sherry, salt, pepper, savory, thyme, sage, nutmeg, cloves, cinnamon and bay leaves. Bring to boil, then reduce heat. Simmer about 25 minutes until most liquid of the liquid cooks off, then remove from heat. Be sure to remove bay leaves!

4. Mix in potatoes and stir well to incorporate evenly. Let cool for ½ hour.

5. On lightly floured surface, roll out pastry dough to make 2 rounds, each ¼" thick. From here, form standard pie crusts. If you don't know how to do that, look it up.

6. Decorate pie top with shapes made of leftover dough, if you like.

7. Brush pie top with egg wash. Cut slits into top to let steam escape, then place pastry decorations onto pie top and finish by brushing with egg wash.

8. Place into preheated 400° oven and bake until hot and golden brown, about 50—60 minutes.

9. Remove from oven and let stand 10 minutes before serving.

Beef Stroganoff

SERVES: 4 | *METHOD: SAUTÉ* | *APPROX. TIME: 30 MINUTES* | *DIFFICULTY: EASY*

This is comfort food, plain and simple. A favourite of mine as a child, and remains so as I've become a potbellied old fart. (You can substitute plain yogurt for sour cream to avoid my potbellied fate.) Kristine and Susan love Stroganoff, as do I, but Jordan and Kaitlyn hate it because of the mushrooms and Kelsey is ambivalent because she thinks she doesn't like beef. However, it's actually illegal to make Stroganoff without mushrooms, and as you know, I'm a law-abiding citizen whenever it feels convenient.

Ingredients

- 1 tablespoon olive oil
- 4 tablespoons clarified butter
- 1 large onion, minced finely
- 3 cloves garlic, pressed
- 1 cup fresh mushrooms, sliced
- 1 cup flour
- 1 tablespoon salt
- 2 teaspoons ground pepper
- 2 lbs. beef tenderloin or sirloin (you must use a tender cut of beef)
- 2 cups beef stock
- ¼ cup dry sherry
- 1 cup sour cream
- 2 tablespoons parsley
- ½ teaspoon tarragon
- ½ teaspoon Hungarian hot paprika
- Salt and pepper to taste

Best Served With

 Spaetzle

Directions

1   Season flour with salt and pepper. Mix well.

2   Slice beef thinly across the grain. Place seasoned flour in bowl, then add beef slices and toss with your hands until well coated. Remove beef from flour and shake off excess.

3   Heat ½ your butter in large frying pan over medium-high heat. Fry onions and garlic until translucent. Add mushrooms and fry until they begin to soften, 2—3 minutes. Remove everything from pan and set aside.

4   Add remaining butter and oil to pan and heat until nearly smoking. Add steak in batches, sautéeing quickly over high heat until browned on all sides, 3—4 minutes each batch. Once beef is brown, add all batches back to pan.

5   Return onions and mushrooms to pan, and stir gently to mix with meat. Add beef stock, sherry, parsley, tarragon, salt and pepper. Cook while stirring occasionally until sauce is thickened and simmering, then add sour cream and cook for 2—3 minutes longer.

6   Serve over buttered egg noodles or spaetzle.

Beef Vindaloo

SERVES: *4* | METHOD: *SAUTÉ & SIMMER* | APPROX. TIME: *2 HOURS* | DIFFICULTY: *TRIVIAL*

Special Equipment

- Blender

Ingredients

- 2 lbs beef
- 3 tablespoons grapeseed oil
- 1 medium onion, chopped
- 4—6 cloves garlic
- 1 tablespoon fresh ginger, minced
- ½ cup red or white wine
- 1 tablespoon turmeric
- 2 tablespoons cumin
- 1 tablespoon coriander
- 6 cloves ground to fine powder (½ teaspoon or so)
- 2 jalapenos, seeds removed
- 1 tablespoon chili powder
- 1 teaspoon dry mustard
- 2—4 cups beef stock, enough to cover mixture
- 3 tablespoons tomato paste
- 1—2 tablespoons sugar to taste
- ½ teaspoon salt to taste

Best Served With

 Naan

Preparation

1   Blend onion and garlic in blender. Add all dry spices, vinegar and ginger, then blend further to make thick and stiff paste for marinade.

2   Remove seeds from jalapenos for a mild recipe. Leave them in if you like pain.

3   Cut beef into 1" cubes and pat dry. Put meat in bowl and coat with spice paste. Marinate for 2 hours, or overnight.

Directions

4   Heat oil in heavy-bottom deep pot over medium-high heat. Remove beef from marinade with slotted spoon, then add beef to hot oil and cook until well browned. Add beef stock, remaining marinade, sugar and tomato paste.

5   Cover pot and simmer over low heat until beef is tender (about 1—1 ½ hours).

6   Serve hot with basmati rice and/or fresh naan.

Braised Beef Short Ribs

SERVES: 8 | *METHOD: SAUTÉ & BAKE* | *APPROX. TIME: 2½ HOURS* | *DIFFICULTY: EASY*

This is one of the all-time favourite meals from my youth. I make this often and the older I get, the more comforting it becomes. I like to use oxtail in place of short ribs. No one else in my home shares my love of oxtail, but one day I'll make them see. One day. And then who'll be the bovine's ass, I ask you?

Ingredients

- 6—8 pieces beef short ribs, bone-in (2 lbs.)
- ¼ cup flour
- 1 teaspoon salt
- 1 teaspoon ground black pepper
- ½ teaspoon mustard powder
- 2 tablespoons vegetable oil
- 4 medium carrots, diced
- 2 stalks celery, diced
- 1 large onion, diced
- 4 cloves garlic, pressed
- 4 cups beef stock
- 1 tablespoon parsley
- 1 teaspoon thyme
- ½ teaspoon tarragon
- 2 bay leaves
- Salt and pepper to taste
- 340g broad egg noodles (1 package)
- 2 cups frozen corn

Directions

1. Mix flour, salt, black pepper and mustard powder into seasoning. Preheat oven to 325°.

2. Pat beef dry and dredge in seasoned flour, shaking off excess.

3. Heat oil over medium-high heat in heavy-bottomed, oven-safe pot (ensure it has a tight-fitting lid) and brown beef on all sides, then remove from pan and set aside.

4. Reduce heat to medium and use empty pan to sauté carrots, celery, garlic and onion about 5 minutes, until onion is translucent. Add beef stock, thyme, parsley, tarragon, bay leaves and bring to boil, then remove from heat.

5. Return beef to pot with other ingredients, cover and place in oven. Cook short ribs for 2 hours, or until meat is tender and pulls easily from bones, then remove pot from oven. Remove beef from liquid and place in large serving bowl to cool.

6. Add egg noodles and frozen corn to sauce and simmer at low-medium heat, stirring occasionally until noodles are cooked al dente. If liquid reaches low level, add water or chicken stock to top up.

7. Once noodles are cooked, plate up with beef, sprinkle with freshly ground pepper and serve hot.

Land of the Rising Dumb
-or-
This Story's a Lot Abalone

In November 2008, I was employed by a Sumitomo-owned firm which distributed Komatsu equipment in Canada. I ended up being part of a group that traveled to Japan for a week to tour Komatsu factories and meet with various company representatives. In this group I was the senior employee. We were joined by a Komatsu America representative, another senior manager named Gary, and seven clients or their reps. It was a great group to travel with, and many laughs and fond memories were created—many because of the food.

I participated in martial arts for years as a kid, and had exposure to Japanese food and culture through living in Vancouver. I knew how wonderful Japanese food could be, but I didn't expect Japan to be such a food-crazed country. They take food very, very seriously, and the service and presentation are art forms in the extreme.

Our entire group was wonderfully shocked by the food, along with the delightful people, the architecture, the cleanliness, the organization... I fell in love with the nation. I hope to return there one day, and when I do, I'll bring Susan to show her in person what I've been raving insufferably about all these years.

I knew we were in for a great trip as we all gathered In Vancouver the evening before the flight. A welcome dinner was organized at Gotham's Steakhouse, where great steaks and fine wine and liqueur were in abundance, along with sick jokes and fits of hysterical laughter, often at someone's expense. Male bonding is best done this way, over steak and liquor. (Female bonding too, I hear.)

Once aboard the Japan Airlines 747, we luxuriated in first class, watching TV, sipping cocktails and eating damn good food. We were also able to walk around to keep the blood flowing, and so lounged around a bulkhead that offered Japanese snacks and a place to set our drinks. At one point, inspecting the snack offerings, I picked up a package containing a dried seafood thingy. I think it was dried squid, but I'm not altogether sure.

With great wisdom and maturity, I commented to the guys in the group, "That looks like foreskin!" to which one of the guys standing there replied, "Funny, it doesn't taste like foreskin."

The trip remained at that level for the duration. Men, liquor and free time; a dangerous combination.

We spent a night on a private floating restaurant and karaoke bar, slowly touring Tokyo Bay and gazing at the rise of downtown Tokyo as its dramatic architecture illuminated the night sky, casting spiritually warming reflections on the water. As the nighttime panorama unfolded, we dined on sushi, sashimi, tempura and other delicacies too numerous to name. With enough liquor to instill courage, we fired up the karaoke machine began and a full-frontal assault on the sensibilities of God and man. What a night— and not a singer in the bunch, except for Sam.

We ate world-class Italian food, some of the best Chinese food I've ever sampled, and fantastic steaks. But the Japanese food! Oh my God! I will savour the memories till the day I die. Teriyaki, shabu-shabu, seafood, tempura, every variety of rice, and my favourite discovery: Japanese curry. The recipe in this book is my recreation of a wonderful curry dish I enjoyed at the Hotel Okura in Tokyo. I had to find and tailor a recipe to honour that memory and the hotel chef who made it possible.

One evening Sumitomo organized a dinner at the Seryna Restaurant. Seryna is a shabu-shabu restaurant, the word meaning "swish-swish." You're served thinly-sliced meats along with seafood and veggies, and essentially you swish the food, fondue-style, in a pot full of hot broth until the item is cooked to your liking. Simple and utterly delicious. Utterly expensive too, but worth every yen—and it was the company's yen, not mine.

The restaurant is on the top floor of the Sumitomo Building in Tokyo, overlooking Tokyo Bay, and I'm not ashamed to say it was an emotion-triggering view. The table was impressive, set up for fourteen of us opposite each other in two rows of seven, with each duo sharing a hot pot between. On my side was our evening's host, Mr. Ishida, a senior Sumitomo executive. Mr. Ishida is a very bright and well-spoken man who spent time in Canada, and his English is top notch. Across from Mr. Ishida sat Gary, a senior manager with Sumitomo (a very bright and funny man).

In this formal setting, as each dish was served, all diners would wait to ensure all others were served before beginning to enjoy theirs. Once the last person received their dish, the rest of us would begin to eat—all together now, an' a one, an' a two, an' a three! Each serving was small, but aesthetically arranged and professionally served, and they kept coming and coming and coming.

Maybe three servings in, I received a little cup about the size of a shot glass, arranged within an artistic tableau and containing a small morsel. Up to this point I'd only been spoiled by the offerings, so I immediately dug in with my chopsticks. But as I bit down on the thing, the It, my internal "This is not going to end well!" alarm went off. I decided that chewing It would only prolong the unpleasantness, but when I tried to swallow it whole, It was not interested in being swallowed. No, It

crawled back up my gullet to be chewed some more, resisting with tenacious force. I began to sweat.

My mind was yelling, "Be still, uvula, be still!" but my uvula had contrarian ideas. Struggling, I imagined myself on the verge of an international and potentially career-limiting dining faux pas. I was in trouble. As I fought this internal battle, I glanced across the table at my shabu-shabu dining co-pilot. I didn't know him well, but as our eyes met, I suddenly knew him deeply—he was having the exact same internal gustatory conflict as I was.

As is the norm where plenty of liquor has been consumed and death seems imminent, combatants bond as one to take on the enemy, and laugh as they head to their last stand. And laugh he did—beginning with an involuntary "Oh fuck!" smile, which became snickers and then stifled yelps of mirth. Respecting the dignity of the environment and our host, we tried to keep our outburst to a silent Marcel Marceau type of laugh, but that was a losing battle also.

I glanced at Gary, who was chatting with Mr. Ishida while struggling with the "It" bobbing in his own gullet. When he observed my tear-streaked face, he gave me a look that said, "You prick! Do you know what you've done now?" Being professionals, we pushed on with our masticating efforts and finally managed swallow our Its in unison.

As we sat shaking, we reached for our sake cups and took shots, then seconds and thirds, not so much in celebration as in abject relief. We stared at our empty It cups, waiting for them to be replaced with something easier to swallow. We waited in vain.

Our kimono-clad server returned with a new course. Another white cup, inside an artful presentation of veggies and greenery—it looked eerily familiar. Another critter, or piece of critter? Another Thing that could neither be identified, reasoned with, or swallowed? Hope is indeed the last refuge of the doomed, and my only hope was to survive the evening without covering Mr. Ishida in projectile vomit.

I politely waited for Gary, who was the first to place It: The Sequel in his mouth. He didn't die, so I followed in turn, as did my fearless tablemate across from me, and then the others. However, Gary had betrayed us all. The texture of It: The Sequel was soft, almost squishy. Vaguely fishy, certainly ocean-sourced. Gelatinous and wiggly. *Probably* dead, for had It been otherwise, our dining party would've produced a cacophony not heard since the Donner Party sat for dinner in the snow bank. Frankly, I was beginning to envy the Donners— at least they'd known what they were eating.

Initially, I blithely clamped down on the critter. I tried to maintain a calm look on my face, although my companions later told me I looked like I was facing a hangman's noose. My brain sensed that It: The Sequel was not to its liking and put my jaw into the feared "mandible lock" position. In my mind I pictured all manner of unpleasantness, from ruining the cauldron of broth in front of me, to sudden unemployment, to endless shame and ridicule and possibly hara-kiri. Two questions flashed through my mind: "Do these windows open?" and "Will my life insurance pay out if they do?"

We were diligent men, but what we needed wasn't diligence—it was help from above. I invoked God's grace to help me get though, and for an agnostic that's saying something. The Lord granted me Providence and began to calm my internal conflict... for precisely two seconds, until I looked at Gary. My stifled laughter became full blown guffaws, my tablemate following suit, and finally Gary himself. This caused Mr. Ishida to look our way and smile politely at the joke he evidently didn't get.

By this point my stomach cramps forced me from the table a moment. I looked back at Gary to see how he was faring, I then had to look away again. Looked again. Turned away. Looked across. Turned away. Looked again. Things got worse. The wave of hysteria put me into a full blown body freeze. I doubled over in pain, my stomach locking up like a Charlie horse. Gary was now on the horns of a dilemma: did he risk unemployment from laughing, or a collapsed diaphragm from keeping it in? He chose to let it go, and this finished the three of us off completely. Gasping. Coughing. Laughing. Wheezing. Laughing. And crying! We cried like eunuchs in a whorehouse.

Mr. Ishida simply smiled. If this had been a test of decorum, we had blown it completely, but when is war ever decorous? The important

Traditional Japanese abalone divers. My trauma was ultimately their fault, but somehow I just can't stay mad at them.

thing was, we had fought It and It: The Sequel to a satisfactory conclusion, together as one.

The next evening we found ourselves at a seaside spa south of Tokyo. We'd ridden the bullet train at 220 miles per hour (a true Bucket List journey), then boarded a small private coach to get us to the resort. After settling into our appointed rooms we gathered on *tatami* (woven straw) mats in a private room, now dressed in our own kimonos, "camel toe" socks and wooden sandals. Yes, Western tourists wearing socks and sandals—the Japanese made us do it, I swear!

We each had our own table and side table with dishes, a tea cup, tea pot, assorted utensils and chopsticks. One the side table sat two pots, both atop cans of alcohol fuel (as I wondered when my own alcohol fuel would arrive). One pot we determined to contain rice and water to be cooked, but we were clueless about the other: it was larger, with a tight-fitting glass lid. We all ventured a guess or two, until finally one of us noticed that his pot's contents seemed to be moving.

We then all looked down through our glass lids. I was shocked to see my dinner was moving also, even clinging to the underside of the glass lid. Now began a guessing game called "Name That Creature." Our companion Mike finally broke the dam of propriety and said, "I don't know what it is, but I've named mine Spot."

I didn't know this until later, but we were participating in *odoriyaki*, or roughly translated, "Dancing Cooking." Other than anthropomorphizing our intended dinners by naming them Spot, Thing and Alice, we could not describe what we were looking at. Not in gentlemanly terms, at least. And am I a gentleman? No.

So I'll lay it out straight: they looked like vulvas. Very large ones, greyish and oyster-like, with enough muscle control to allow the 'lips' to grasp glass. What kind of Kegel exercises could allow such a thing? Once we noticed this uncanny resemblance, we were stuck for any further profound or pithy observations. We could only sit in Freudian silence, wondering what would be asked of us next.

Luckily the servers for the meal were all women in kimonos, beautiful and attentive. No sooner had one of us emptied our sake cup when one of these lovely ladies would magick a new one out of thin air. Not wanting to offend our hosts by refusing their hospitality (because we were nothing if not polite guests) we guzzled sake by the gallon.

While we drank, we offered up more suggestions of what It was, and what we each would do with our Its when it came time to do what It required of us. Frankly, you really had to be there, and you really had to drink a lot. I will not wax vulgar any further, but it was funny stuff. Very, very funny. Man stuff. Funny man stuff.

Our attendants came by with long matches to light the burners beneath the rice pots. After a number of delicious courses, by which time the rice was ready, our faithful attendants reappeared and lit the burners beneath our wiggling and clinging acquaintances.

This is when things got disturbing. As the pot heated, Spot, Thing, Alice and the other doomed critters began to squirm and wiggle like drunk white guys at a disco (I'm very familiar with these moves). We all watched with misgivings as our individual dinners meet their demises. Certainly it was a cruel way to go, though the rising steam brought with it a pleasant seafood smell that made us salivate, however guiltily.

Then with theatrical aplomb our attendants re-emerged to kneel in front of each of us. No, it's not what you think. Wielding long slender forks and knives, they moved the lifeless creatures from our pots to wooden cutting blocks, removed the meat from the shells (they had shells, who knew?) and sliced them into bite-sized pieces.

We learned that the critters were abalone, a type of sea snail with a clam-like shell and a powerful, labia-like muscle. I had eaten them (abalone, I mean) as part of a Chinese dinners before, but I'd never seen one whole, much less alive.

The other guys looked more confused than I did, sitting quietly in apparent dread. But having some familiarity with abalone, I dug into mine and finished it off in short order. My companions on both sides passed on their servings, so I ate theirs also. And despite the psychological trauma, they were delicious.

We decided that the best way to remove the disturbing images from our minds was to drink more sake. After a round of drinking games (Japanese folks love good booze just like us Canucks) a geisha performance began. Now, for many people when they hear geisha, they think escort or prostitute, but the geisha is not that at all. They're hostesses, trained in the art of conversation, dance and song. To entertain us, one geisha began to dance and sing while an older performer strummed a single-stringed instrument as accompaniment.

Traditional Japanese music is an acquired taste. To this day I have not acquired it. I'm used to western music, and even in that realm, Pink Floyd is about as adventurous as I get. It seemed to me that the plucking of the single string was a random act intended to put the singer off balance vocally and physically, and if that was the intent, it succeeded.

Throughout the performance, our guide described the intended meaning of the dance and the lyrics, and named the guitar thingy as an *ichigenkin*. He also informed us that the ichigenkin is strung with cat gut, to which Gary shouted, "Finally! Someone found a good use for a cat!"

Nowadays, having traveled a little and sampled the foods of far-flung cultures, I have a fond admiration for those on television who make their living doing just that. No one did it better than Anthony Bourdain (RIP). We'll live vicariously through Anthony's exploits for a long time to come, and I've seen him eat things that would normally be sent to the compost heap. When I watch an episode where Bourdain eats some deep-fried pig anuses or some unidentifiable thing in some Asian location, I ask myself, "I wonder if I could do that?"

Sometimes the answer is, "Oh, that's right—I did."

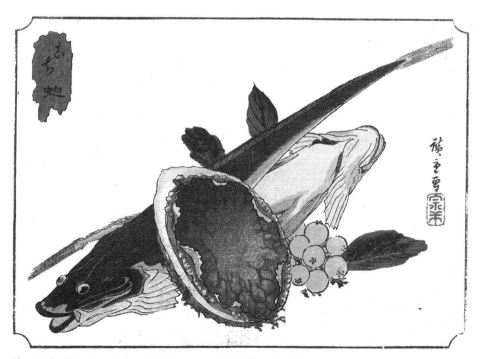

The middle thing is an abalone. You know what it looks like. We all know what it looks like.

Japanese-Style Beef Curry

SERVES: 4—5 | *METHOD: SAUTÉ & SIMMER* | *APPROX. TIME: 2½ HOURS* | *DIFFICULTY: TRICKY*

This dish is not sweet per se, but it's sweeter than some other curry dishes. If it's not sweet enough at first, add honey 1 tablespoon at a time to the beef mixture until it's to your liking. Likewise, if you want the dish spicier, add more ground cayenne pepper or red pepper flakes. These are neutral spices that work well with Japanese curry. Be sure to add your improvements to the beef before you add the roux so they can cook and infuse a few minutes.

Special Equipment

- Blender

Ingredients

- 1½ pounds stewing beef
- 3 medium onions, sliced thin
- ½ teaspoon salt
- 6 cloves garlic, pressed
- 2 tablespoons ginger paste
- 1 can crushed tomatoes or tomato sauce (14 oz.)
- 5 cups beef stock, unsalted
- 2 bay leaves
- 2 pieces whole star anise
- 2—3 tablespoons garam masala
- 1 medium apple, peeled and grated
- 3 tablespoons honey
- 2 teaspoons ground cayenne pepper
- 3 tablespoons olive oil
- Salt and pepper to taste

Beef Directions

1 Dice beef into 1" cubes. Heat large non-stick pan and add 1 tablespoon oil. Place cubed beef into pan and fry for 10 minutes until browned on all sides. Remove from pan and set beef aside.

2 Return pan to heat. Add 2 tablespoons oil, onions and ½ teaspoon salt, then cook on low-medium heat for ½ hour, stirring occasionally until caramelized. (You may need to crank the heat to finish them, but be careful not to burn).

3 Once well-browned and caramelized, add ginger paste, apple and garlic. Sauté for 10 minutes, being careful not to burn or crisp the mixture. Add tomatoes and 2 cups of beef stock to mixture and bring to a gentle boil.

4 After all ingredients are well cooked and very soft, allow to cool. Puree cool mixture with a hand blender or jar blender.

Do not put hot liquid into a blender. The heat may shatter the blender jar and ruin your good looks forever. Ruins the dinner too! For this reason and others I prefer a hand blender, also known as an immersion blender.

Japanese-Style Beef Curry
(CONTINUED)

5 Return pureed mixture to pan and add browned beef, bay leaves, star anise and remaining beef stock. Simmer for 2 hours or longer until beef is very tender. Keep topping the simmering mixture with water or beef stock to maintain consistency.

6 While beef is simmering, prepare curry roux.

In all cooking, and in particular with tricky recipes like roux, the French term "mise en place," or "everything in place," should be your habit. Have every tool and ingredient you'll need ready beforehand so you don't get distracted by a search for missing elements while you're cooking.

Curry Roux Directions

7 In small frying pan, melt ¼ cup butter and heat until it quits foaming (you may substitute olive or grapeseed oil for a healthier variation). Add ¼ cup flour and cook the mixture over medium-low heat, stirring constantly, until it becomes light brown in color.

8 Take the pan off heat. Add 1 tablespoon garam masala, 1 tablespoon yellow curry powder and 1 tablespoon cayenne pepper.

9 Return to medium-low heat and stir constantly until mixture is a rich brown colour.

✕ *Careful not to burn it! Burnt curry roux can wound your olfactory senses for life and strip paint from the ceiling (you'll also know it's burnt if you begin to see little black flecks in it).*

10 Remove roux from heat and set aside to cool.

11 Take beef mixture off stove and remove bay leaves and star anise. Place beef back on heat and add curry roux 2 tablespoons at a time, stirring well to avoid clumping. Keep adding roux until the mixture has very rich, medium-thick, gravy-like consistency.

12 The finished dish should be a deep chocolate brown and so fragrant that Japan Airlines may circle overhead in a holding pattern waiting for a share. Cook for 5 minutes longer over medium heat, stirring gently, then remove.

13 Serve with steamed Japanese rice or Arborio rice and oven-roasted vegetables such as carrots, parsnips and sweet potatoes. Many recipes call for root vegetables in the sauce to cook up like a stew, but I prefer to serve them on the side.

✕ *This dish also goes great with peas, lentils, chives, fried onions and numerous other veggies. Experiment to your liking!*

Japanese-Style Beef Curry, Even Easier

SERVES: *4—5* | METHOD: *SAUTÉ & SIMMER* | APPROX. TIME: *2½ HOURS* | DIFFICULTY: *TRICKY*

Store-bought Japanese curry is actually pretty good, or at least it can be turned into such with a little creativity. I use stewing beef or chuck when making this, so it needs to cook for a couple hours to tenderize, but the flavour is worth the wait. I've also substituted chicken for the beef occasionally and it was fantastic as well. Using beef broth (commercial or homemade) adds a depth to the flavour without additional salt. The roux is salty enough on its own.

Ingredients

✕ *1 lb. stewing beef or chuck, cut into 2" cubes*

✕ *½ package Japanese curry roux*
BART RECOMMENDS:
Kokumaro hot curry

✕ *4 cups sodium-free beef broth*

✕ *4 cups vegetables of your choice*
(carrots, peas and celery are great)

Directions

1   Brown beef in a large heavy pot over high heat.

2   Once beef has browned, add water or beef stock and bring to a boil. Once boiling, turn down heat to simmer and cook for 1 hour or until beef starts to get tender.

3   Heat up oil in frying pan. Sauté carrots and celery on high to get a nice brown. Do not overcook or allow to get soft.

4   Once beef begins to get tender, add curry roux blocks to stock and stir well until the roux is melted and stock begins to thicken. Stir to prevent sticking. Add as much roux as you need to get the consistency you prefer.

5   Sauté carrots and celery before adding the peas.

6   Add vegetables to the thickened gravy and simmer until carrots are soft enough to eat. Stir occasionally.

7   Once, carrots are cooked, add peas just before serving. No one likes wimpy peas.

8   Place over steamed rice and serve hot. Enjoy!

Texas-Style Chili

SERVES: 8 | *METHOD: SAUTÉ & SIMMER* | *APPROX. TIME: OVERNIGHT* | *DIFFICULTY: EASY*

Yes, pork in a Texas-style chili. How novel!

Ingredients

- 1 lb. ground pork
- 1 lb. ground beef
- 1 tablespoon canola oil
- 2 large onions, minced finely
- 5 cloves garlic, pressed
- 1 litre (4¼ cups) beef stock
- 1 teaspoon pepper
- 2 tablespoons chili powder
- 1 tablespoon dried chili flakes
- 1 tablespoon ground cumin
- 1 tablespoon ground oregano
- 2 tablespoons hot Hungarian paprika
- 1 can tomato sauce (28 oz.)
- More tomato paste as desired

Directions

1. Add oil to deep heavy pot over medium heat. Add pork and beef, then brown well. Drain excess fat. Add all remaining ingredients and bring to boil, then turn down to low simmer for 1 hour.

2. After 1 hour, check consistency of chili, and if desired, add tomato paste to flavour and thicken further. Simmer for 1 more hour.

3. Let cool to room temperature, then place in fridge overnight to set flavours. Serve next day.

4. If you like, you can add red kidney beans, but I prefer Texas-style, which is just meat. Serve with steamed white rice or corn tortillas for a hot, incredibly filling winter food.

Mexican Shredded Beef

SERVES: 4—6 | *METHOD: BAKE* | *APPROX. TIME: OVERNIGHT* | *DIFFICULTY: MEDIUM*

You may substitute pork in this recipe, but you'll need a twist. After you marinate, place pork onto a hot barbeque and grill long enough to develop a nice dark char. In fact, you should burn it, just a little. Then place back in a casserole dish with marinade and finish cooking as per directions above. A bit of char makes a big difference, turning an average pork cut from bland to grand.

Ingredients

- 2 lbs. boneless beef (blade or chuck roast)
- 1 tablespoon ground cumin
- 2 teaspoons ground coriander
- 1 tablespoon chili powder
- 4 cloves garlic, pressed
- 2 teaspoons sugar
- 1 teaspoon salt
- ½ teaspoon ground pepper
- ½ teaspoon red pepper flakes
- 1 cup of salsa sauce (red or green)
- 1 cup water
- 1 tablespoon hot red pepper sauce (avoid vinegar-based sauces such as Tabasco)
- 1 package soft corn tortillas

Directions

1 Cut roast into 2" cubes and place in casserole dish. Add rest of ingredients to meat pieces and mix with your hands until meat is fully coated. Place in fridge overnight to marinate.

2 When you want to cook, preheat oven to 400°.

3 Remove meat from fridge and stir again to ensure all pieces are evenly coated. Place into casserole dish, cover, and cook in oven for 1 hour. Then turn down heat to 300° and cook for another 2—3 hours. Gently stir meat every hour to ensure that heat and flavour are even.

4 Once beef is cooked to fall-apart-tender, remove from oven. Move beef to large bowl using slotted spoon. Refrigerate remaining liquid to cool until grease has congealed on surface. Scrape away fat, then add fat-free liquid back to beef.

5 Using forks, shred beef to a uniform consistency. You want shredded beef to be moist, but not soupy.

6 Now prepare corn tortillas. Place tortilla on heated non-stick frying pan and cook for 20—30 seconds per side. If you don't have a tortilla serving dish, place warm tortillas on a plate, then cover with towel to keep warm until ready to serve.

7 Serve tortillas with beef and a bib.

Mexican Shredded Beef

(CONTINUED)

A Happy Accident

On vacation in Idaho with the family, I was visiting (read: drinking wine) with our friends, and not paying attention to the pork steaks on the barbeque. They got charred. I mean inedibly so, blackened and chewy, like melted hockey pucks.

Panicking that I may have screwed up our whole meal plan, I saved the steaks from the barbeque and sorted out the good from the cremated. There were just enough good ones to feed us, thank God!

But the wine was giving me ideas anyway. After dinner, I took the scorched steaks and tossed them in a pot with 2 cans of La Victoria Verde Enchilada Sauce, adding a tablespoon of cumin powder and one chopped onion.

Not knowing what to expect from the taste other than "maybe charcoal," I let the concoction simmer for 2 hours and took it off the stove to cool a little.

One taste and I was in heaven. The burned bits had rendered down into a heavenly smoked flavour. I convinced the others to try some on fresh corn tortillas, and after they'd stopped stuffing their faces and regained the ability to speak, they agreed it was fantastic.

From a near disaster did excellence spring forth. It's a regular recipe of mine to this day. Yes, this anecdote is about pork, but it works with beef too.

Entertaining guests with another Bart Rant as my pork steaks burn.

Osso Buco

SERVES: 8 | METHOD: SAUTÉ & BAKE | APPROX. TIME: 2½ HOURS | DIFFICULTY: EASY

The name makes osso buco sound exotic, but it's just good old-fashioned comfort food. It's like a stew in that it tastes better the second day, so perhaps make it ahead of time if you really want to impress someone on the day of serving. Veal shanks are tough to find, so most often I use pork or beef. Any reddish meat will create a delicious base for this recipe, including beef and lamb.

Ingredients

- 4 tablespoons olive oil
- ½ cup all-purpose flour
- 6 veal shanks, about ½ lb. per shank
- 1 large onion, minced
- 2 large celery stalks, diced
- 2 large carrots, diced
- 4 cloves garlic, pressed
- 3 bay leaves
- 1 teaspoon thyme
- 1 teaspoon basil
- ½ teaspoon rosemary
- 1 teaspoon salt
- 1 teaspoon ground pepper
- 1 cup dry white wine
- 1 cup full-body red wine (optional, but I do it)
- 1 large can (28 oz.) tomatoes, drained and chopped
- 4 cups low-sodium beef or chicken stock
- 1 tablespoon parsley, chopped

Directions

1. Preheat oven to 350°.

2. Heat large Dutch oven over medium heat, then add olive oil to heat up.

3. In shallow bowl or plate, combine flour with salt and pepper. Dredge shanks in seasoned flour until fully coated, then fry in hot oil until well-browned on all sides. Remove shanks from pan and set aside.

4. Add onions, celery and carrots to Dutch oven and cook until softened. Now add garlic, bay leaves, thyme, rosemary, salt and pepper, and stir for a minute until spices are mixed.

5. Add wine and stir more, making sure you scrape pot surfaces to return browned goodness into the mixture. Add stock and chopped tomatoes and bring to a boil.

6. Place browned shanks back into Dutch oven with stock. Cover with lid and place into preheated oven. Cook for 1½—2 hours, or until shanks are very tender.

7. Serve with rice, roasted potatoes, buttered egg noodles, linguini or whatever other starch floats your boat.

Barbeque Beef Ribs

SERVES: *4—6* | METHOD: *BAKE & BBQ* | APPROX. TIME: *4 HOURS* | DIFFICULTY: *MEDIUM*

....

Ribs are expensive, but worth the effort. They're not what your cardiac surgeon or nurse dietician would recommend, but a few times a year? What could go wrong? Well, as it turns out, a lot. But that's another story. As of this writing, I'm still alive and tempting fate to this day.

Boning Up on Rib Knowledge

Before I get to the recipe, there are a few things that, if you're doing this for the first time, you should definitely know.

Firstly, you'll need long rib bones. Also called barbeque bones, long ribs, standing ribs, beef ribs, prime rib, or big ribby beefy boys. I made up the last one. But they all refer to the same thing, and I'll refer to them in the simplest possible terms—beef ribs —because I'm at heart a simpleton and I don't like to venture too far away from my comfort zone.

Selecting beef ribs isn't hard because it's a standard cut without much variation. Refer to earlier in this meaty chapter for details on how to inspect, select and trim cuts of beef.

In addition to regular beef ribs for barbeque, I often use beef short ribs. While sold in 4-inch "short" pieces, they're not called short due to their length, but rather because they're cut from the *short plate*, a particular cut from the belly of the cow. Short ribs make for great barbeque, and are almost always available even when regular beef rib is not.

Got it straight so far? If in doubt, go to your trusted butcher shop for help. You can find individually-cut ribs, but I recommend avoiding those. Instead, ask for your ribs as a slab, to make removing the "silver skin" membrane easier on you. You can also ask the butcher to remove the membrane for you in-store, because it's a shitty task best left to an expert.

What's the silver skin? It's a chewy membrane on the back of your rib rack, which needs to be removed or it'll prevent your spices and flavouring from penetrating the meat. Oh, it's too late? You've got a silver skin to deal with? No matter.

Place your membranous ribs side-down. Work a rounded-tip knife between the end bone and the membrane and work at the edge until you've lifted enough membrane to grab ahold of. With a firm grip using a dry paper towel, slowly pull the membrane from the meat. It's easy to mess this up, so don't get frustrated if it doesn't come off all in one piece.

Yes, it's a very annoying chore that can take several attempts before it's done. But you can't skip it. There is no benefit to attempting to cook or eat the silver skin. It's inedible. Don't be a hero.

Once the membrane's removed, you can trim the bones by cutting away the visible surface fat. (That's anything white that doesn't look like meat.) Once you've removed as much fat as possible, cut the ribs into individual pieces by cutting between the bones. If you do it right, you'll have a pile of meaty ribs in front of you, all your fingers intact, and no need for stitches or painkillers.

Done? Congrats! You can start cooking.

CONTINUED NEXT PAGE

Barbeque Beef Ribs
(CONTINUED)

Special Equipment

✕ *Barbeque grill*

Ingredients

✕ *18 trimmed beef bones, about 2 slabs*

✸ *3 tablespoons Creole seasoning*

✕ *2 tablespoons garlic powder*

✕ *2 tablespoons onion powder*

✕ *2 tablespoons celery salt*

✕ *1 tablespoon mustard powder*

✕ *1 teaspoon sugar*

✕ *2 tablespoons Montreal steak spice (optional)*

Preparation

1 Fully mix all dry ingredients in medium bowl.

2 Place ribs on baking sheet, equally spaced. Sprinkle dry ingredients over ribs, turn upside-down, and repeat until ribs are coated on all sides.

3 Let ribs rest in fridge for a couple hours to allow the rub to do its thing.

4 Preheat oven to 375°.

Directions

5 Place ribs in deep roasting pan, bone side down. Cover with tight-fitting lid or aluminum foil, then seal tightly.

6 Roast for 2 hours. Check at the 2-hour mark by poking a rib with a fork. Meat will pull apart easily when it's done. If not, allow to cook ½-hour longer.

7 Once ribs are tender, remove from oven and place on wire rack over baking sheet. Fat will drip off as it cools.

8 When ready to eat, place ribs on preheated barbeque grill over medium flame. Cook 3 minutes, turn over and repeat another 3 minutes, then baste with your favourite barbeque sauce.

Be warned! Once barbeque sauce is applied, the meat becomes more susceptible to burning (due to the sauce's sugar content). Pay attention. Keep your tongs in hand and put the liquor down for these 4 critical minutes!

9 Grill 1—2 minutes each side.

10 Serve hot with your choice of side dishes.

The Sauerbraten Incident

The Sauerbraten Incident of my youth is the most mentally and spiritually scarring, and thus the most-retold, story of all my bad food experiences. The events herein are true. The names have been changed, but not to protect the innocent—because there are no innocents left.

Before I go further into the story, I need to include a traditional sauerbraten recipe for your review. For this, I travel (electronically) to Germany, the country of the dish's birth...

Sauerbraten (German Sour Pot Roast)

SERVES: *8* | METHOD: *SAUTÉ & BAKE* | APPROX. TIME: *3 FUCKING DAYS* | DIFFICULTY: *MEDIUM*

Special Equipment

- Dutch oven or slow cooker
- Sieve

Roast & Sauce Ingredients

- 4 lbs. boneless beef roast
- 3 tablespoons butter
- 2½ cups onions, diced
- 2½ cups carrots, diced
- 1¼ cups celery, diced
- 2 tablespoons flour
- ½ cup water
- ¾ cup gingersnap cookies, crumbled

Marinade Ingredients

- 1 cup dry red wine
- 1 cup red wine vinegar
- 2 cups cold water
- 1 medium onion, sliced thinly
- 1 tablespoon black peppercorns, crushed
- 1 tablespoon juniper berries, crushed
- 2 bay leaves
- 1 teaspoon salt
- 2—3 tablespoons Spice House Sauerbraten Spice

CONTINUED NEXT PAGE

Sauerbraten (German Sour Pot Roast)

(CONTINUED)

Directions

1   Combine all marinade ingredients in large saucepan. Bring to boil over high heat. Remove from heat and allow to cool to room temperature.

2   Place beef in deep, non-reactive (glass or ceramic) bowl. Pour marinade over beef until at least half-submerged. Add more wine if necessary. Cover tightly with foil or plastic and refrigerate for 2-3 days, turning meat in the marinade at least twice a day.

3   On third day, remove meat from marinade and pat dry with paper towels. Strain marinade through fine sieve and reserve the liquid. Discard spices and onions.

4   In Dutch oven, heat butter until bubbling stops. Add meat and brown on all sides, turning frequently to brown evenly. Transfer to platter and set aside.

5   For roasting, add onions, carrots, and celery to same pan you cooked meat in. Cook over moderate heat until soft and light brown (5—8 minutes). Sprinkle 2 tablespoons of flour over vegetables and cook, stirring constantly, 2—3 minutes or until flour begins to colour.

6   Pour in 2 cups of your saved marinade and ½ cup of water. Bring to boil over high heat. Return meat to pot, cover tightly, and simmer over low heat for 2 hours, or until meat is soft. Alternatively, bake in 350° oven for 2 hours.

7   Transfer roast to heated platter and cover with foil to keep warm while sauce is made.

8   Pour leftover braising liquid into large measuring cup and skim fat from surface. You'll need at least 2 ½ cups for sauce. If additional liquid is needed, add more marinade.

9   Combine liquid and gingersnap crumbs in saucepan and cook over moderate heat, stirring frequently for 10 minutes until crumbs are dissolved and sauce is thickened. Depending upon amount of liquid, you may need to add additional cookie crumbs.

10   Strain sauce through fine sieve, pressing down hard with wooden spoon to force as much of the vegetables and crumbs through as possible. Return sauce to pan, adjust seasoning and simmer over low heat until ready to serve.

11   Slice roast, pour sauce over slices on platter and pass remaining sauce separately.

Helpful Hints

✕   *Traditionally, sauerbraten is served with dumplings, boiled potatoes, spaetzle, and red cabbage. This recipe requires advance planning and time (3 days!), but it has incredible flavour and aroma.*

✕   *You may adjust the amount of ginger snap cookies to give the sauce your preferred consistency. Ginger snaps are used as thickener instead of flour, so you don't run the risk of having a pasty, starchy sauce.*

Recipe Source: TheSpiceHouse.com
Submitted by Alexander Rhoads

The Incident

Okay. There you have a sauerbraten recipe, one of many available on the internet. If you look at the recipe it seems innocuous, possibly tempting, even palatable. But you may have also noticed something weird about it.

First off: this recipe includes ginger snaps. Ginger snaps, as in, the cookies! In a beef gravy! To thicken and flavour it! Oh my God! That should have been the first clue that this recipe should have been left alone, barren, cast out like a leper, buried forever below salted earth.

Ginger snap gravy. My swallower shifted into reverse just typing this. Be still, my uvula, be still.

You may be asking, at this point, why anyone would add any amount of ginger snap cookie crumbs to fucking *gravy*. Well, some believe there's a reason. Good gravy does taste savory, and "savory" is actually a complex mix of flavours, including sweetness. A small amount (small!) of brown sugar or molasses in a dark gravy may be just the thing you need to complete an otherwise flat-tasting recipe.

In addition, sweet dessert flavours like ginger, in minuscule amounts, can add a certain complexity to savoury dishes, especially beef. Yes, it's true! Ginger is a staple of savoury Asian cooking, obviously. I have a lasagna recipe in this book with nutmeg. And the most delicious chili you've ever eaten possibly had cinnamon and even chocolate in it. I'll leave you to collect the pieces of your blown mind.

So that's the theory. Solid, I suppose, as theories go. Now look at the recipe previous to this ramble. The amount of ginger snaps required is ¾ of a cup. That's three-quarters. Not even a full cup. This little observation will be important soon.

Listen, my parents are smart people. Intelligent, articulate, well-meaning, educated, informed, well-traveled and well-read. They're also great cooks—you know, normally. Knowing this, I've asked them many times what could have possibly gone so wrong on that fateful day. To this day my parents answer, somewhat

warily, that they can't fully recall. I don't know if this is just a face-saving evasion or full-blown PTSD.

But one thing is clear: Somehow, and I will never know how, they read "¾ cups of ginger snaps" as "34 cups of ginger snaps."

Thirty-four cups of ginger snaps.

Come on. *Come on.*

I realize that, at the time, they were young parents, still honing their culinary skills. Perhaps there was even alcohol involved, or one of those other intoxicants that were so popular in the late '60s. Giving them the maximum benefit of the doubt, it's possible a critical forward-slash (/) was missing from the cookbook due to a typo. Typo's are always a hazzard with cokobooks.

Still, that doesn't excuse a damn thing. As a little volume called *Mein Kampf* once proved, just because it's in a book doesn't mean it's a good idea.

Even more baffling: On some level, my parents both understood that 34 cups of ginger snaps, in relation to the recipe's other ingredients, was unbalanced. Apparently they knew that "mushed cookie with beef drippings" wasn't an ideal outcome. But instead of questioning the initial recipe, they figured they'd simply increase the amounts of other ingredients to compensate.

So, in mid-cooking, they both absconded to the grocery store for more Oxo cubes, vinegar, sour cream, wine vinegar, vegetables, spices, eye of newt and wings of bat to add to *thirty-fucking-four* cups of ginger snaps.

After they returned, chaos reigned. My sisters and I approached the kitchen to determine the reason for all the frantic clattering and clanging. We stood at the doorway, watching our parents try to get their flaming train derailment back on track somehow. We shuddered—knowing, even at our tender ages, exactly how it would end. For a time, mom and dad worked feverishly side-by-side, chopping and broiling and bubbling. Without comment Dad left suddenly, returning twenty minutes later with another truckload of groceries. Taking breaks to bark at each other, my parents continued their hideous Frankenstein experiment of stirring, pouring and cursing.

The pots and pans stacked up like rusted cars in a junkyard. The smell of ginger began to permeate the air, the very walls. As my parents' creation grew in size and scope, so too did our concern. Piles of dishes and bowls, empty cookie boxes, bags and cans began to cramp our already-modest kitchen.

My parents did not falter or flinch or quit. They were invested in the sunkest of sunk costs. And to our increasing horror, so were we.

The process of realization was as follows:

1. *The horrifying pile of dishes would need to be washed, and we were the cleaning staff.*

2. *My parents never threw food out, and the sheer amount was growing ominously.*

3. *The mingled reek of vinegar, sour cream, ginger snaps, beef and human terror smelled less like a recipe and more like an Al-Qaeda attack at an Applebee's.*

4. *The pots and pans were bigger than we were. I questioned our physical ability to wash them, to say nothing of our willingness.*

5. *Did I mention my parents never threw food out? Increasingly, it looked like we'd be eating this alleged food until we all ended up drinking it from straws at a retirement home.*

6. *Baby Sister started to wail. Her voice is a harbinger of doom in several world mythologies.*

7. *The creation atop the stove developed an audible heartbeat.*

8. *Thump-thump, thump-thump.*

9. *My eyes began to water from the sting of ginger in the air.*

10. *Baby Sister fainted just from the smell. Slightly Larger Sister began to gag and retch.*

11. *Mom and Dad never threw food out. We were doomed to eat it forever. Not only doomed, but damned, in the manner of Sisyphus—to never be free.*

12. *The heartbeat on the stove began to whisper, terrible things, things I cannot repeat...*

Finally the order was given to set the dinner table. It—Stephen King's It—was ready. With the grim precision of the house band aboard the Titanic, we assembled the necessary plates, glasses, knives and forks. Mom brought the roast, gravy and noodles to the table and we all sat down.

Things looked fine. Looked. "Okay, let's eat!" Dad said.

"Ronnie, should we?" Mom asked warily, spooning up some of the offering. I watched as the creation stared at me. I could count the heartbeats as ripples in the gravy.

Thump-thump, thump-thump, thump-thump.

Mom finished serving up the fetid glop with beef and noodles, then placed the plate in front of Baby Sister and the rest of us. Each of us stared at our plates the way cattle rustlers on the gallows stared through their nooses.

"Eat!" the master commanded. He placed his own forkful of ichor into his mouth, then chewed slowly, deliberately. I thought I saw his shoulders heave. Just little, almost imperceptibly, but they moved. Convulsed, even.

"What's wrong, Dad?" I squeaked out.

"Tickle in my throat," he choked. "Now eat your dinner, or it'll be your breakfast." He heaved again.

My sainted mother and father preparing the sauerbraten.

Baby Sister, the youngest and most skittish, tentatively tasted her gravy-slathered noodles. Before her jaw could move a second time, she retched and immediately spewed the ginger-poisoned slop back through her mouth and nose onto the table. Then she began, as Baby Sisters often do, to cry.

Everyone stared, realizing what this meant: The train wreck had arrived right on time. I observed through teary eyes, knowing my father would force me to eat the gelid, whispering mass in front of me. We trembled, hesitated.

"What's the problem?" asked Dad.

Mom answered, "She's got the same problem we're all do. It's the gravy."

"There's nothing wrong with the gravy."

"It's speaking to me," I offered. "A language from the Black Times, before the sun was created."

"There's no problem with it," said Dad, convincing nobody. "It tastes just like Grandma used to make."

It's possible that Grandma simply enjoyed tormenting Dad with such recipes. Mom yelled at him, "They don't have to eat it!"

"Why not? It's perfectly fine! What's that sound going thump-thump over and over again?"

As Mom and Dad had a Nietzschean argument about the nature of fate and death, Slightly Larger Sister placed a tiny sample of the controversy into her mouth. Startled by mom's outburst, she jumped, accidentally swallowing the entire forkful.

Instantly she gagged and spat with the sound of a liquid cannonade. I ducked out of the way. The projected mass hit the window behind me and coated the back of my head with wet ricochet.

The culinary train wreck grew in scale as more dining cars toppled off the rails and into the void, taking all the screaming passengers—that is to say, us—with it. By that point, my gag reflex had gone into double-overdrive, high-range reverse. We, the children, shuddered and sobbed like reverse Dickensian orphans, begging *not* to eat.

At this point, Baby Sister cried, "No more, Mommy! I'll never be bad again!"

Dad didn't believe her (and knowing my sister, who would?). "Everyone eat your damn dinner!"

In fear for our lives, we obeyed. There was no turning back. I only prayed that my sensitive taste buds would perish with relative quickness in the flames.

We each of us fought individual battles that instant, lost in the fog of war with our German foe. Imagine if the alien from *The Thing* attempted to shapeshift into a gingerbread man but changed his mind halfway through. Then you'll have a rough idea of what we faced before our forks.

I cannot describe the flavour to you. I will not. It is *haraam*.

We offered a symphony of sound: crying, retching, coughing, gasping and other, worse noises as our entire bodies rebelled. My mom balanced a weeping Baby Sister in one hand and a two-six of vodka in the other. Dad silently writhed and heaved, his stoic facade burned away by ginger and regret.

The gravy began to move, howling with a thousand mouths, demanding a small child as sacrifice. Apparently we had been judged by the gravy, and found wanting. We were not strong enough. Angry, it started to crawl towards me, reaching out with black gingery tendrils.

My Dad's favourite phrase was, "Stop crying or I'll give you something to really cry about!" Which is what he yelled at that moment—but the threat didn't work this time. Because he had already given us the thing to really cry about. The God-Emperor, the Cthulhu of things to cry about. And oh, how we cried.

I heaved some more. Baby Sister screamed ever-louder. Slightly Larger Sister slumped off her chair and tried to crawl away. The gravy, sensing the sudden movement, began to give chase. I screamed, "Run!"

Slightly Larger Sister rose to her feet and bolted like Forrest Gump. If she hadn't fainted in the hallway only moments later, she might still be running to this very day.

Dad had run out of commands. Short of physically spooning the slop down our gullets, which would have resulted in a much bigger mess than he probably wanted to make, he could no longer force us to eat. He himself gasped for air, chewed, gagged, chewed and gagged again.

The din began to dull, and we realized Dad and his gravy had been defeated.

Mom quietly whispered, "What do we do now?"

Nobody answered.

I was finally able to pull my swallower from reverse and into neutral. Slightly Larger Sister had escaped the blob, Baby Sister held it at bay with a fork, and I had no life-force left for it to steal.

Dad warned all of us, "Be quiet and stay still. It can sense fear."

We froze in place, as still as the guests of honour at a wake, but the gravy had heard my Dad and turned its pseudopods toward him. As we gathered our wits, the gravy mass slowly burbled and wrapped around Dad's left leg. I heard hissing as the cloth of his pants started to corrode.

Dad finally looked up. His voice cracking through a strained smile, he asked, "How about we make it a pizza night?" Then he leaned in and whispered, "Run."

We bolted. Dad gave his leg a kick and a shimmy to free himself of his captor. The gravy roared and thrashed, spraying a cloud of defensive ink. Mom smashed at it with an umbrella to protect the rest of us. Slightly Larger Sister, awake now and far ahead of us, raced to the car door with Baby Sister toddling close behind.

In the nick of time, we escaped!

We didn't return from the pizza joint until some hours later. A terrified neighbour had called the authorities, and then the authorities had called *their* authorities, and now the street was cordoned off. Through a maze of quarantine tents and fumigation pipes I could see the sauerbraten, thrashing in a sealed tank, being carefully loaded by a hazmat crew into an armoured military truck.

Men in black suits accosted our family, forcing us to sign papers we didn't understand. (I may be breaking federal laws just telling you this story.) When the commotion died down, the armoured truck, with a police escort, slowly crested a rise at the end of the street and disappeared. We knew not where the sauerbraten was headed—but we knew it was away, far, far, away. And that was enough for us.

We never attempted sauerbraten ever again. Since that day, I've never even come within ten miles of a sauerbraten. God willing, I never will.

I know the sauerbraten was defeated. I know it can't hurt us anymore. But sometimes, on nights when the air is still, and the moon casts strange shadows on the ceilings, I can still hear a faint sound, as if from far away, or far underground.

And I can smell ginger.

Thump-thump, thump-thump, thump-thump...

The End...?

Chicken, Turkey and Other Fowlness

Flocking to Dinner

I love chicken for its versatility and its taste. Chicken can stand quite a bit of abuse (especially the rubber chickens in my punishment dungeon), but there are limits. Chicken breast often gets cooked carelessly and ends up dry and tough—a sad fate, since the chicken has given its all to be part of the meal, and the least you could do is give it an honourable send-off.

I'll use breast meat in dishes where I can control its finished temperature and resultant juicy disposition. However, as a result of my short attention span, and its resulting implications in cooking, I prefer skinned and deboned chicken thighs, or drumsticks if thighs aren't on hand (thighs on hand? Does that sound right?).

Two or three pieces per person is usually sufficient, so dark meat is a cheap option, and it's adaptable, so it's perfect for beginning cooks. It can still be edible after abuse, overcooking, and other extreme malfunctions. It's fattier and thus juicier than breast meat, so it's harder to screw up. That said, I always trim as much fat as I can before cooking, which renders dark meat chicken a lower-fat option than pork or beef while offering a uniquely delicious flavour.

Chicken is the biggest staple meat in my home due to its low cost, versatility, and the fact that Kelsey will actually eat it. In years past, Jordan and Kristine would eat any meat served to them, and though Kaitlyn is more health-conscious, even she couldn't resist my pork ribs. Kelsey, on the other hand, was not a fan of red meat for most of her life. Chicken became a staple for her and thus for all of us. After four children of willful dietary preferences, I now lack the strength to argue otherwise.

Besides, chicken is healthier. My doctor insists I eat healthier, as this is the only cure for my advanced Dic-Doo disease, and it's hard to keep to dietary restrictions. Indulgence and guilt are my most faithful dining companions, and chicken helps a little with that.

In cooking chicken, it helps to be slow and low-key. I recommend you cook chicken boneless breast to 160° and no hotter. With bone-in breast, thigh and leg meat, you might cook to 170°. Remember too that chicken loves sauce, be it red, white or rosé, and that poultry can be used in place of pork or beef in almost any recipe. Chicken is an ugly critter, but versatile—just like you.

To all of you, but especially Kelsey: Enjoy!

Roasting Chicken and Turkey

Nothing says dinner like roasted beast. Previously I brayed on about roast beef, and now it's the bird's turn. For chicken, first you need to know that frying and roasting chickens are the same thing, with the exception of their ages. Fryers are younger birds and more delicate, overcooking more easily due to their smaller mass.

How big a bird to you need? When selecting a buzzard to serve your guests, generally go with one pound per person. The fancier you get—fresh, free-range, varied diet—the better your bird will taste.

Fresh, never-frozen birds roast better than defrosted ones, and don't let anyone tell you different. However,,you can reinvigorate a frozen bird with the right brine preparation. A good brine will elevate the shittiest bird to roasted excellence. I provide a brine recipe and instructions next, following these mind droppings.

Birds are more prone to foodborne illness than beef. So treat it like pork—as in, with paranoia. Until the moment you put the buzzard in the oven, try to keep the meat as cold as possible.

Cooking any bird is best accomplished by a spatchcock method, whereby you split the backbone and splay the buzzard out, skin-side up, and it roast flat in the pan. It's easier than it sounds and will completely change the way you cook a bird. If necessary, I'll assist you in spatchcocking the buzzard. Just call! No job is too messy!

The temperature you want to remember is 170°. This is how hot a bird needs to get before it's done, whether you're reading the centre of your stuffing or the fleshiest, thickest part of the thigh. Anything less than 170° is inedible—unlike beef, you simply can't eat rare chicken. Not even as part of a rebellious caper. It's just *bad*.

What about stuffing? I prefer to roast my birds unstuffed due to the spatchcock method. I cook the stuffing separately from the bird, and then mix in some pan drippings just prior to serving. It's far easier, less time-consuming, and tastes exactly the same. But if you insist on stuffing a bird the old-fashioned way, your stuffing must be cold. Never, ever, never jam warm stuffing into a bird. I'm not kidding. Fuck around and find out!

Generally, you'll want to oven-roast your bird under a roaster lid or foil covering until the last ½ hour, at which point, you'll remove the covering to let the skin crisp. However, there are times where you roast birds uncovered the whole time. The recipe will tell you.

Also, invite me for dinner once in a while. Please! Don't make me beg! Susan says I'm not allowed to beg anyone else but her!

The Leg Bone's Connected to the...

Deboned whole chicken legs aren't something you can typically buy at the grocery store, particularly not with the skin still on. But you can easily do it yourself. I learned this technique from Jacques Pepin's TV show. It's proven useful, as chicken legs come on sale often and can be used in many different recipes.

Place a chicken leg skin-side down and run a knife to the bone along down the interior length of the leg. From this incision, work the meat away from the bone slowly, being careful not to damage the skin. Eventually the bones and joints will shuck out, and you'll end up with a piece of butterflied chicken with the all-important skin still on.

You can also save the bones and joints for making stock later, which, if you've been reading this book in order for some reason, you know about already.

Earning Your Wings

It's a pain in the ass to debone chicken wings, but you'll love the result. Cut the lower section (drumette) from the upper (wingette). Leave the wingette and tip together.

Place the wingette flat on your cutting board. Work the tip of a paring knife under the skin and work the tip around to separate the meat from the bone, being careful to not cut through the skin. Flip wingette over and repeat process. Continue to work the knife until you feel the bone coming loose under the skin.

Now, gently pull back skin with your fingers to expose the bones and joint. Grip bones and wiggle back and forth to separate from the joints. Once separated, pull bones out, leaving the skin and meat whole.

Deboning wings is a process best undertaken while sipping red wine or sake. At least for me, because I'm a professional. (Do not do this. I am not responsible if you accidentally debone your hand.)

Brined Turkey or Chicken

SERVES: VARIES | *METHOD: MARINATE* | *APPROX. TIME: VARIES* | *DIFFICULTY: EASY*

There are many ways to make a delicious brine. It's a great opportunity to experiment! Jordan has made brined poultry for many years and swears by an Asian-inspired concoction that includes Sichuan peppercorns, miso paste, rice wine and soy sauce. Obviously he's been living in Vancouver too long.

Special Equipment

- 1 large stewing pot
- OR
- 1 large camping cooler

Ingredients

- 1 cup coarse kosher salt
- ½ cup brown sugar
- 1 cup boiling water
- 1 gallon (3.8 litres) ice water

If you need more or less brine to fully submerge your bird, keep the same ratio of ingredients.

Directions

1. Remove and discard any restraints or twine from bird. Remove organ sachet and neckbone if present, but keep them for later if you wish to use in gravy.

2. Trim away large areas of excess skin and fat around poultry's body cavity. Optionally spatchcock carcass here and remove backbone.

3. Rinse poultry thoroughly and drain well. Place prepared bird into clean, insulated cooler or large stewing pot, along with enough cold brine to cover bird completely. If buzzard is floating, place heavy casserole dish on it to submerge it.

4. Maintain cold temperature throughout brining process. A large enough stewing pot is ideal if it fits in fridge, but if not, use sealed ice bags in large plastic cooler.

5. If using cooler, check every few hours to ensure brine is still cold (34°—38° is best). If ice has melted, replace as necessary.

6. For roasting chicken under 5 pounds, brine around 8 hours. For turkey up to 12 pounds, brine for 24 hours. For turkey over 12 pounds, brine up to 48 hours.

7. Once time has elapsed, remove bird from brine, rinse well with fresh cold water and pat dry with paper towels.

8. Roast bird per instructions in other recipes until correct temperature of 170° has been reached.

9. Enjoy! You'll never roast non-brined poultry ever again.

KFC-Style Chicken Batter (Please Don't Sue Me)

SERVES: VARIES | *METHOD: BLEND* | *APPROX. TIME: 5 MINUTES* | *DIFFICULTY: PFFFT!*

Special Equipment

✕ *Spice grinder or blender*

Ingredient Note

✕ *All ingredients should be dried*

Ingredients

✕ *1 cup flour*

✕ *1 teaspoon salt*

✕ *2 tablespoons paprika*

✕ *1 tablespoon onion salt*

✕ *1 tablespoon garlic powder*

✕ *1 teaspoon celery salt*

✕ *1 teaspoon rubbed sage*

✕ *1 teaspoon ground oregano*

✕ *½ teaspoon rosemary*

✕ *½ teaspoon dried thyme*

✕ *1 teaspoon chili powder*

✕ *1 teaspoon black pepper*

✕ *1 teaspoon basil leaves, crushed*

✕ *1 teaspoon marjoram leaves, crushed finely*

Directions

1   Mix all ingredients *except salt and flour* in spice grinder or blender. Once blended, store in well-sealed glass jar.

2   When ready to use, mix together a ratio of 2 tablespoons of spice mix, 1 cup flour and 1 teaspoon salt.

3   Cook as per your normal fried chicken recipe.

Chicken & Dumplings

SERVES: **4** | *METHOD:* **SIMMER** | *APPROX. TIME:* **2—3 HOURS** | *DIFFICULTY:* **EASY**

Chicken Ingredients

- ✕ *1 large stewing or frying chicken (about 3 lbs.)*
- ✕ *10 cups sodium-free chicken stock*
- ✕ *1 large onion, chopped*
- ✕ *3 large carrots, chopped*
- ✕ *3 stalks of celery, chopped*
- ✕ *2 parsnips, cored and chopped*
- ✕ *2 cloves garlic, crushed*
- ✕ *2 bay leaves*
- ✕ *Salt and pepper to taste*

Dumpling Ingredients

- ✕ *2 cups flour*
- ✕ *1 teaspoon baking powder*
- ✕ *1 teaspoon salt*
- ✕ *½ teaspoon white pepper*
- ✕ *1 large egg*
- ✕ *½ cup milk or water*

Chicken Directions

1. Cut chicken into manageable pieces. Place in deep pot with onion, garlic and bay leaves. Add stock to cover the chicken, bring to light boil, then turn down heat and simmer until meat is tender, 2—3 hours for stewing chicken or 1 hour for fryer chicken.

2. Remove chicken from stock and set stock aside for later. Let chicken cool, then strip meat from bones. Now place all veggies (and more onion and parsley if desired) into broth pot. Cook for 15 minutes more until veggies are edibly soft.

Dumpling Directions

3. Sift together flour, baking powder, and salt. Add milk and egg, and work into a stiff dough. Let rest for ½ hour.

4. Roll out to desired thickness (about ¼" is best) on floured surface, then cut into 1" squares.

5. Add dumplings one at a time to lightly boiling broth. Stir gently to keep dumplings from sticking to bottom of pot.

6. Once all dumplings are added, turn heat down to low-medium and gently simmer for 10 minutes. Dumplings will float, then settle again as they cook. Once dumplings settle, turn off heat, add deboned chicken and stir gently.

7. Let sit covered for 10 minutes to let dumplings tenderize. Stir gently again before serving in soup bowls.

Chicken Cacciatore

SERVES: **5** | *METHOD:* ***SAUTÉ & BAKE*** | *APPROX. TIME:* ***1 HOUR*** | *DIFFICULTY:* ***EASY***

Ingredients

- 8 chicken thighs, skin removed
- 2 mild Italian sausages (pre-cooked and chopped)
- 2 tablespoons olive oil
- 1 large onion, minced
- 4 cloves garlic, pressed
- 3 carrots, minced
- 4 oz. mushrooms, sliced thinly
- ½ cup dry white wine
- 1 can tomato sauce (14 oz.)
- 1 tin tomato paste (5 oz.)
- 1 cup chicken broth
- 1 teaspoon oregano
- ½ teaspoon rosemary
- ½ teaspoon sage
- ¼ cup chopped parsley
- Salt and pepper to taste

Directions

1. Remove skin from chicken thighs, rinse pieces, then pat dry and season with salt and pepper.

2. Heat oil in large skillet over medium heat. Brown chicken pieces well on both sides. Remove chicken and place in deep baking dish.

3. Add mushrooms, onions, garlic and carrots to hot skillet and sauté until soft. Once sautéed, add tomato paste and sauce, white wine, chicken broth, sausage and herbs into mixture and simmer for 10 minutes.

4. Add this sauce to baking dish with chicken. Bake uncovered at 375° for 45 minutes.

5. Serve hot with cooked pasta or gnocchi.

Chicken Diablo

SERVES: 4 | *METHOD: SIMMER* | *APPROX. TIME: 1½ HOURS* | *DIFFICULTY: EASY*

This honey-mustard chicken was a childhood favourite that earned an entry because it came from dear 'ol Mom. We dined on this with steamed rice often. Childhood memories are so powerful, and this recipe tastes as great now as it did back then. Love you, Mom!

Ingredients

- 1 broiler chicken
- 4 tablespoons butter
- ½ cup honey
- ½ cup prepared mustard (regular yellow stuff, if you don't know)
- 1 teaspoon salt
- 1 teaspoon curry powder

Directions

1. Melt butter in pan on medium heat, then add all other ingredients and stir as liquid simmers off until you've got a thick liquid.

2. Cut chicken into edible pieces and arrange evenly in baking dish. Pour liquid mixture over chicken.

3. Bake uncovered 1 hour at 375°.

4. Serve with white rice or potatoes of your choice.

Chicken Fingers

SERVES: 4 | *METHOD: DEEP FRY* | *APPROX. TIME: 30 MINUTES* | *DIFFICULTY: CAREFUL!*

Serves 4—6 normal people. Or… you know. You know what my family is like. They've chained me here in this kitchen. Chicken fingers. They demand more chicken fingers, always more chicken fingers. I long to see blue skies again. Please help me.

Special Equipment

✕ *Deep fryer*

Ingredients

✕ *1 lb. chicken breast (boneless and skinless)*

✕ *1 large egg*

✕ *1 cup milk*

✕ *1 cup all-purpose flour*
   OR
   50/50 rice-potato flour mix

✕ *2 cups corn flakes, crushed into crumbs*
   OR
   2 cups bread crumbs

✕ *1 teaspoon salt*

✕ *1 teaspoon black pepper*

✕ *1 teaspoon garlic powder (not garlic salt)*

Directions

1 Preheat deep fryer to 350°.

2 Mix egg, milk and ½ teaspoon salt in medium bowl and beat like a mule in a rock quarry.

3 Mix corn flakes, ½ teaspoon salt, pepper and garlic powder in steep-sided pan (a pie plate works great for this).

4 Cut chicken breast along grain into ½" strips. Place strips into plastic bag along with flour in small batches. Shake to coat all pieces thoroughly.

5 Remove flour-coated chicken and shake off excess flour. Dredge chicken in milk-egg mixture and roll until thoroughly coated. Place each wet chicken piece into corn flake mixture one at a time and roll until fully coated with crumbs.

6 Place crumb-coated chicken into deep fryer at 350° for 3 minutes. The pieces will float when cooked.

7 Serve hot along with hollandaise sauce or whatever dipping sauce you like.

Chicken Paprika

SERVES: 4—6 | *METHOD: BAKE* | *APPROX. TIME: OVERNIGHT* | *DIFFICULTY: MEDIUM*

This dish goes really well with cold weather, or coolish weather, or warmish weather. Or even hot weather, if you're a true twisted freak. How about some fava beans and a nice Chianti while you're at it?

Ingredients

- 2 lbs. chicken thighs, skinned and deboned
- 1 cup sour cream
- 1 quart chicken broth
- 1 large onion, minced
- 3 large carrots, chopped
- 2 stalks of celery, chopped
- 3 tablespoons Hungarian paprika
- 3 garlic cloves pressed
- 1 teaspoon salt
- ½—1 teaspoon black pepper
- ½ teaspoon ginger powder
- 2 bay leaves

Best Served With

 Spaetzle

Directions

1 In deep 3-quart pan, add 1 tablespoon olive oil and chicken pieces. Brown chicken on both sides over medium-high heat, then remove from pan and set aside.

2 Add garlic, onion, celery and carrot to pan. Sauté until onions are translucent, about 4 minutes.

3 Add pepper, ginger, pepper and salt to onion mixture and cook for 1—2 minutes until mix is blended and dark red. Add broth and chicken to pan and simmer for 30 minutes.

4 Remove now-cooked chicken from sauce and set aside. Thicken sauce with flour roux or corn starch slurry to reach gravy-like consistency.

5 Once sauce is thickened, add sour cream to mixture and bring to just bubbling. Add chicken back to sauce.

6 Serve immediately over spaetzle or noodles.

Lemon Chicken

SERVES: 4—6 | *METHOD: BAKE* | *APPROX. TIME: OVERNIGHT* | *DIFFICULTY: MEDIUM*

Most often, the "lemon chicken" people order in a Chinese food restaurant is a heavily- battered, deep fried chicken with a vaguely lemon-like flavour poured over it. Yuck. This, my friends, is much better.

Special Equipment

✗ Deep fryer

Chicken Ingredients

✗ 2 lbs. chicken thighs, skinned and deboned

✗ ½ cup cornstarch or tapioca starch

✗ 3 tablespoons all-purpose flour

✗ 1 teaspoon salt

✗ 1 teaspoon pepper

✗ ½ cup water

✗ 2 egg yolks, beaten

✗ 2 tablespoon toasted sesame seeds (optional)

Lemon Sauce Ingredients

✗ 1½ cups water

✗ 4 medium lemons for juicing

✗ 3 tablespoons brown sugar

✗ 1 tablespoon white sugar

✗ 2 tablespoons cornstarch

✗ 3 tablespoons honey

✗ 1 tablespoon toasted sesame oil

✗ 1 teaspoon chicken bouillon powder (optional)

✗ 1 teaspoon fresh ginger, grated

Chicken Directions

1 Squeeze lemons into juice. About ½ cup juice should result. Set aside.

2 Combine cornstarch, flour, salt and pepper in large bowl. Mix water and egg yolks together. Once blended, add to dry ingredients and mix well with whisk.

3 Dredge chicken pieces in batter until well coated. Refrigerate 30 minutes.

4 Preheat deep fryer to 350°. Cook chicken one piece at a time, about 5 minutes each, until golden brown. Remove chicken from hot oil and place on paper towel-lined plate to drain.

Lemon Sauce Directions

5 Combine all sauce ingredients together in a saucepan. Mix well.

6 Cook over medium heat, stirring constantly for 5 minutes until sauce boils and thickens. As it cooks, sauce will turn from milky yellow to clear yellow. Once clear, turn heat to lowest simmer until ready to use.

7 Pour hot lemon sauce over cooked chicken and serve hot. Optionally sprinkle toasted sesame seeds on top prior to serving.

Three-Meat (Chicken, Sausage, Shrimp) Gumbo

SERVES: **8** | *METHOD:* **SAUTÉ & SIMMER** | *APPROX. TIME:* **45 MINUTES** | *DIFFICULTY:* **EASY**

I always thought gumbo was exclusive to the Louisiana bayou area of the US, but after reading up on it, it seems it's a staple in numerous regions of the South. Every chef down there will assert that theirs is the true and authentic version. I make no such claims, other than to say that mine is the best.

Many versions of gumbo include oysters, but mine does not. Me and oysters have a thing, and that thing is, I don't ingest them unless they're smoked and canned, or unless I'm extremely drunk and attempting a dare. If you like oysters, use them. The bayou chefs are far away and they can't hurt you. Probably.

Ingredients

- ½ cup all-purpose flour
- ½ cup unsalted butter for clarifying
- 5 cups chicken broth
- 1 tablespoon vegetable oil
- 2 celery stalks, minced
- 2 garlic cloves, pressed
- 1 jalapeno, minced finely
- 1 red pepper, minced
- 1 medium sized onion, minced
- 1 lb. boneless, skinless chicken thighs

- ½ lb. Andouille sausage
  OR
  ½ lb. chorizo sausage
  OR
  ½ lb. pre-cooked hot Italian sausage
- 2 tablespoons parsley
- 1 tablespoon thyme
- 1 teaspoon sage
- 3 bay leaves
- ½ teaspoon salt, or more to taste
- ½ teaspoon ground pepper
- ½ lb. fresh okra, cleaned (optional, but also not optional, you know?)
- 1 lb. medium shrimp, shelled and deveined

Preparation

1. Clarify butter. Cut 2 sticks good quality, *unsalted* butter into quarters. Add butter to glass measuring cup and microwave on high 2 minutes. Remove from microwave and let stand for 1 minute. Spoon foamy layer off top and discard, saving only the fat below.

Directions

2. Cut okra across into ½" rounds and set aside.

3. Cut chicken and sausage into bite-sized pieces. Brown together over medium-high heat, then remove from heat and set aside.

Three-Meat (Chicken, Sausage, Shrimp) Gumbo

(CONTINUED)

4   Cut okra across into ½" rounds and set aside.

5   Cut chicken and sausage into bite-sized pieces. Brown together over medium-high heat, then remove from heat and set aside.

6   In large heavy-bottom pot, melt butter over medium-low heat. Gradually stir in flour and cook, stirring with a whisk, about 10 minutes or until mixture is a mahogany to chocolate brown. Be very careful that you don't burn this! Trust me, you'll know.

7   Remove pot from heat to allow the roux to cool slightly. Add celery, garlic, red pepper, jalapeno and onion. Cook until vegetables are tender, stirring occasionally.

8   Add chicken broth to veggie roux mix, stirring well. Bring to boil, then turn down heat to simmer. Add herbs, salt, and black pepper.

9   Cook for 10 minutes. Then spoon cooked sausage and chicken into sauce and simmer over low heat, stirring occasionally. Add okra at this point, then simmer for 10 more minutes.

10   After, add shrimp and simmer until fully cooked (3—5 minutes depending on shrimp size).

11   Remove from heat and serve over steamed rice.

Another variant of three-meat gumbo.
I shan't be preparing this one.

Pollo Loco-Style Chicken (Crazy Chicken)

SERVES: 4 │ *METHOD: SIMMER* │ *APPROX. TIME: 1½ HOURS* │ *DIFFICULTY: EASY*

While travelling in the States, especially California, we've come to love eating at the Pollo Loco restaurants. I've attempted to replicate their secret recipe many times and this as as close as I've gotten. While it isn't exact, I'd call it a respectful homage.

You ask my kids, they'd all rather eat at this fast food place than any burger joint in the land. The first time we tried Pollo Loco was on a family visit to Los Angeles in the early '90s. We'd been driving around doing the expected touristy things. We didn't spot any celebrities, or even any also-rans, but we grew hungry in our gawking attempts, so we stopped at the first chicken joint we found—a local franchise called Pollo Loco. We all fell in love with their unique, thoroughly Californian take on chicken.

Frankly, Pollo Loco saved our lives that day. Celebrity stalking is hungry work.

Ingredients

- ¼ cup vegetable oil
- 4 limes for juicing (½ cup)
- 4 oranges for juicing (1 cup)
- 4 cloves garlic, pressed
- 1 medium onion, minced finely
- 1 tablespoon cumin
- 1 teaspoon oregano
- 1 large pinch saffron
- ½ cup hot water
- 1—3 lbs. frying chicken
- 1 package corn tortillas

Preparation

1. Soak saffron in hot water and, set aside. Put all remaining ingredients in glass bowl. Add saffron and water to mix and whisk together. Cool in fridge 1 hour.

Directions

2. Cut chicken into bite-sized pieces and place in a large pan or zip-lock bag. Add marinade. Ensure all pieces are fully coated, preferably submerged, and place in fridge for a minimum 6 hours. Overnight is best.

3. Remove chicken from marinade. Place remaining marinade in a pot and cook at medium heat to reduce to thick consistency, for basting chicken later.

Pollo Loco-Style Chicken (Crazy Chicken)
(CONTINUED)

4 Place chicken in roasting pan and cook at 375° for 35 minutes. Once time has elapsed, remove chicken from oven and place on hot barbeque grill. Use your reduced marinade as a sauce to coat chicken on the grill.

5 After 7 minutes, turn chicken over and repeat. Make sure chicken doesn't burn! Now remove from heat to cool.

6 Heat your corn tortillas by enclosing in damp paper towel and microwaving for 15 seconds, or place each tortilla on a heated non-stick pan for about 30 seconds per side.

7 Strip cooled chicken from bones. Add meat to tortilla with salsa, guacamole, beans and rice. Or just eat it out of the pan, like a dog. Treat yourself.

I'll show you who's loco, you feathered fuck!

Butter Chicken

SERVES: *4* | METHOD: *SIMMER* | APPROX. TIME: *OVERNIGHT* | DIFFICULTY: *MEDIUM*

Chicken Ingredients

- 2 lbs. chicken thighs, skinless and boneless
- 1 cup plain yogurt (Greek style is best)
- ¼ cup liquid honey
- 1 teaspoon cayenne
- ½ teaspoon salt
- 2 tablespoons ginger paste
- 2 tablespoons lemon juice
- 2 tablespoons garlic paste
- 1 tablespoon paprika
- 1 teaspoon mustard powder
- 1 teaspoon garam masala

Sauce Ingredients

- 4 tablespoons olive oil
- 1 cup tomato sauce
  OR
  1 cup chopped canned tomatoes
- 1 cup water
- 2 green chilis (Serrano or habanero), chopped
- 1 cup cream or whipping cream
- 1 tablespoon ginger paste
- 1 tablespoon garlic paste
- 1 tablespoon red chili powder
- 2—3 teaspoons garam masala (or more! I like more!)
- 2 tablespoons honey
- 2 teaspoons cumin
- 1 teaspoon turmeric
- 3 tablespoons butter
- Salt to taste

Butter Chicken

(CONTINUED)

Preparation

1   Cut chicken into 1" strips. Mix yogurt, chili powder, salt, ginger paste, garlic paste, lemon juice, mustard powder, honey, paprika, and 1 teaspoon garam masala in large bowl. Add chicken, mix thoroughly until coated, and marinate for 4 hours or overnight.

Directions

2   Once marinated, place chicken on skewers and broil or barbeque for 10—12 minutes, or until almost done with a hint of char. Remove from heat and set aside.

3   Heat olive oil in a pan. Place ginger-garlic paste and cut green chilis and sauté for two minutes. Mix in tomato puree, red chili powder, garam masala, water, honey, sugar, cumin and turmeric. Bring to a boil, lower heat and simmer for 20 minutes.

4   Remove mixture from heat and let cool for 20 minutes. Then place in blender and puree until mixture is smooth and creamy.

5   Return pureed mixture to pan and heat until bubbling. Add cooked chicken pieces. Add salt to taste.

6   Simmer for 5 minutes, then add cream and butter. Simmer 5 minutes longer and remove from heat. Serve with naan or rice, especially saffron or coconut rice!

Notes

Kaitlyn can eat more butter chicken than... who eats a lot of butter chicken? An entire UK football team? I normally make a double-batch, or even triple. As we gather to eat, Kaitlyn is rendered speechless by an inordinate volume of drool. But that's just the beginning.

Imagine with me as I try to paint the picture. There's a large truck on the street in front of your house—we call it a vacuum truck in these here parts. It's parked beside a storm drain, with a large hose stuck down the grate.

At the signal of a guy in a hard hat, the truck revs up and the vacuum starts. The noise is incredible. A sucking, ravenous, wet roar that shakes the whole neighbourhood. Your good china rattles in its cabinets. Dogs flee, cats take refuge under the beds, jittery old men grab their trusty Winchesters from the closets.

The noise pummels the whole of the earth until finally, with a glub, clang and filthy slurp, the drain is empty and the truck is full. The workers gather up their supplies. The truck, groaning under the weight of countless tonnes of muck, trundles slowly away, its wheels splayed, axles gone bowlegged.

An eerie quiet falls over the neighbourhood. Weeks later, the birds return.

This process is what this family endures whenever I serve butter chicken. I've filmed Kaitlyn's horrifying culinary depravity for posterity and eventual release in theaters when my retirement fund runs out. John Waters keeps leaving me voice-mails about it.

Chicken Teriyaki

SERVES: *4* | METHOD: *MARINATE & BAKE* | APPROX. TIME: *OVERNIGHT* | DIFFICULTY: *TRICKY*

This dish is worth the effort to plan ahead and babysit as it broils. I found this recipe on the internet and after tasting it, I realized it was a perfect duplicate of a delicious meal I had in Tokyo. No, not that meal. A different one, thank God.

Marinade Ingredients

- ½ cup cold water
- 2 tablespoons dark soy sauce
- 2 tablespoons brown sugar
- 2 tablespoons mirin
- 4 chicken legs

Teriyaki Sauce Ingredients

- 2 tablespoons honey
- 2 tablespoons dark soy sauce
- 2 tablespoons mirin marinade
- 2 tablespoons sake or dry sherry (sake is best)

Preparation

1   Combine water, soy sauce, brown sugar and mirin in large, leak-proof plastic bag. Add chicken, press out as much air as possible before sealing, place bag in large bowl to guard against dripping, and refrigerate overnight.

Directions

2   Preheat oven to 425°. Debone chicken legs (use a tutorial if you must) but leave skin on.

3   In small saucepan over medium heat, add honey, soy sauce, mirin and sake. Bring to rolling boil until sauce reduces by half. Once reduced, remove from heat and set aside. It will thicken nicely as it cools.

4   Place wire rack on baking sheet lined with aluminum foil, then set chicken pieces skin-side down onto rack. Place baking sheet into oven in top-third position.

5   Bake for 5 minutes, then turn oven up to broil setting. Broil chicken for 3 minutes longer.

6   Remove chicken from oven and flip pieces over, skin-side up. Return to oven and broil for 8 minutes longer. Watch closely to make sure chicken doesn't burn!

7   If chicken skin starts to burn, move baking sheet from top-third to lower position, keeping broiler on. Baste with reduced teriyaki sauce just prior to removing from oven.

8   Serve with steamed rice along with dipping dish of extra teriyaki sauce.

Thai Red Curry Chicken

SERVES: 6 | *METHOD: SIMMER* | *APPROX. TIME: 30 MINUTES* | *DIFFICULTY: EASY*

According to Kaitlyn, if she had to pick 5 foods to live on for the rest of her life, my Thai curry chicken would be one of them. When I make this dish, the whole family will eat it for 2 days straight without complaint. In fact, the complaining only begins when there's none left. At that point, God have mercy on me. God have mercy on us all.

Ingredients

- 2 tablespoons grapeseed oil
- 2 lbs. chicken thighs (boneless and skinless is best)
- 3 cloves garlic, pressed
- 1 medium onion, minced finely
- 3 teaspoon ginger paste
- 2—3 tablespoons Thai red curry paste (3 is best!)
- 1 stalk lemongrass, cut into large pieces for easy removal
- 2 cans coconut milk (400ml)
- 1 fresh lime
- 2 tablespoons sugar
- 3 tablespoons fish sauce
- 1 red pepper, julienned (toothpick-thin)
- 1—2 cups chicken stock

Directions

1. Juice lime into small bowl and set aside. Cut chicken thighs into bite-sized pieces and season with salt and pepper.

2. Add oil to large non-stick skillet and heat on high until just beginning to smoke. Add chicken to skillet and brown well on all sides, then remove remove from pan.

3. Into hot pan add garlic, ginger, red curry paste and onion. Sauté until onion is tender, about 2 minutes. During sauté, add chicken broth to deglaze the pan and concentrate your chicken flavour.

4. Add lemon grass, coconut milk, lime juice, sugar, and fish sauce. Bring to simmer, then add browned chicken pieces. Simmer for 15 minutes, or until liquid reduces by a third.

5. Finally, add red peppers and cook 1 minute. Serve piping hot over steamed rice.

Exploding Chicken (with Country Gravy)

SERVES: 6 | *METHOD: SAUTÉ & BAKE* | *APPROX. TIME: 3 HOURS* | *DIFFICULTY: MEDIUM*

Chicken Ingredients

- ✕ 12 pieces chicken legs and thighs
- ✕ 1 quart buttermilk
- ✕ 1 cup cooking oil

Chicken Coating, Round One

- ✕ 1 cup all-purpose flour
- ✕ Salt and pepper to taste

Egg Wash

- ✕ 2 large eggs
- ✕ 2 cups milk
- ✕ 1 teaspoon salt

Chicken Coating, Round Two

- ✕ 4 cups flour
- ✕ ½ cup fried chicken spice
- ✕ 1 tablespoon salt

Chicken Coating, Round Two

- ✕ 2 cups chicken stock
- ✕ 2 cups heavy cream

Preparation

1   Wash chicken parts thoroughly, then soak in 1 quart buttermilk for 2 hours.

Directions

2   Preheat your oven to 350°. Remove chicken from buttermilk but don't allow to dry too much.

3   Place your first round of flour, salt, pepper, and chicken into large plastic bag, then shake vigorously to coat evenly.

4   Mix egg wash ingredients well in large bowl. Remove chicken from plastic bag, shake off excess flour and dip coated chicken into egg wash, turning over until evenly coated.

5   Place chicken into your second seasoned flour mixture, shake to coat well, then remove and put aside. Don't throw out flour mixture yet—you'll need it later.

6   In large skillet, pour 1 cup of cooking oil, or enough to cover bottom of pan ¼" deep. Heat on medium-high heat, then place seasoned chicken into oil to fry. After 3 minutes, turn over and cook for 3 more minutes.

7   Remove chicken from skillet (don't get rid of the oil yet!), place on baking sheet, and cook in the oven for 40 minutes at 350°.

Exploding Chicken (with Country Gravy)
(CONTINUED)

Country Cream Gravy

1 Drain oil from skillet into a bowl, leaving browned flour bits behind. Add ¼ cup spiced flour mixture to skillet and cook on medium heat to make a roux, adding some oil back if roux is too dry.

2 Cook roux for 3—4 minutes, but don't brown. Now add your chicken stock and heavy cream, whisking thoroughly to ensure smoothness.

3 Cook for 5 minutes, then remove from oven and season with salt and pepper to taste.

4 Serve chicken with gravy, mashed potatoes and a defibrillator.

The Tale of the Exploding Chicken

Many years ago, on a chilly October evening, I was preparing this meal for the family. As I was cooking, Susan, Jordan and Kristine were watching CNN's coverage of the San Francisco earthquake, which had only occurred an hour or so before. It was a terrible scene, and emotions were running high in the house.

Me, I still had a dinner to make. So alone in the kitchen I was, preparing Country Chicken Gravy, the final part of my spread.

I removed the tray from the oven and removed the chicken from the tray. I placed the tray on the stovetop and turned on the burner to begin the roux. All normal stuff. But here's where my plan went wrong: I was using a Pyrex pan. On the bottom, it said, "Safe for stovetop, oven, microwave and freezer." Or at least I thought it said stovetop.

I added the flour to the oil and began to stir. I then whisked the cream into the hot roux, creating a gravy that began to bubble nicely. You know, normal stuff. It was at this point that science of tempered glass entered my kitchen.

As the gravy bubbled, I stepped back a foot or two to catch a glimpse of CNN. The moment I looked back at the bubbling gravy I watched in fascination as the Pyrex pan seemed to expand noticeably and then shrink.

Then with a very loud bang, it exploded.

Hot sharp glass and torrents of gravy rocketed in every direction. I somehow avoided taking shrapnel, but the ceiling, floor, walls, stove, fridge, counter tops weren't so lucky. My entire goddamn kitchen became a wet, steaming, down-home, country-style catastrophe.

At the sound of the bang, Susan and the kids raced to the kitchen. Talking about it later, Susan had expected to see me on the floor, full of shards like a trench fighter in the Argonne, but instead she saw me standing stunned and quite unharmed with glass and gravy dripping off my clothes, right at the epicentre of the thermo-cream explosion.

We began the clean-up once the shock wore off and my ears stopped ringing. Cleaning took a couple of hours (note: stucco ceilings are a terrible thing to install in a kitchen).

Once we finished cleaning, we realized our dinner problem hadn't been solved. The chicken, mashed potatoes and veggies had sat within the radius of the explosion. Not willing to risk biting down on glass shards, we were forced to dispose of them uneaten.

Exploding Chicken (with Country Gravy)
(CONTINUED)

Have fun explaining Exploding Chicken to your insurance company.

Another pizza night in the wake of disaster! Such is the Boos family tradition. At the pizza place we rehashed the main event of our day and began to find the humour in our own little disaster, although not the larger one we'd witnessed on TV.

By the end of the night, one of us had provided a name for my mistake that has stuck even to the present day, just like the gravy residue on the walls. I had failed to make a meal that night, but I had succeeded in making the world's first Exploding Chicken.

Lessons learned that day:

✗ *Turns out, Pyrex does not actually say "Safe for stovetop" on the bottom.*

✗ *Pyrex expands and contracts rapidly when placed on a burner on the stovetop.*

✗ *Pyrex can explode with enough force to hurl large amounts of liquid considerable distances.*

✗ *Bart should not be left alone in the kitchen with Pyrex.*

✗ *Pyrex is very good quality stuff if used correctly, but where's the story in that?*

✗ *A good pizza can salvage any disaster.*

✗ *Stucco ceilings suck ass.*

✗ *Earthquakes are scary, man. And distracting.*

✗ *Use steel pans to cook gravy, not fucking Pyrex.*

Panang Curry Chicken

SERVES: 4 | *METHOD: SAUTÉ & SIMMER* | *APPROX. TIME: 40 MINUTES* | *DIFFICULTY: EASY*

Ingredients

- 2 lbs. boneless, skinless chicken thighs
- 2 cups rice
- 2 cans coconut milk (350ml)
- 2 tablespoons Panang curry paste
- 3 tablespoons brown sugar
- 2 tablespoons nuoc mam (Vietmanese fish sauce)
- ½ fresh lime
- 1 cup chicken stock (optional)
- 1 lb. long beans or green beans, chopped
- ½ cup roasted unsalted peanuts

Preparation

1 Cook rice according to package instructions. Chop peanuts the easy and fun way: place into plastic bag and smash with heavy pan until thoroughly crumbled. Juice lime into small bowl and set aside. Cut chicken thighs into bite-sized pieces.

Directions

2 Heat oil in deep non-stick pan. Brown chicken over medium heat for 5 minutes. Add coconut milk, curry paste, sugar, lime juice and fish sauce to pan, bring to a boil, then turn down heat to low and simmer for 10—12 minutes.

3 Next, add beans and simmer for an additional 12 minutes. As mixture cooks it will thicken, so add chicken stock or water, if necessary, to reach your preferred consistency.

4 Bring back to a boil and remove from heat, then serve with cooked rice.

5 Sprinkle crushed peanuts over mixture when it's plated.

Brown jasmine rice is especially good here.

CONTINUED NEXT PAGE

Panang Curry Chicken
(CONTINUED)

Notes

The first time I cooked this, I served it to an eager audience of Kaitlyn, Kelsey and Susan. It was like feeding a nest of baby birds, except with less regurgitating. But as I went in for my second helping, I felt a sharp pain in my forearm and nearly dropped the serving spoon.

I looked down at my forearm only to see Kaitlyn's fork jutting from the fleshy part of my arm. In a voice I've never heard before or since, a guttural gurgle from the gulfs of Hell, Kaitlyn simply said, "Leave it. It's mine."

So I left it, and it was hers. No second helping for me, or for anyone else except Kaitlyn. These are the *good* reviews, people. You see what I have to live with?

So, take it from my daughter, my curry chicken is really, really good. Good enough to make you stab your own father to protect your share. So the lesson from this dish is: if you're dining with my family, wear Kevlar, or preferably that suit of armour like Grizzly Man had. And cook extra. And whatever you think "extra" means, double it. Consider yourself warned.

By all means, join us for dinner, but I hope you can dodge a fork better than I can.

Kaitlyn feasts.

Stuffed Chicken Legs

SERVES: 4 | *METHOD: SAUTÉ & SIMMER* | *APPROX. TIME: 40 MINUTES* | *DIFFICULTY: EASY*

Ingredients

- 8 chicken legs, whole
- 8 squares aluminium foil (8" × 8" is ideal)
- 8 slices honey ham, sliced thin
- 16 large basil leaves
- ½ cup mushrooms, diced finely
- 2 shallots, diced finely
- ¼ cup celery, diced finely
- ¼—½ cup grated cheese (Swiss, edam, jack or other white cheese)
- ¼ cup fine bread crumbs
- 1 clove garlic
- 1 tablespoon olive oil
- 1 pinch dried sage
  OR
  1 teaspoon chopped fresh sage
  OR
  1 teaspoon herb(s) of your choice
- Salt and pepper to taste

Directions

1 Preheat oven to 375°.

2 Debone chicken with butterfly method and refrigerate ½ hour.

3 Sauté shallots, garlic and celery until translucent. Add mushrooms and sauté until all water has been evaporated and the mixture is nicely incorporated. Remove from heat and allow to cool to room temperature.

4 When mixture is cool, place into mixing bowl. Add grated cheese, bread crumbs, salt and pepper. Mix well.

5 Place chicken piece skin-side down and place 1 slice of ham, 2 basil leaves and 2 tablespoons stuffing onto meat's widest part. Roll up like cigar and fold ends over at halfway point. Your roll should be sealed and uniform now.

6 Place stuffed chicken on foil sheet and roll up, making sure it's sealed, and twist ends closed. Repeat making rolls with remaining chicken until there's none left.

7 Evenly space chicken rolls on baking rack and bake for 20 minutes. Remove from oven, allow to cool for 15 minutes, then remove chicken from foil.

8 Space chicken evenly on non-stick baking sheet and return to oven for 10 minutes or until skin is crispy and golden brown.

9 Remove from heat and prepare to have an out-of-body experience.

Chicken Grand-Mère Farcie

SERVES: *3* | METHOD: *MARINATE & BAKE* | APPROX. TIME: *OVERNIGHT* | DIFFICULTY: *TRICKY*

Chicken

- ✕ 6 chicken legs
- ✕ 6 squares aluminum foil (8" × 8" is ideal)

Marinade Ingredients

- ✕ 1 cup fish sauce
- ✕ 1 cup sugar
- ✕ 1 cup water
- ✕ ¼ cup chopped cilantro
- ✕ 1 large fresh lime for juice (about 3 tablespoons)

Stuffing Ingredients

- ✕ ½ lb. ground pork
- ✕ ½ lb. raw shrimp, cleaned and deveined
- ✕ 1 small onion, minced finely
- ✕ 2 cloves garlic, pressed
- ✕ 1 small carrot, grated
- ✕ 1 can (8 oz.) water chestnuts, drained
- ✕ ½ oz. dried wood-ear mushroom
- ✕ 3 dried shitake mushrooms
- ✕ 2 tablespoons fish sauce
- ✕ 2 teaspoons sugar
- ✕ 1 teaspoon black pepper

Preparation

1   Heat oil in deep non-stick pan. Brown chicken ovJuice lime and mix all marinade ingredients in large bowl or container. Debone chicken with the butterfly method (but leave skin on). Submerge chicken into marinade, then refrigerate at least 8 hours or overnight.

2   The next day, closer to your time of cooking, rehydrate dried wood-ear and shitake mushrooms by placing in steel bowl, covering with boiling water and soaking for 1 hour.

Directions

3   Drain mushrooms, remove and discard stems from shiitakes, then place all mushrooms into blender. Add water chestnuts to blender, mince with mushrooms (but don't puree), then remove.

4   Next place shrimp into shrimp into blender and pulse a few times until shrimp is ground, but not pureed. Place minced shrimp into bowl with ground pork.

5   Add water chestnut-mushroom mix to pork mixture. Add remaining ingredients and mix well.

6   Place covered bowl in fridge until ready to prepare the ballotines. That's what you're making now: a *ballotine*, a French term for stuffed boneless poultry.

Chicken Grand-Mère Farcie
(CONTINUED)

7   Remove chicken from marinade and allow to drain. Remove and discard lemongrass pieces.

8   Preheat oven to 350°.

9   Lay chicken piece flat, skin-side down on foil square. Place 3 tablespoons of stuffing onto chicken piece, then roll up into sausage shape.

10   Roll foil around chicken, then twist foil ends to seal and compress package slightly. Repeat with next chicken piece until all 6 are done.

11   Place wrapped chicken ballotines onto baking sheet. Roast in oven for 30 minutes or until the internal temperature reaches 170°. Then remove chicken from oven and let cool for 15 minutes.

12   Turn oven up to 400° at this point.

13   Once cooled enough to handle, remove foil from chicken, then evenly space on oil-coated oven rack, over tray to catch drippings.

14   Roast in 400° oven for 10—12 minutes or until skin is golden brown. Remove and serve hot.

Notes

There was once a restaurant in Vancouver years ago named The Green Hut, on the corner of Robson and Broughton. The only Vietnamese restaurant in the West End at the time, it is still the best I have ever eaten, anywhere. The signature dish was something called Chicken Grand-Mère Farcie.

I've looked for it on the menu of every Vietnamese restaurant I've been, without success, so I set upon reconstructing it from memory. The recipe here was the outcome. Chicken Grand-Mère Farcie, Pseudo-Vietnamese style.

A *ballotine* is a stuffed deboned poultry dish, normally a deboned leg or chicken breast, sometimes a whole chicken. Stuffings can vary with fruit, nuts, bread, vegetable and other meats.

Traditional ballotines are trussed with string, but with the advent of aluminum foil, we can skip that arduous chore. I first saw Jacques Pepin do it on TV years ago, and who are we to question him?

Vietnam was a French colony until the French did what the French do, which is surrender and beat a hasty retreat. The high point of French occupation, if any military occupation has a high point, was a food fusion before that term was fashionable: a culinary art that the Vietnamese embraced and infused with local ingredients and recipes.

The French left lots of other stuff behind in Vietnam as well—misery, poverty, exploitation, emotional scars for generations... for that, there are other books you can look into.

The French occupation also proved a warrior spirit in the Vietnamese population, a feature that the Americans later discovered to their chagrin. The Viets remain a lovely people with extremely beautiful women, all of whom can deliver a lethal left hook.

If you want to travel without leaving the comfort of your kitchen, this recipe is the way to do it.

Thai-Style Stuffed Chicken Wings

SERVES: **8** | *METHOD:* **STEAM & BAKE** | *APPROX. TIME:* **2 HOURS** | *DIFFICULTY:* **MEDIUM**

You can buy bamboo steamer baskets at most Asian markets, and they often come in sets. When purchasing, make sure the steamers fit flush over the cooking pots you intend to boil with, without unwanted gaps. (In other words, measure your pots before you shop.) Steamers are inexpensive, last for years—mine are over a decade old—and impart a light flavour you can achieve no other way.

Special Equipment

- Deep fryer
- Bamboo steamer, large

Chicken Ingredients

- 4 pounds chicken wings (about 24), deboned
- 1 cup wheat flour
- 1 tablespoon granulated garlic
- 1 teaspoon salt
- 1 teaspoon ground pepper

Filling Ingredients

- ½ lb. ground or minced pork
- ½ lb. raw shrimp, shelled and deveined
- 2 bundles mung bean noodles
- 1 small can water chestnuts
- 4 dried shitake mushrooms,
- ½ oz. (¼ cup) dried wood ear, soaked
- 3 cloves garlic, pressed or minced
- 1 tablespoon fresh basil, minced
- 1 tablespoon tapioca starch
- 2 tablespoons dark soy sauce
- 1 tablespoon light soy sauce
- 1 tablespoon fish sauce
- 1 tablespoon dried chili flakes
- 1 teaspoon white sugar
- 1 teaspoon ground pepper
- ½ teaspoon kosher salt

Thai-Style Stuffed Chicken Wings
(CONTINUED)

Directions

1 Add mushrooms and wood ear to large bowl and add boiling water. Let soak for 20 minutes until rehydrated. Drain, then remove and discard mushroom stems.

2 Place dry noodles in different bowl and add hot water. Soak for 10 minutes, then flush under cold running water until noodles are cool. Drain well, then chop into inch long strands. Set aside.

3 Place shrimp in blender, pulse 4-5 times, until shrimp is ground well, but not pureed. Transfer shrimp to new bowl and add ground pork.

4 Put fungi, water chestnuts, mint and basil in blender and pulse until minced finely. Add to pork mixture.

5 Add mung bean noodles to pork mixture, along with all other filling ingredients. Mix well until all ingredients are well incorporated. Refrigerate 1 hour to allow full flavour penetration. This will give you time to debone chicken wings, as described earlier in this book.

6 Use teaspoon to stuff deboned chicken cavity tightly with filling, leaving no air pockets. Do not overfill because wings will shrink as they cook.

7 Place stuffed wings on a plate, then place into a large steamer.

8 Steam chicken over high heat for 10 minutes, then check meat's internal temperature. At 170° they're fully cooked.

9 Remove from heat and set onto tray lined with parchment paper. Cool for 20 minutes. Wings are now ready for the next part!

10 Preheat deep fryer to 350°. In separate bowl, blend flour, salt, pepper and granulated garlic together until fully mixed. Dredge cooled chicken wing in flour mix until fully coated and shake off excess.

11 Space out coated chicken on baking sheet or cutting board. Repeat dredging process until all wings are evenly coated.

12 Move wings to deep fryer basket and gently lower into fryer for 5 minutes, or until skin is golden brown. You may have to do this in batches. When wings are cooked, they'll start to float, so let float a minute or so.

13 Remove from fryer and serve with dipping sauce of your choice, or simply dash with black pepper and kosher salt.

✕ *In-fucking-credible! And in-fucking-credibly painful if you don't let them cool down before you eat them.*

Chicken Piccata

SERVES: *4* | METHOD: *SAUTÉ & BAKE* | APPROX. TIME: *1 HOUR* | DIFFICULTY: *TOUGH*

Ingredients

✕ *8 chicken thighs*

✕ *2 cups all-purpose flour*

✕ *1 teaspoon sea salt*

✕ *1 teaspoon ground pepper*

✕ *4 tablespoons unsalted butter*

✕ *4 tablespoons vegetable oil*

✕ *1 large lemon, fresh-squeezed for juice*

✕ *¼ cup dry white wine*

✕ *½ cup low-sodium chicken stock*

✕ *3 tablespoons capers, rinsed*

✕ *3 tablespoons fresh parsley, minced*

Directions

1 Place 1 chicken thigh between 2 pieces of plastic wrap. Pound chicken flat with a meat tenderizer or heavy pot until about ¼" thick—flattened chicken is now called an *escallope* (scallop). Season both sides with salt and pepper.

2 Mix flour, salt and pepper well and spread on wide bowl or plate. Dredge chicken in flour until fully coated and shake off excess. Set aside. Preheat your oven to 350° now.

3 In large skillet over medium heat, melt 2 tablespoons butter along with vegetable oil. Once oil begins to bubble, add half your chicken (4 escallopes) and fry for 3 minutes each side until lightly browned.

4 Remove chicken and transfer to oven proof plate, then place into oven to keep warm. Fry remaining chicken and add it to oven also.

5 Keep frying pan drippings and remainders in place for the next part.

✕ *Once you place chicken in pan to fry, don't lift, peek or poke it. If you feel you need to "work it" simply shake the pan a little, but otherwise leave it alone. This will allow evenly-browned chicken.*

6 Add lemon juice, white wine, chicken stock, parsley and capers to frying pan over medium heat and bring to boil. Scrape all flavourful brown bits and drippings from pan and mix into simmering liquid. Cook for 5 minutes or until liquid reduces by half.

Chicken Piccata

(CONTINUED)

7 Taste sauce and add salt and pepper as
you like. Whisk in your last 2 tablespoons
of butter. Sauce will thicken, and is ready
once butter is fully incorporated.

8 Remove chicken from oven. Plate
2 pieces of chicken with generous
drizzle of sauce and serve.

✕ *Some cooks will add the fried chicken
back into the sauce to sautée further, but
I prefer my chicken a little crispy instead.
Try it both ways and see what you like.*

Notes

Years ago Susan and I were in Reno. At a casino
whose name I can't recall, I was waiting around for
a seat at a blackjack table, and I ended up hooked
to a one-armed bandit beside two elderly women.

We made small-talk as I fed the coin-eating monster,
and I was soon distracted by a loud clamour of
bells and lights. I turned to my new elderly friends
to see what they'd won, but they were in turn
looking at me. So I looked at my slot machine and
realized that the clamour was all mine. Imagine
my surprise when I found out I'd won $1,600!

I sat there with a dazed smile on my face, then
hit the *cash out* button, causing silver dollars
to pile up noisily on the tray below. The old
lady next to me leaned over, slapped my arm
and said, "Isn't it fun when that happens?"

Without thinking I replied, "You bet! Heck,
I think it's even better than sex."

Without missing a beat, the lovely woman
patted me gently on the shoulder and said,
"Darlin', then you must be doin' it all wrong!"

She and her friend began to laugh hysterically,
and so did I. As I shoveled coins into the plastic
bucket, I offered the ladies a drink on me, at which
point the other sweet granny chimed in, "No need
to fill us with liquor, young man, we'll take you to
our room sober." I nearly dropped my bucket.

With uncanny timing, my wife appeared at my
side. Seeing me making time with my newfound
friends, she asked what was happening. The
lovely lady to my left told her, "Oh nothing
that you would want to be part of!"

I nearly fell off my stool. I was laughing too hard to
protect my winnings, so Susan scooped up a few
hundred bucks and left me to my own devices.

I gave both of them a kiss on the cheek as I prepared
to leave, but before I stepped away, the lovely lady that
offered to take me to their room pressed further: "You
ain't gonna leave us wanting, are you, young man?"

Stunned for a reply, I offered a retort from an old joke,
"At your age, that kind of thing could be dangerous."

She looked me in the eye, and with a twinkle
in hers, responded, "You look like a healthy
young man. But if you die, you die!"

I didn't get the ladies' names or origins, but they
left a positive mark on my soul forever and for
that I'm grateful. In fact, I *do* nearly die from
giggles every time I think of that memory.

What does this have to do with chicken
piccata? Nothing. Enjoy!

Singapore Rice Noodles & Chicken

SERVES: **4** | *METHOD:* **SAUTÉ** | *APPROX. TIME:* **30 MINUTES** | *DIFFICULTY:* **MEDIUM**

This is another perennial favourite that the kids attacked like tigers in a rice paddy. In my house, I don't think any leftovers ever made it to the fridge. it's a fragrant marriage of simple ingredients that you can expand upon to make it your own. I like it hot and just a little sweet, but not sugary, hence the provided recipe. You can include bean sprouts, different meats or seafood, tofu or anything you like.

Ingredients

- 6 oz. dried rice vermicelli
- ½ lb. cooked shrimp, small
- 1 tablespoon oil
- 2 cloves garlic, pressed
- 6 dried Chinese mushrooms, rehydrated
- ½ medium onion, minced finely
- 8 oz. chicken, chopped (not ground!)
- 2 tablespoons curry powder
- ½—1 teaspoon cayenne powder
- 1 tablespoon fish sauce
- 1 tablespoon soy sauce
- ½ cup chicken stock
- 1 teaspoon sugar
- 1 large carrot, julienned
- 1 large sweet red pepper, julienned
- 1 cup broccoli, chopped

Directions

1. Rehydrate Chinese mushrooms with hot water if necessary. Chop off and discard stems.

2. Chop broccoli into florets and julienne stems. Chop chicken into bite-sized pieces. Julienne carrot and peppers to matchstick size.

3. Submerge rice vermicelli in boiling water for 5 minutes, then place in colander and rinse under cold water to avoid clumping. Drain very well and set aside.

4. Heat oil in wok or large frying pan over high heat. Sauté onions and garlic for 2 minutes. Add meat and sauté for 3 minutes further.

5. Reduce heat to medium and add curry powder, sugar and cayenne. Sauté for 2 minutes until curry gets fragrant.

6. Return heat to high. Add carrots, broccoli, fish sauce, soy sauce and chicken stock. Sauté for 2 minutes to blend all ingredients. Bring liquid to boil.

7. Add shrimp and red peppers and stir gently for 2 minutes, then add noodles and toss gently to coat fully in sauce. Once all ingredients are hot and well-mixed, move to serving platter and serve immediately.

Pork Me Harder

-or-

This Little Piggie Went to Market

Ham, bacon, ribs, shank, hocks, fresh, smoked, braised, stewed or roasted… where does it end, except in my gullet? What a versatile beastie the old pig is. It's the method actor of the protein set.

Pork can stand in for chicken, beef or even lamb in many recipes. Emeril says pork fat rules and he's not wrong. On average, I prefer pork roast to most beef roasts. Pork even pairs well with Yorkshire pudding, which is the litmus test for a roast in my books.

Pork must be cooked well-done, so it needs fat and moisture to keep the meat soft and flavourful at that heat. I prefer shoulder and leg cuts (butt, shank), blade steaks and sirloin because of their fat marbling. I find chops and tenderloin too lean for my taste; over the years, I've choked down enough tough, dried-out chops that I avoid them entirely, even in the store.

You can use whatever cut you wish. You don't have to be like me, although being me is great, really. But to make the effort of purchasing and cooking pork, only to scorch yourself a dried hunk of meat, is to dishonour the pig's memory. And I've certainly known some pigs in my time. Some aren't too bad, if they let you off with a warning.

These little piggies went to market, but strangely, they weren't very talkative all the way home.

Crispy Mapo Tofu

SERVES: 4 | *METHOD: SEVERAL!* | *APPROX. TIME: 45 MINUTES* | *DIFFICULTY: MEDIUM*

Special Equipment

- Deep fryer (optional)

Ingredients

- 1 block firm tofu, drained and cut into 1" cubes
- 2 tablespoons canola oil
- 8 oz. ground pork
- 2 cloves garlic, minced
- 3 shiitake mushrooms, minced finely
- 2 tablespoons fermented chili bean paste
- 1 tablespoon fermented black beans
- 1 tablespoon chili garlic paste
- 1 cup chicken stock
- 2 teaspoons white sugar
- 2 teaspoons dark soy sauce
- 2 tablespoons tapioca starch
  MIXED WITH
  ¼ cup cold water
- 3 tablespoons pickled daikon (Chinese radish) (optional)

Tofu Coating Ingredients

- 3 tablespoons corn starch
  OR
  3 tablespoons tapioca starch
- ½ teaspoon salt

Directions

1   Heat oil in wok or deep-sided, non-stick frying pan over high heat. Add pork and stir-fry until brown but not dry. Reduce heat to medium, add garlic and cook for 2 minutes.

2   Add fermented chili bean paste, black beans, and sauté for about 1 minute, until oil is a rich red colour.

3   Add chicken stock, sugar, soy sauce, chili paste, mushrooms and optional radish. Simmer 5 minutes. Add corn-starch-water mix slowly, stirring well until sauce is thick enough to coat a spoon.

If you don't want to deep fry, skip the following steps. Merely add cut tofu to sauce directly and simmer for 5 minutes prior to serving. Don't overstir, or tofu will crumble and you'll end up with an unappetizing slurry resembling dog food.

Still tastes good, though.

4   While sauce simmers, mix tapioca starch and salt to make coating. Coat tofu cubes evenly with starch mix and shake off excess.

5   Place tofu into preheated deep fryer at 350° until golden brown, then remove from hot oil and drain well.

6   Plate browned tofu over steamed rice, pour sauce on top and serve.

Bart's Asian Braised Pork

SERVES: 8 | *METHOD: MARINATE & BAKE* | *APPROX. TIME: 3+ HOURS* | *DIFFICULTY: EASY*

I've been making this for years and never divulged the recipe, despite begging from everyone who's tried it (often with my salad rolls). But now I'm growing old and feeble, and my resolute objection to sharing the recipe has drooped along with my body parts. So here it is.

My children were real pains in the ass whenever I cooked this. Once it came out of the oven, the smell drew them like rats to piper music. I needed to guard the pork zealously to ensure there was enough left for the salad rolls at dinner. That's why I cooked four pounds of it! But I am only one man, and the children are wily. They would feign doing chores (in retrospect, this was a dead giveaway), and once I turned my back, they pounced.

Preparation

1. Add all ingredients with pork into bowl and mix well. Cover and allow to marinate in the fridge for 2 hours minimum. Overnight is best.

Directions

2. Preheat oven to 350°.

3. Place mixture into casserole pot, cover with lid and put in oven to bake. Every 30 minutes, stir and toss the mixture so it doesn't bake into one big lump.

4. Bake for 1 hour, then turn down heat to 275° and bake for about 2 hours longer.

5. At about 2½ hours, check for tenderness by removing a pork cube and pressing it with a fork. If it breaks into shreds easily, it's done.

6. Remove pork from oven, then move pork to metal colander over your casserole pot. Drain pork into pot and set liquid aside to settle and cool.

Ingredients

- 4 lbs. pork shoulder, cubed 2" x 2"
- ¼ cup soy sauce
- 2 tablespoons Asian fish sauce
- 1 tablespoon white sugar
- 2 tablespoons sesame oil
- 1 tablespoon Sriracha sauce
- ½ teaspoon white pepper

7. After about 15 minutes, hardened fat will collect on top of liquid. Scrape off and discard this.

8. Place drained pork into a bowl and mash with the back side of a fork until all cubes are well shredded.

9. Pour remaining, now-fatless liquid over shredded pork.

10. Use in salad rolls, or serve warm with some hot sauce as an entree.

Chinese-Style Barbeque Pork

SERVES: **6** | *METHOD:* **BAKE** | *APPROX. TIME:* **2 DAYS** | *DIFFICULTY:* **EASY**

Ingredients

- ✕ *3 lbs. pork shoulder, cut into strips (3" × 3" thick and 6" long)*
- ✕ *1 cup hoisin sauce*
- ✕ *½ cup brown sugar*
- ✕ *½ teaspoon five spice powder*
- ✕ *1 teaspoon red food colouring (optional)*

Goes Great With

- ☸ *Hot and sour soup*

Directions

1. Place all ingredients in plastic freezer bag, mix well, squeeze air out and seal. Place in fridge for a minimum of 24—48 hours. Longer is better. Squeeze and rotate bag twice per day to keep marinade blended.

2. After appropriate time has elapsed, remove pork from marinade and set on wire racks placed over baking sheet.

3. Place in 375° preheated oven and roast for 10 minutes. At the 10 minute mark, turn pork over and cook for another 10 minutes. Repeat again at 20-minute mark.

4. At 30-minute mark, check internal temperature with meat thermometer. If it's 170°, it's done. If not, flip pork again and cook for 10 minutes longer.

5. Remove pork from oven and let cool on rack for 20 minutes.

6. Slice and serve as a meal entree, serve as a side dish or in soup (I suggest hot and sour soup). Be prepared to fight off roving marauders if they should happen to smell it roasting.

Cuban Pork

SERVES: **5** | *METHOD:* **BAKE** | *APPROX. TIME:* **4—6 HOURS** | *DIFFICULTY:* **EASY**

Ingredients

- 2½ pounds pork shoulder, cubed 1" × 1"
- 4 cloves garlic, pressed
- 2 large limes for juicing
- ½ teaspoon salt
- 1 orange for juicing
- 2 tablespoons vinegar
- 1 tablespoon ground cumin
- 1 tablespoon lemon juice
- 2 tablespoons sugar
- Ground black pepper to taste

Directions

1. Mix all ingredients in large, oven-safe covered dish. Refrigerate 4—6 hours or overnight.

2. Remove from fridge. Drain off marinade into bowl for later.

3. Bake pork in covered dish at 375° for 2 hours, stirring every 30 minutes to distribute heat evenly. Remove from oven.

4. Place leftover marinade in soup pot and bring to boil, then lower heat and simmer for 10 minutes to reduce volume by ⅓.

5. Once reduced, strain liquid through cheesecloth or fine mesh and serve hot over cooked pork with rice and black bean soup. Simply delicious.

Thai Green Curry Pork

SERVES: 4 | *METHOD: SAUTÉ* | *APPROX. TIME: 1 HOUR* | *DIFFICULTY: EASY*

Ingredients

- 2 tablespoons canola oil
- 2 shallots

  OR

  1 medium onion, finely chopped
- 3 tablespoons Thai green curry paste
- 1½ pounds pork, cubed
- 1 can coconut milk
- 2 cups chicken stock
- 2 tablespoons fish sauce
- 1 tablespoon sugar
- 1 small lime (for juicing and lime zest)
- 1 cup green beans
- 1 large red pepper, julienned
- 1 bunch cilantro (optional)

Directions

1   Juice lime and grate 1 teaspoon of zest (about ½ your lime). Add oil to pan on medium-high heat and bring to smoking point. Brown pork on all sides, then remove from pan and set aside.

2   Add shallots and curry paste to pan with pork drippings. Sauté for 2 minutes but don't brown! Remove from heat and set aside. Deglaze hot pan with chicken stock.

3   Add coconut milk, fish sauce, sugar and lime juice to pan. Bring to low boil and reduce heat to simmer for 10 minutes. Add browned pork and simmer for 30 minutes over low heat.

4   Add beans and cook for 10 minutes. Add red pepper, lime zest and optional cilantro just prior to serving.

5   Serve with jasmine rice.

Vietnamese Barbeque Pork

SERVES: 4 | *METHOD: GRILL* | *APPROX. TIME: OVERNIGHT* | *DIFFICULTY: EASY*

This is candy on a plate, a signature of Vietnamese restaurants we frequent. The marinade is similar to spring roll dipping sauce, and complements other Vietnamese cuisine well.

Ingredients

- 2 lbs. pork shoulder
- ½ cup white sugar
- ½ cup fish sauce
- ¼ cup water
- 2 tablespoons white vinegar
- 1 fresh lime (for juicing)
- 2 teaspoons chili garlic paste

If You Screw Up, See Also

 Mexican shredded beef

Directions

1. Hand-squeeze ½ your lime into bowl. This should result in about 2 tablespoons juice.

2. Trim pork of fat and slice across grain into thin slices. Place all ingredients with lime juice in medium bowl. Cover and marinate in fridge for 6 hours or overnight.

3. Remove pork from marinade and drain well.

4. To avoid pork sticking to grill, as marinated meat does, grease hot grill with oil-soaked paper towel just prior to placing meat on barbeque.

> *Use tongs for this, or risk having all the hair on your arm scorched off. How do I know this? Take one guess. Caveman Oog do indeed know fire hot.*

Exercise caution. Keep pot of water on hand to dunk your used paper towel if it ignites. And maybe save some extra slices of pork for the fire department when they show up.

5. Grill over low heat on barbeque until cooked through, 1 minute per side if sliced thin. Be vigilant and make sure flames don't char your pork. Don't overcook! (If this happens, see my Mexican shredded beef recipe.)

6. Serve immediately.

Lazy Bastard Barbeque

There are a million ways to grill pork ribs. I'm not bold enough to suggest that my way is the best, even though it is. They're also the easy way, and people don't call me Lazy Bastard for nothing.

Unless you own a good quality smoker and know how to use it, you'll be forced to utilize the family barbeque, either gas or charcoal. Charcoal is best, but since most of us use gas grills, we'll concentrate our technique there. Such is the way of the Lazy Bastard.

Spare ribs (side ribs) are popular for their tremendous flavour, but I find that most butchers boost the cut's weight by including more fat and cartilage than necessary. For that reason, I prefer side ribs—less fat, less gristle, less waste. By the time you trim all the tips, cartilage and fat from your spare ribs, you're left with much less meat, and it would've been the same price as buying back ribs from the get-go, so just do that instead.

Some butchers call back ribs "baby back" ribs, though that name leaves an unpleasant picture in my overactive imagination. They're so named by virtue of how they're cut: shorter and smaller than spare ribs. I've seen them called Canadian back ribs or Canadian baby back ribs, and it's all the same shit.

You want annoyance about names? The mere act of calling something "barbeque" has caused as much Southern bloodshed as the Civil War. You know a word is contentious when nobody can even agree on how to spell it.

In my remote Upper Canadian world, "barbeque" means grilling on a gas or charcoal grill (also known as… you guessed it, a barbeque). But in the South, "barbeque" means using a smoker, which is a hot chamber filled with wood smoke that cures and cooks meat in a low-heat environment over an extended period of time. Up here we merely call this "smoking" and it tends to be rather primitive in technique compared to the South.

Down South, barbeque is an art form practiced by maestros for adoring fans, and I'm one of those fans. I won't go on about all the glorious barbeque I've enjoyed in my travels through Georgia, Oklahoma, Tennessee and Kansas. If you haven't been there, it would be rude to brag, and I'm an exceedingly humble man.

Sadly, Southern barbeque hasn't caught on in Canada, and that's a pity. I do love to smoke meats, especially sockeye salmon—I've dreamt for years of owning a big barbeque trailer like the ones you see on *BBQ Pitmasters*. So if you purchased this book instead of stealing it, you may be contributing to fulfilling my long-held dream.

But chances are I gave you this book as a gift. So, frankly, you owe me.

Grilling is an art of its own, and there are many great cookbooks, TV shows and websites to consult. I suggest you begin with Bobby Flay's cookbooks or website, as he's one of the grilling gods. Read up, because good barbeque takes planning. The meats have to be grill-ready, not simply thrown from the fridge to the fire.

To recap: You grill on a barbeque, barbeque in a smoker, and smoke on a… I haven't thought this through. But it's important to know the difference to avoid confusion and banish ignorance.

Mind you, a perpetual state of ignorance is a blissful place to be. And this book isn't intended for Americans anyway. They already think they know everything.

As we say in my industry: Let's get back to the porking. There's still debate about the merits of parboiling your grill ribs versus cooking dry. Both methods can work. If you prefer to barbeque only, you can use a dry rub from the start. Me, I simmer the ribs beforehand. It doesn't sacrifice much flavour, but it tenderizes the meat to perfect softness and reduces grilling time, which lessens the chance of drying out and burning. Plus it's lazier, and such is the Lazy Bastard way.

I won't argue with purists over this. We can agree that slowly barbequing over wood smoke in a trailer is indeed the best way, but it's not the most accessible way. I'm not making *BBQ Pitmasters* ribs until I'm making *BBQ Pitmasters* money.

Pork Rib Barbeque

SERVES: *6* | METHOD: *SIMMER & GRILL* | APPROX. TIME: *4 HOURS* | DIFFICULTY: *ACHTUNG!*

Directions

1 Remove silver skin from ribs, if present. See instructions in chapter introduction if unsure.

2 Add salt, onion, bay leaves and ¼ cup barbeque rub to large pot. Bring to boil, then lower heat to simmer for 1½ hours or until ribs are tender. Remove ribs from water and set on baking sheet to cool.

3 Rub ribs with olive oil and liquid smoke, then coat lightly with barbeque rub.

✕ *Liquid smoke is a contentious ingredient and a little goes a long way. Flavour purists may substitute 1 teaspoon of chipotle pepper instead.*

4 Wrap in plastic wrap, then set in the fridge for 1 hour. This allows meat's fat and collagen to harden again, making grilling much easier.

5 Remove from fridge when ready to cook, unwrap and let sit at room temperature for ½-hour. This will help it dry a little and reach a consistent temperature on the grill.

6 Preheat barbeque on low heat. Grease grill with oil-coated cloth or paper towel just before grilling.

Ingredients

✕ *6 racks back ribs (silver skin removed)*

☸ *¼ cup Bart's Barbeque Rub*

✕ *1 tablespoon salt*

✕ *1 large onion, minced*

✕ *3 bay leaves*

✕ *¼ cup olive oil*

✕ *½ teaspoon liquid smoke*
  OR
  1 teaspoon chipotle pepper

7 Grill ribs for 6 minutes, turning once at 3-minute mark.

8 Once grill has done its thing, cover ribs with your favourite barbeque sauce. Grill another 2 minutes per side, letting barbeque sauce char slightly for a smoky flavour.

9 I said *slightly*. Don't burn!

10 Remove from barbeque and serve immediately.

Do Not Overcook the Seafood
-or-
Do Not Overcook the Goddamned Seafood

Crustaceans, bivalves, mollusks, fish and other fine critters are all regular visitors to my home, although unfortunately for them it's a one-way trip. I can't think of much seafood that I won't eat. Granted, there are many undiscovered creatures lurking in the deep and I cannot confirm their deliciousness at this time.

Dungeness Crab

Of all the offerings the seas and lakes have supplied our table, Dungeness crab is the family favourite by far. If I was to wax poetically about the Dungeness it would end up a lengthy superlative description and I don't want to come across as verbose, so I'll simply state that we like them a lot. An awful lot. Cooked with black bean sauce, boiled and slathered with garlic butter, shelled and served with a piquant cocktail sauce… oh, right. Verbose. Moving on.

Growing up on the Pacific Coast, Dungeness was a regular treat for my family. Not because we were rich, sadly, but rather because we had laid crab traps in a very productive area, and we monitored it every day. Dungeness crabbing is a bountiful fishery, if they're harvested lawfully and sustainably—by taking mature males from the traps, and tossing females and young'uns back to the water. (Early in my life, I was taught the necessary life skill of distinguishing between male and female crabs. It's easier with crabs than it is with Starbucks baristas.)

Our freezer was often full to bursting with crab, so we shared our largesse with friends, family and neighbours. Our next-door neighbours in turn rewarded us with tonnes of fresh vegetables from the market garden they owned in Richmond. Our neighbours loved us for that, and never complained when we, well-mannered teenagers that we were, threw parties with crowds that numbered in the hundreds. This negotiation tactic is called acquiescence by crab.

My favourite crab dish included a black bean garlic sauce, which Mom and Dad were experts in preparing due to endless practice on us. I learned the recipe from them. I don't know where they learned it from—perhaps Bob? At the moment it remains a delicious mystery.

For most people (including us, these days) Dungeness crab is an expensive treat, even a luxury. Here on the frozen tundra, our fishmonger normally wears a mask and demands our money at gunpoint as part of the purchasing ritual. Occasionally, when money is tight, I simply offer myself to the fishmonger in return for a few pounds of Dungeness, and he or she (it doesn't matter to me, I lie back and think of black bean sauce) takes advantage of my vulnerable nature. Days later I'll still feel violated… but also satiated.

As many a divorce lawyer can tell you, it can be dangerous to bring crabs home. My previous paragraph notwithstanding, it was simply a naive mistake, and it wasn't those kind of crabs, you ghouls. Sometimes we'd purchase live crabs from the seafood section and, while I cooked, I tried to entertain the kids by letting them free the crabs and wander about the kitchen awhile. I wouldn't let my kids get a cat, but as pointy-clawed, taciturn creatures go, a crab is pretty much the same, right?

So the crab wanderings were routine entertainment for my kids... except for the one time they decided to introduce our dog to the crab. Now, I don't have to go into explicit detail to have you conclude that this introduction didn't end well. Suffice to say, the crab caught the dog's nose in its claw, and the ensuing brawl brought the rest of the house to near-collapse until I was able to pry the two combatants apart.

Once order was restored, the crab was sent to its final reward and the dog to its kennel. The children learned a life lesson that day, and I doubt they've ever arranged a playdate between a dog and a crab since.

I used to toss the live crabs into boiling water to cook them whole. Although it's inhumane, it was the only way I knew, until one day a coworker convinced me to try cleaning them first (in the sense of cleaning a fish) before cooking. I tried it later and he was right. From that day forth, I've always cleaned the crabs before boiling. The meat tastes better when the innards aren't cooked with it.

Of course, it's a little more work. First you have to tape or cable-tie their claws, or risk losing a finger to the fight. Turn your crab upside-down and notice the tapered tail flap at the back. Now simply jam a long knife into its butthole and spear it through the centre of its body up to the eyeballs. Yes, this is the most humane way to go, if you're a crab—this method cuts the crab's nerve ganglia, which is as close to painless and stress-free as it's possible to get.

Note that the knife-butt method only works on crabs, not lobsters (which have much longer nerve ganglia) or any other animal. Believe me. You can't imagine the fight I had with the moose.

When your crab is dead, twist the knife to pry the stomach shell off the body, then wash the innards from the body cavity under cool running water. After that, grasp the crab and break it down the middle, leaving 2 big pieces, with 4 legs and 1 claw arm attached to each piece. Place into a large pot of rapidly boiling, salted water and cook for 8 minutes. Remove from water and let drain. Serve hot, warm or chilled. Simple and delicious!

Other Beasts of the Sea

Scallops and shrimp need to be cooked with care, meaning not too long. Shrimp are ready when they turn red, and depending on their size, they can cook in seconds. Overcooked shrimp are tough and chewy, and what's worse, they cost the same as properly-cooked ones.

Note this advice for scallops, clams and mussels as well. Most seafood and fish is best served slightly rare, not undercooked, but on the razor edge of it. You can achieve this by cooking quickly at very high heat, whether with the stovetop, grill or oven. Scallops and shrimp are full of moisture, which can boil and toughen the meat quickly unless you flash-cook them. A short application of high heat merely sears them, and lets the radiant heat penetrate for a time after removing from the heat source. This cooks them slightly further but keeps them moist and tender.

This is why you add shrimp and scallops to a chowder or gumbo at the very, very end. And the same goes for clams and mussels, which are done the second the shells open in the heat. So, what's the secret to cooking seafood? That's right, don't overcook the seafood! Let's repeat together: Don't overcook the seafood! Timing and practice, and many buckets of rubbery overcooked shrimp you'll choke down in shame, will eventually make you an expert on this.

Oysters, on the other hand, are best left raw. I can't eat a cooked oyster unless they're canned and smoked and decidedly non-oyster-like. My preference is raw on the half-shell, sprinkled with a little lemon juice, hot sauce or horseradish—maybe preceded by a half-bottle of rum to get me in the zone.

Other seafood may be eaten raw, especially sushi, though of course this varies by your location and the trustworthiness of your seafood supplier as far as food poisoning is concerned.

What's that secret again? Don't overcook the seafood! I think we're done here.

Spicy Baked Fish

SERVES: 4 | *METHOD: BAKE* | *APPROX. TIME: 30 MINUTES* | *DIFFICULTY: EASY*

This is without a doubt my favourite way to cook fish fillets in an oven. (You can also grill them, but that requires more practice and a good grill.) So what if it smoulders a bit? The false alarm charge from the fire department is well worth it.

You're going to want a clay or ceramic baking sheet for this. The best I've ever used is from Pampered Chef. it's a flat, shallow-sided clay baking sheet that we use to cook everything from cookies to fish to chicken to smaller, weaker trays. it's by far the best baking sheet ever built. I'm not being paid to say this, although if Pampered Chef is reading this, get in touch.

Special Equipment

- Ceramic casserole dish
  OR
  Clay baking sheet

Ingredients

- 4 large fillets of your favourite fish
- ¼ cup grapeseed oil
- ½ large lemon for juicing
- 2 tablespoons Creole spice
- 1 teaspoon sriracha hot sauce
- ½ teaspoon salt
- ½ teaspoon sugar
  OR
  1 teaspoon honey (my preference)
- ½ teaspoon ground black pepper

Directions

1. If using frozen fillets, defrost fully. Debone and skin if necessary.

2. Preheat oven to 450°. Place large, shallow casserole dish or clay baking pan in oven for 15 minutes to preheat.

3. Juice lemon and combine with all other ingredients in large bowl. Toss well to coat fish with mix evenly.

4. Once baking dish is hot, open oven and pull out rack. Evenly space fish flat on baking dish (use tongs, obviously).

5. Depending on choice of fish, cook for 4—8 minutes, or until fillet becomes flaky in the middle.

   Don't worry if there's a bit of smoke toward the end; that's just liquid smouldering at the edges.

6. Remove from oven, plate and serve.

Almost Bouillabaisse

SERVES: 4 | *METHOD: BAKE* | *APPROX. TIME: 45 MINUTES* | *DIFFICULTY: EASY*

It's called 'almost' bouillabaisse because bouillabaisse has fish, and I prefer shell-fish alone here. But your mileage may vary—it's delicious with salmon as well.

Bouillabaisse has a lot of liquid, so serve with spoons! Large ones! Or straws! Or hearty fresh-baked bread like sourdough, ciabatta or French baguette to dip. Anything to assist you in vacuuming up the broth, because there won't be a drop left when you're finished.

Ingredients

- 2 large onions, minced finely
- 10 garlic cloves, pressed
- 2 tablespoons olive oil
- 1 can crushed tomatoes (28 oz.)
- 2 tablespoons dried parsley
- 1 teaspoon dried thyme leaves
- 3 bay leaves
- 1 large pinch saffron, crushed
- 1 cup dry white wine
- 2 tablespoons dry sherry
- Salt and pepper to taste
- 1 lb. fresh Manila clams, cleaned
- 1 lb. fresh mussels, cleaned and beards removed
- 1 lb. large shrimp, shells on
- 1 large Dungeness crab

Directions

1 Pre-cook Dungeness crab according to introduction instructions and break up into 10 pieces.

2 Heat oil in large soup pot over medium heat. Add onions and garlic and sauté until onions are soft.

3 Add tomatoes, thyme, bay leaves, pepper, parsley, wine, sherry and saffron. Simmer for 10 minutes.

4 Turn heat to medium-high, then add shellfish to broth. Cover pot with tight-fitting lid. At 4 minutes, stir mixture to ensure even coating and cooking. Cook for 3 minutes longer, or until all clams and mussel shells have opened.

5 Serve immediately from cooking pot or large, deep-sided serving platter.

Coquille St. Jacques

SERVES: *4* | METHOD: *MULTIPLE* | APPROX. TIME: *1 HOUR* | DIFFICULTY: *MEDIUM*

Ingredients

✕ *1 lb. scallops, washed and drained*

✕ *1 small onion, minced*

✕ *¾ cup dry white wine*

✕ *1 cup chopped mushrooms (I prefer morels)*

✕ *¼ cup butter*

✕ *¼ cup flour*

✕ *⅓ cup grated Parmesan cheese*

✕ *½ teaspoon tarragon*

✕ *½ teaspoon marjoram*

✕ *3 medium potatoes*

✕ *1¼ cups half-and-half cream*

✕ *2 egg yolks, beaten well*

✕ *1 teaspoon white truffle oil*

✕ *½ teaspoon salt*

✕ *½ teaspoon white pepper*

Directions

1 Peel potatoes and boil until fork-tender. Remove from heat and drain, saving 1 cup potato liquid.

2 Whip potatoes with 2 tablespoons butter, ¼ cup cream, egg yolks, white truffle oil salt and white pepper. Set aside to cool.

3 To medium saucepan add wine, 1 cup potato liquid, tarragon and marjoram. Bring to a boil.

4 Add scallops and simmer for 2 minutes. Add mushrooms, simmer another 2 minutes, then remove from heat. Remove scallops from liquid to prevent overcooking. Set liquid aside for later.

5 At medium heat, melt ¼ cup butter. Sauté minced onion until transparent, then stir in flour to make roux. Cook until smooth and lightly bubbling. Don't allow to brown!

6 Stir in saved liquid from before, then add Parmesan cheese and remaining cream. Stirring constantly, heat until boiling, then reduce heat to very low and simmer 3 minutes.

7 Pipe whipped potatoes around edges of oven-proof serving plates (shell shapes are best) to form bowls. Place cooked scallops in the middle, then pour sauce on top. Pipe remaining mashed potato over top to cover. Sprinkle Parmesan on top if you like.

8 Place plates in 400° oven for 12 to 15 minutes, or until potatoes are golden brown.

Honey Chili Shrimp

SERVES: 2 | *METHOD: BAKE* | *APPROX. TIME: 4 HOURS* | *DIFFICULTY: TRICKY*

Sriracha sauce is a must—use no substitutes. You can find this in most grocery stores in the Asian food section. Once you get into this little miracle sauce, you'll marvel at what foods you can jack up with it.

Ingredients

- 1 lb. large shrimp (8-12), shelled and deveined
- 2 tablespoons sriracha sauce
- 1 tablespoon sesame oil
- 1 tablespoon soy sauce
- 3 tablespoons liquid honey
- 1 lime for juicing

Preparation

1 Squeeze lime for juice. Add all ingredients to large glass bowl and mix well until shrimp are evenly coated in marinade. Cover bowl and refrigerate 4 hours.

Directions

2 Remove shrimp from marinade and place on barbeque grill or hot skillet. Cook until just barely done, as overcooking is a sin (and not even one of the fun sins).

3 Serve immediately and watch the look on the faces of those around you. Almost X-rated. And from something so simple and easy to prepare!

Dungeness Crab & Black Bean Sauce

SERVES: 4 | *METHOD: MULTIPLE* | *APPROX. TIME: 1 HOUR* | *DIFFICULTY: MEDIUM*

Crab Ingredients

- ✕ 4 Dungeness crabs (3 lbs. each)
- ✕ 12 quarts water
- ✕ ¼ cup kosher salt

Sauce Ingredients

- ✕ 2 tablespoons dried black beans
- ✕ 2 tablespoons canola or grapeseed oil
- ✕ 2 tablespoons fresh garlic, pressed
- ✕ ½ cup water
- ✕ 2 tablespoons tapioca starch or corn starch
- ✕ 2 tablespoons oyster sauce
- ✕ 2 tablespoons sake or dry sherry
- ✕ 1 tablespoon sesame oil
- ✕ 2 teaspoons sugar

Preparation

1. Place dried black beans in 1 cup hot water and let soak for 15 minutes. Drain and rinse, then set aside. If you don't have dried black beans, use 2 tablespoons prepared black bean sauce and omit oyster sauce.

Directions

2. Prepare crab according to instructions in chapter introduction. Add kosher salt and water to large pot and bring to rolling boil. Once boiling, add crab. Once water boils again, cook for 4 minutes, then remove crab and set aside.

3. Combine water, tapioca starch, sake, oyster sauce, black beans, sesame oil and sugar in small bowl, mix well, and set aside.

4. In large wok or frying pan over medium-high heat, add oil and then garlic. Sauté until lightly brown. Once garlic is browned, add black bean sauce mix. Bring sauce to boil.

5. Once sauce thickens, add cooked crab and toss well to fully coat. Cook for about 3 minutes to ensure crab is fully reheated. If sauce gets too thick, add a bit of hot water and stir well.

6. Once crab is hot, plate and serve immediately with steamed rice.

Dungeness Crab & Black Bean Sauce
(CONTINUED)

Notes

One crab per person may seem like a lot, but it's not. Not in my house, anyway.

For this recipe you'll need to cover the carpet, chairs, ceiling and walls with sheets. In fact be prepared to call a disaster cleanup crew after dining. Saying this meal can be messy is like saying the Titanic incident was a fender-bender. Crab juice will spray when the shells are cracked, so this is full-on, sloppy, splattery, sticky kind of affair (the best kind of affair, I hear). Use wet-wipes, or perhaps eat in a barn you can easily hose off. And wear impact-resistant glasses.

When I made this for the kids, we literally covered the dining room in sheets as I suggest above, and even so, the carnage was unbelievable. I've never blown up crabs with firecrackers, but I feel like I know what it looks like.

This was also the first meal I ever cooked for Susan. When preparing that feast, I suggested she go into the bedroom and change her shirt beforehand, and offered her a t-shirt for that purpose. She was a little apprehensive, no doubt dreading a different outcome, but she humoured me—a good sign!

Once the meal was finished, she looked at the t-shirt and agreed that changing had been a very good idea. I'm convinced that was the meal that sealed our fate. To this day I don't really know if it's me she really likes, or just my crab and black bean sauce. Regardless, we're a package deal, so she's stuck with me.

If you're feeling flush after a lottery win, a successful bank heist, or the death of a rich but generous uncle, you might even try substituting lobster in this recipe. I've done this a scant handful of times, and it is simply incredible.

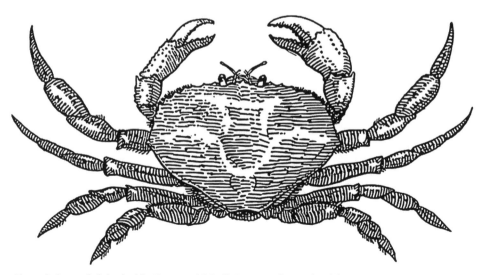

The crab that sealed the deal for Susan and I. Sadly it was too late to thank him.

Lobster Ravioli

SERVES: **6—8** | METHOD: **BLEND & BOIL** | APPROX. TIME: **1 HOUR** | DIFFICULTY: **MEDIUM**

The perfect marriage of lobster and pasta. If the lobsters were told this was to be their fate, they'd surrender to the fisherman en masse, just so they could be first in line to meet you in the kitchen.

Special Equipment

- Blender
- Pasta roller machine (optional)
- Ravioli cutter (optional)

Filling Ingredients

- ½ lb. lobster meat, uncooked
- ½ cup ricotta cheese
- ¼ cup parmesan cheese, grated
- 2 tablespoons shallots, minced
- ½ teaspoon Tabasco hot sauce
- ½ teaspoon Worcestershire sauce
- 2 tablespoons dry sherry
- ½ teaspoon dried parsley, minced
- 1 teaspoon salt
- ½ teaspoon ground pepper

Pasta Ingredients

- 2 lbs. pasta dough

See Also

- Alfredo sauce
- Creamy tomato vodka sauce

Directions

1 Add all filling ingredients to blender and blend to a paste consistency.

2 Roll dough into strips about 4" wide, 12" long and ¹⁄₁₆" thick (thin enough to see light through it when lifted).

3 Every 3" of pasta strip, add 1 teaspoon filling to centre. Your strip should allow 3 or 4 in a row.

4 Line baking sheet with parchment and sprinkle with corn flour.

5 Fold over pasta to cover filling mounds. Cut around each filling mound with jar lid or ravioli cutter. Check seams to ensure they're sealed. Evenly space ravioli on parchment.

6 Repeat until you run out of ingredients. You should have a lot of ravioli at that point. If needed, store raw ravioli in fridge up to 24 hours.

7 Time to cook! Add ravioli to 6 quarts boiling, salted water. Cook at rolling boil for 5 minutes or until ravioli is al dente.

8 Remove cooked ravioli from water, drain well, and add to sauté pan with sauce of your choice.

9 Heat sauce to desired temperature and serve with dusting of Parmesan.

Oven-Baked Fish

SERVES: 6 | *METHOD: BAKE* | *APPROX. TIME: 30 MINUTES* | *DIFFICULTY: EASY*

Special Equipment

✗ Cooking spray
  OR
  Olive oil sprayer

Ingredients

✗ 2 cups flour

✗ 1 tablespoon salt

✗ 1 tablespoon pepper

✗ ¾ cup bread crumbs

✗ ¾ cup cornflakes

✗ ¼ cup Parmesan cheese

✷ 1 tablespoon Creole spice mix

✗ 6 pieces white fish (4—6 oz. each)

✗ Ground black pepper to taste

✗ 1 large egg

✗ ½ cup milk
  OR
  ½ cup water

✗ 6 tablespoon vegetable oil

Directions

1 Preheat oven to 450°. Combine bread-crumbs, cornflakes, spice mix and Parmesan cheese in large plastic bag and shake to mix. Then pour mix out into large bowl.

2 Mix flour, salt and pepper in medium sealable container. Place fish inside with flour mix and shake vigorously to coat fish in mixture.

3 Make egg wash by beating 1 egg into ½ cup milk or water in shallow dish.

4 Dip flour-coated fish in egg wash, then roll in breadcrumb mixture and coat evenly.

5 To ensure coating browns evenly, spray triple-coated fish very lightly with Pam or an olive oil sprayer.

6 Place fish on preheated, oiled cooking tray, then place in oven for 4—8 minutes, depending on the thickness and type of fish. When flaky to the touch of a fork, remove fish from oven.

Poached Salmon

SERVES: 4 | *METHOD: POACH* | *APPROX. TIME: 20 MINUTES* | *DIFFICULTY: BE CAREFUL*

I like to use no-sodium chicken stock in place of the water to add additional flavour to the poaching liquid. Keep it mild and the fish will be wonderful. I also prefer fresh sockeye or coho salmon for this dish.

Fish

- 2 lbs. salmon

Poaching Liquid Ingredients

- 4 cups water
- 2 cups white wine
- 1 tablespoon salt
- 1 teaspoon pepper
- 2 tablespoons butter
- 1 shallot, quartered
- 1 whole garlic clove, pressed
- 1 teaspoon dried tarragon

Best Served With

 Mock Mornay sauce

Directions

1. If using fresh whole salmon fillets, remove bones using needle-nose pliers and cut into serving-sized pieces (about 4 oz. each). You can also use pre-cut salmon fillets for this recipe if you're a coward.

2. Place all poaching liquid ingredients in deep-sided frying pan or wide pot, bring to boil, then reduce heat and simmer for 10 minutes to open up herb and spice flavours.

3. Now place salmon into simmering liquid and poach for 4—8 minutes, or until flesh resists pressure from pressing a finger on it.

   Don't overcook the fish! If you over-cook, you haven't made poached salmon, you've made cat food!

4. Serve to the delight and amazement of guests.

Shrimp Grapanay (The Keg's Shrimp Gratinée)

SERVES: 6 | *METHOD: SAUTÉ & BAKE* | *APPROX. TIME: 30 MINUTES* | *DIFFICULTY: EASY-ISH*

Technically this dish is called "shrimp au gratin" but for some reason it was called "shrimp gratinée" on the Keg's menu at the time. In our house, we call it Shrimp Grapanay to commemorate Kelsey's cute pixie voice when she was a baby. When we dined at the Keg in Prince George, this was all she wanted to eat, and Grapanay is what she called it. I still smile at the memory every time I cook it. Kelsey loves her Shrimp Grapanay to this day.

Ingredients

- ✗ *1—1½ lbs. medium shrimp*
- ✗ *½ cup melted butter*
- ✗ *¼ cup white wine*
- ✗ *6 cloves garlic, pressed*
- ✗ *¼ teaspoon tarragon*
- ✗ *¼ teaspoon rubbed sage*
- ✗ *½ teaspoon white pepper*
- ✗ *2 tablespoons fresh-squeezed lemon juice*
- ✗ *⅔ cups shredded cheddar*
- ✗ *⅔ cups shredded mozzarella*

Directions

1. Peel and devein shrimp if necessary.

2. Preheat oven to 400°

3. Melt butter in sauté pan. Add garlic and sauté until garlic is translucent. Then add wine, tarragon, sage and pepper. Simmer for 5 minutes, stirring constantly, then remove from heat. Stir lemon juice into sauce.

4. Divide shrimp into 6 servings and space evenly on oven-proof serving plates. Place 2 tablespoons of butter garlic mixture on top of each shrimp dish. Mix two cheeses and sprinkle ¼ cup on top of each plate.

5. Place plates in oven for 10—14 minutes depending on size of shrimp. Don't overcook!

6. Remove from oven and serve immediately.

- ✗ *A loaf of fresh French bread and a salad make this a complete meal fit for royalty. Or someone you're trying to impress.*

Stuffed Sole

SERVES: **6** | *METHOD:* **SAUTÉ & BAKE** | *APPROX. TIME:* **45 MINUTES** | *DIFFICULTY:* **EASY**

Kristine loves this dish, and since she moved away we seldom make it for dinner. But I make it every once in a while to remind me of her, and that's what good cooking is all about.

Ingredients

- 6—12 sole fillets, skinned and deboned
- 4 tablespoons butter
  OR
  4 tablespoons grapeseed oil
- 2 tablespoons flour
- 1½ cups fish, chicken or vegetable stock
- 3 oz. button mushrooms, minced finely
- 6 oz. peeled, cooked shrimp
- 4 oz. cooked crab meat
- ¼ cup heavy cream
- 2 tablespoons white wine
- 2 tablespoons panko bread crumbs
- Salt to taste
- Pepper to taste

Directions

1   Preheat oven to 400°.

2   On stovetop, melt 4 tablespoons butter in pan and add flour. Cook for 3 minutes over gentle heat or until liquid turns colour of pale straw. Add stock and bring to boil.

3   Add mushrooms and cook until sauce thickens. Add cream and bring to gentle boil, then remove sauce from heat. Add brandy, shrimp, crab and breadcrumbs. Mix well and set aside to cool.

4   Place sole fillet on work surface, then spread filling on skinned side. Roll up and place in buttered baking dish, then repeat until all fillets are evenly spaced in dish. Spoon melted butter overtop and sprinkle with paprika.

5   Bake for 8—12 minutes until fish is just firm. To avoid overcooking, check fish's texture every 2 minutes after 8-minute mark.

6   Once cooked, remove from oven and let rest for 3—4 minutes before plating up. Best served with rice pilaf and steamed veggies.

Thai Green Curry Prawns

SERVES: 4 | *METHOD: SAUTÉ & BOIL* | *APPROX. TIME: 45 MINUTES* | *DIFFICULTY: MEDIUM*

I also like to grill the shrimp after coating them lightly with melted butter, about 1 minute per side, before adding to coconut sauce. It elevates the flavour to something otherworldly.

Ingredients

- 2 lbs. large uncooked shrimp (about 20)
- 1 tablespoon vegetable oil
- 2 large shallots, finely chopped
  OR
  1 medium onion, finely chopped
- 2 tablespoons Thai green curry paste
- 2 cans coconut milk (400ml each)
- 2 cups chicken stock
- 3 tablespoons fish sauce
- 1 teaspoon sugar
- 1 small lime (for juicing and lime zest)
- 1 cup green beans
- 1 large red pepper, julienned
- 1 bunch cilantro (optional)

Directions

1   If necessary, peel and devein shrimp.

2   Juice lime and grate 1 teaspoon of zest (about ½ your lime). Set aside.

3   Oil up non-stick pan on medium-high heat. Add shallots and curry paste to pan and sauté for 2 minutes. Don't brown! Deglaze with chicken stock.

4   Add coconut milk, fish sauce, sugar and lime juice. Bring to gentle boil, then reduce heat to simmer for 20 minutes. Add beans and simmer for 10 minutes over low heat until beans are slightly tender.

Add chicken stock in minute amounts throughout the cooking process to ensure the desired amount of liquid is maintained.

5   Add prawns, red pepper and cilantro if desired, and cook 4 minutes. Serve with steamed jasmine rice.

Linguini & Clams

SERVES: **6** | *METHOD:* **SAUTÉ & BOIL** | *APPROX. TIME:* **30 MINUTES** | *DIFFICULTY:* **EASY**

This tastes so good it should be more difficult to make. Oh well. You can still tell your guests it was an ordeal. They'll believe you.

Ingredients

- 1 can baby clams, large
  OR
  4 lbs. fresh clams, steamed and shelled
- ¼ cup extra virgin olive oil
- 2 tablespoons butter
- 1 small onion minced finely
- 3 large garlic cloves, pressed
- 3 tablespoons fresh parsley, chopped
- 1 teaspoon hot chili pepper flakes
- ½ cup dry white wine
- ¼ cup heavy cream
  OR
  ¼ cup half-and-half cream
- ¼ cup fresh grated Parmesan cheese
- 1 lb. linguini noodles, uncooked
- 8—10 fresh basil leaves
- ½ fresh squeezed lemon (for juicing)

Directions

1. Drain clams and set liquid aside for later.

2. In large skillet over medium heat, add 2 tablespoons of olive oil, garlic and onions and sauté until soft. Once onion mixture is cooked, add clam nectar (juice for the uninitiated), white wine, cream and chili flakes. Simmer 5—7 minutes, reducing by one fourth.

3. In large pot, bring water to boil and add 4 tablespoons salt. Add linguini to boiling water. Once water returns to boil, turn down heat to medium to maintain a light boil (not a simmer, or your pasta will become mushy).

4. Once pasta is cooked al dente, remove from water and drain well. Add pasta to sauce. Now add the delicate ingredients: clams, basil leaves, butter, lemon juice and tomatoes. Toss to coat pasta evenly.

5. Plate and serve immediately with sprinkle of grated Parmesan.

Miscellaneously Delicious

I didn't know where to catalogue the following recipes. These family faves are an eclectic mix that don't have much in common—much like most families, I suppose. They're hard to place into other sections by the nature of the ingredients. Sushi, pierogi, jambalaya and other ethnic delicacies are all scattered among the entries here.

Perhaps I should have organized this book according to the Dewey Decimal System to keep you happy! But nope. I'm a free spirit, a rebel, a maverick. However, my editor (my son, the reason this book is late) has provided you ingrates an index at the back of this book. If you need to find something, look there!

Lettuce Wraps

SERVES: 4 | *METHOD: SAUTÉ & DEEP FRY* | *APPROX. TIME: 1 HOUR* | *DIFFICULTY: TRICKY*

I make these often, usually when I have some leftover barbeque duck from the Chinese market. If no duck is available, I use barbeque pork (see recipe elsewhere in the book) in its place. Your Chinese sausage can be either the cured variety or fresh-barbequed, both found at the Chinese market or Asian meat section at your market.

Ingredients

- 1 lb. Chinese barbeque pork, minced
  OR
  1 lb. Chinese barbeque duck, de-boned
  OR
  1 lb. cooked chicken, minced
- 6 oz. Chinese sausage, minced
- 2 tablespoons sesame oil
- 6 dried shiitake mushrooms
- 3 cloves garlic, pressed
- 1 bunch green onions, sliced fine
- 1 large head iceberg lettuce
- ¼ cup canned water chestnuts, minced
- ¼ cup canned bamboo shoots, minced
- 1 cup celery, minced
- 2 tablespoons soy sauce
- 1 tablespoon nuoc mam (Vietnamese fish sauce)
- ½ teaspoon sugar
- 1 teaspoon corn starch
- ½ teaspoon white pepper
- 2 oz. mung bean (cellophane) noodles

Preparation

1 Hydrate shiitake mushrooms by soaking in warm water until soft, then remove stems and mince finely.

2 Pre-make starch slurry by mixing corn starch with 2 teaspoons water.

3 Separate lettuce leaves, rinse well, and chill in fridge until ready to eat.

Directions

- *You must use Asian cellophane noodles (also called glass noodles, made from mung bean or potato starch), especially if you intend to deep fry. Rice vermicelli, which is otherwise similar, will not work here! Don't even try it!*

4 First, deep fry noodles. Place one small bundle at a time into preheated deep fryer at 375°. Once they puff up fully, remove from oil and place on paper towel to drain.

5 When cool, break them up a little to make manageable portions. Set aside in bowl for now.

Lettuce Wraps

(CONTINUED)

6   In large non-stick frying pan or wok over high heat, add oil, garlic, mushrooms and green onions. Sauté until onions wilt. Add water chestnuts, bamboo shoots, celery, soy sauce, fish sauce, sugar, starch mix, white pepper and meats.

7   Stir fry on high for 3 minutes until ingredients are hot and thick-textured (the secret is to stir-fry, not boil, hence the quickness). When celery is hot but still crisp, you're done. Don't overcook!

8   Once hot enough, serve immediately.

9   To eat, place 2 tablespoons of meat mixture and 2 tablespoons of fried noodles onto 1 lettuce leaf. Drizzle 1 teaspoon of hoisin sauce over filling, then fold lettuce leaf over like a taco and place into normal orifice. No, the other one. No, the *other* other one.

10   Okay, fine, just eat it with your mouth.

Deep frying... again. Again! My family will not let me rest. The rats nibble at my shoes. What does sunlight feel like? I don't remember. If you can read this, I'm still down here. Send help!

Chicken Jambalaya

SERVES: **6** | *METHOD:* ***SAUTÉ*** | *APPROX. TIME:* ***1 HOUR*** | *DIFFICULTY:* ***EASY ENOUGH***

Ingredients

- 2 lbs. chicken thighs, boneless skinless
- 1 lb. Andouille sausage
  OR
  1 lb. cooked hot Italian sausage
- 1 lb. raw small shrimp (about 80)
- 1 large onion, minced finely
- 1 red bell pepper, minced
- 6 cloves garlic, pressed
- 4 ribs celery, chopped
- 2 small cans tomato paste
- 1 can crushed tomatoes (28 oz.)
- 6 cups chicken stock
- 2—3 tablespoons Creole seasoning
- 2 bay leaves
- Salt to taste
- 2 cups rice, uncooked (par-boiled rice like Uncle Ben's won't get mushy on you)

Directions

1. Debone and skin chicken thighs if necessary, then cut into bite-size pieces. Peel and devein shrimp if necessary.

2. On high heat, sauté chicken on all sides, sprinkling with pinch of Creole seasoning. Once cooked, remove from pan and set aside.

3. Add sausage to pan and sauté until browned. Remove from heat, pour off and discard fat. Return pan to heat and sauté onions, garlic, peppers and celery until onions are cooked. Add tomato paste. Stir constantly until dark red colour is achieved.

4. Once vegetables are cooked and tomato paste is dark red, deglaze pan with 2 cups stock, scraping bottom of pan to mix up any browned bits. Stir until vegetables, paste and stock are well mixed. Add Creole seasoning, tomatoes and salt to taste.

5. Cook over low-medium heat for 10 minutes. Now add meat and rest of stock. Stir in rice, combining thoroughly. Reduce heat to low and cook another 20 minutes, or until rice absorbs all remaining liquid.

- *If mixture begins to dry out and gets all gloopy-like (advanced cooking term!) add more stock.*

6. 5 minutes before serving, add shrimp, making sure all shrimps are covered by hot mixture. Remove pan from heat to let ambient food heat cook shrimp.

7. Serve and enjoy!

Sushi

I love sushi, rice rolls (maki and nigiri) and sashimi. Sadly, I seldom get to enjoy really good sushi at the local joints that purport to be sushi restaurants. Fast food sushi leaves me wanting, as do most sushi restaurants that seem to have sprung up in every town, big and small, throughout the land. Just because the guy behind the counter wears a kimono does not make him a sushi chef. Madame Butterfly wore a kimono, and she wasn't what she said she was either.

In Japan, chefs take their sushi to a level we don't find in North America normally, and if you do find such a chef, their cuisine will be bank-breaking expensive. This is because making sushi takes time just to get to a satisfactory level of accomplishment, and to get to expert level takes decades.

To become familiar with (and worship) expert sushi, get to know the work of the late Anthony Bourdain. He went to the best places on the globe and sat a-table with the best sushi makers in the world. You can live vicariously through him if you like, and if that's not enough, you can try your hand making sushi yourself.

Now, if you aren't rich enough to go to a world-class sushi joint (and if you're reading this book then most likely you're not), chances are you'll have to make some yourself.

I've attended and hosted a few make-it-yourself sushi parties, and while not world-class, they have been tasty enough. A sushi party is easy to host now, as many stores, seafood shops and Asian markets have all the supplies necessary to make the basics. I won't get into detailed instructions on how to roll maki, form a nigiri base or slice fish. You can locate step-by-step instructions on YouTube and other such websites, because some things are best done by observation.

My foremost advice is to find the best frozen fish you can. Generally speaking, frozen fish is frozen at sea, where it's at the peak of its quality. Fresh, never-frozen fish is difficult to find unless you live by a fishing port, and geographically speaking, most of us don't. Frozen is fine and don't let the coastal elites tell you otherwise!

Up here in the north, there are small-portioned sushi fish packages available that thaw quickly in the fridge and keep everyone safe from a bellyache. I suggest looking for those to start with. Depending on your ambitions (and I am the Lazy Bastard, after all) it's less wasteful and stressful than buying and attempting to trim a whole fish yourself, and the smaller portions will leave you free to experiment and find the flavours that work for you.

Tempura

METHOD: **DEEP FRY** | *APPROX. TIME:* **20 MINUTES** | *DIFFICULTY:* **BE CAREFUL!**

When hosting a sushi party, make some tempura as well. It's easy to make and complements the sushi nicely. I recommend using only fresh oil like canola or other neutral-flavoured oil, and eat the results as soon as it's cooked. You can batter and deep fry almost anything for tempura, so be daring and don't let good taste, common sense or the police stop you.

Special Equipment

✕ *Deep fryer*

Things You Should Fry

✕ *Japanese sweet potato*

✕ *Kobocha squash*

✕ *Jumbo prawns (shelled, tails left on)*

Batter Ingredients

✕ *1 cup all-purpose flour*

✕ *2 tablespoons corn starch*

✕ *1 egg, beaten well (it was a bad, bad egg)*

✕ *1 cup ice water*

Dipping Sauce Ingredients

✕ *1 tablespoon dashi soup base powder*

✕ *1 cup warm water*

✕ *2 tablespoons mirin sweet rice wine (no substitutions)*

✕ *2 tablespoons good quality sake*

✕ *¼ cup soy sauce*

Directions

I   Blend flour and corn starch together. In medium bowl, beat egg until it confesses to the Lindbergh Baby kidnapping.

2   Add ice water, mixing well. Add flour slowly to water-egg mixture and gently stir with a fork until mixed well and only smallest lumps remain.

3   Preheat deep fryer to 350°.

4   Dip seafood or veggies into batter, coating evenly. Place battered items in preheated deep fryer at 350° and fry until golden (3—4 minutes).

5   Serve with dipping sauce and sushi rolls of your choice.

Sushi Rice

METHOD: *BOIL* | APPROX. TIME: *30 MINUTES* | DIFFICULTY: *TRIVIAL*

Directions

1   Cook rice per package instructions. Once cooked, move rice to large bowl and let cool.

2   Mix vinegar, sugar and salt together until solids have been fully dissolved.

3   Drizzle vinegar solution slowly over cooked rice. Stir rice well to ensure vinegar is well-distributed and rice is evenly flavoured.

4   Let cool to room temperature. Use in your favourite sushi design.

Ingredients

- 3 cups sushi rice
- ½ cup rice vinegar, warmed to lukewarm
- 1 teaspoon fine kosher salt
- 4 tablespoons white sugar

Keep sushi rice covered as you work. Sushi rice is best used and rolled when warm, and as such, its moisture will continue to evaporate (and dry out your rice) unless it's covered.

Sushi Egg (Tamago)

METHOD: *SAUTE* | APPROX. TIME: *10 MINUTES* | DIFFICULTY: *EASY*

Ingredients

- 2 eggs
- 1 tablespoon dashi soup stock
- 1 teaspoon sugar
- ½ teaspoon salt
- 1 teaspoon sesame oil

Directions

1   Mix all ingredients well with whisk or hand blender and add to non-stick pan over very low heat. Cook like a crêpe, gently, and don't brown.

2   Once egg is cooked and set, roll omelette onto plate and gently fold into deck of cards shape, then refrigrate uncovered to cool.

3   Once tamago is cool, cut into small strips and use in your favourite sushi or maki design.

Pasta & Pierogi

I can't imagine this world without pasta or pierogi (or perogies as many call them). I prefer fresh-made pasta to the dried store-bought variety, but the latter is a simple affair compared to making it from scratch at home, suiting the Lazy Bastard ethos. However, when making pierogi from scratch, I'll save the leftover dough for pasta noodles. When dried, they keep for a long time, and handily beat store-bought varieties for flavour.

My family eats pasta often. Years of carb-loading has increased the diameter of my equator substantially, but I regret nothing. It would be a disaster for me to be gluten-intolerant, and I pity those who are, such as my poor daughter Kristine. On her behalf, I've discovered that pasta made from quinoa is almost as good as wheat. One hundred times more expensive, sure, but it's worth it for a gluten-free person to have pasta back in their life.

Pierogi are a food memory that evokes a lot of warm memories for me. My grandmother made them, my mom made them, I make them, and my kids make them. I like a variety of fillings, and prefer them just boiled. My family prefers the cheddar cheese and potato variety, and they prefer them pan-fried after boiling for a slightly browned, crispy exterior.

I have to admit I'll eat them to excess any way they're served: with bacon, onions, cream sauce, sour cream, or any other creamy, savoury or bold topping. Add them to a chicken soup or stew. Or skip the fore-play and simply pop one in your mouth when it's freshly boiled—but take my advice and wait for it

to cool. A boiling-hot pierogi will cause uncomfortable burns, embarrassing speech impediments and drooling for a week or so, possibly costing you that promotion or hot date. Ask me how I know.

I've included my Grandma Evelyn's recipe here, a classic from my youth. However, I've also found a recipe that uses sour cream in the dough, and it produces the most tender and flavourful pierogi dough I've ever tasted. It's a recent finding for me, but the critics (there are always critics at my table, they're called children) all agree it's excellent. I include the recipe for that here as well. Sorry Grandma Evelyn! I still treasure your pierogi memories!

When we make pasta or pierogi, we make a day of it to create a large amount, which we freeze or dry to preserve for a later date. This is our flour-covered quality time for bonding and eating (these two things are intertwined, of course). I use my Grandma's pasta roller to thin the dough for both pierogi and pasta, and I recommend you use one as well. It provides a controllable, uniform thickness, which is a bit trickier to achieve with a regular rolling pin. But if a rolling pin is all you have, by all means use it.

Pierogi go best with cabbage rolls and boiled garlic sausage, but you can serve them with almost anything. Susan's cabbage rolls are wonderful and they add to the sensual enjoyment of the pierogi. We also schedule cabbage roll-making days as well, and freeze them to enjoy at a later date. This is what a romantic date looks like in middle age, folks! Get used to it, or better yet, get started early.

Grandma's Pierogi & Pasta Dough

SERVES: **6** | *METHOD:* **MIX? KNEAD? IT'S JUST DOUGH.** | *APPROX. TIME:* **4+ HOURS**

Directions

1 In large mixer, add flour and salt. Hand-mix with whisk first to ensure salt is evenly incorporated. Attach mixer's dough hook, turn mixer to medium speed and add eggs 1 at a time until all 6 eggs are mixed in. Add oil and continue to mix.

2 Mixture should start to take on crumbled texture. Add water 1 oz. at a time, allowing to mix briefly at intervals, until dough forms firm ball and pulls cleanly away from sides of bowl.

Never allow too much water or you'll get a soft, gooey dough, and will have to increase your flour ratio to fix it, possibly screwing up the whole works.

3 Allow finished dough to mix another few minutes to shorten hand-kneading time later.

4 Once dough is ready, turn out onto work surface and knead for at least 5 minutes. When surface of dough becomes smooth, it's ready.

5 Coat kneaded dough with a little oil, wrap tightly in plastic wrap and place in fridge. Refrigerate dough for at least 4 hours before use.

✕ *Dough should be slightly stiff to work with at first, and should shrink a little at first when you roll it out. I use a pasta machine for this part, but the trick with a pasta machine is not to rush the process.*

Special Equipment

✕ *Electric mixer*

✕ *Pasta roller*

Ingredients

✕ *5 cups all-purpose flour*

✕ *2 teaspoons salt*

✕ *6 large eggs*

✕ *3 tablespoons canola oil*

✕ *1 cup cold water*

6 Place about ¾ cup dough in your hand. If using pasta machine (and this recipe is very hard without it), flatten dough out to allow easy insertion at highest opening setting.

7 Run rolled dough through each setting at least twice before turning the dial to a thinner setting. Turn handle slowly but steadily. If your cranking speed is good, rolled dough will have a nice smooth surface when it exits the roller. If it looks mottled or torn, you're turning too fast.

8 Continue passing dough sheet through smaller rollers until desired thickness is reached. On my machine the #3 setting seems to be perfect for ravioli and noodles, and #6 for pierogi. The same will (probably) be true for you.

Sour Cream Pierogi Dough

METHOD: ***IT'S DOUGH. DOUGH!*** | *APPROX. TIME:* ***2 DAYS***

Special Equipment

- ✕ *Electric mixer*
- ✕ *Pasta roller*

Ingredients

- ✕ *5 cups all purpose flour*
- ✕ *1 teaspoon salt*
- ✕ *2 eggs*
- ✕ *1 cup sour cream*
- ✕ *¼ cup canola oil*
- ✕ *1 cup water*

Directions

1. Follow same instructions as Grandma's dough in previous recipe, adding all ingredients to mixer progressively with small amounts of water until dough is finished in mixer.

2. Remove dough from bowl and knead for 8—10 minutes by hand.

3. Cover in plastic wrap and put in fridge for maximum 48 hours (this dough improves with time, but not too much time).

✕ *This dough is incredible, and is now my standard pierogi dough.*

Pierogi Dill Sauce

METHOD: ***SAUTÉ*** | *APPROX. TIME:* ***20 MINUTES***

Directions

1. Sauté onions and garlic in a small pot over medium heat, until onions are translucent.

2. Add sour cream, heavy cream and dill. Simmer until sauce thicken to desired consistency.

3. Season with salt and pepper to taste. Serve hot overtop your pierogi. You're welcome.

Ingredients

- ✕ *1 medium onion, minced*
- ✕ *1 tablespoon butter*
- ✕ *2 cloves garlic, pressed*
- ✕ *½ cup sour cream*
- ✕ *½ cup heavy cream*
- ✕ *1 tablespoon fresh dill, minced*
- ✕ *Salt and pepper to taste*

Grandma's Cheddar & Potato Pierogi

*METHOD: **BOIL*** | *APPROX. TIME: **1 HOUR***

Directions

1. Boil and mash potatoes the usual way. Add cheese, salt and pepper to hot mashed potatoes and mix well. Set aside to cool.

2. Divide dough into 3 pieces and roll one piece at a time to ⅛" thickness. Use thin-rimmed glass, jar lid or round cutter (we use a gadget called a Perogy Zipper) to cut circles from dough.

3. Place rounded tablespoon of filling on each round. Lightly moisten edge of ½ dough round with water, then fold over to half-moon shape. Pinch edges together to seal and crimp.

4. Place on baking sheet lined with parchment paper to prevent sticking. Repeat process until dough and/or filling run out.

5. In large pot of boiling salted water, cook pierogi in batches, for 4—5 minutes, or until they float to top. Stir gently to prevent pierogi from sticking to pot or each other.

6. With slotted spoon, move pierogi to colander to drain. Rinse with cold water and gently shake colander with vegetable oil drizzle to prevent pierogi from sticking.

7. Mince 6 strips of bacon and 1 large onion separately. Fry bacon on medium-high. As fat starts to render, toss in minced onion and fry both until bacon is slightly crispy and onions are caramelized. Remove from heat and set aside in bowl.

Special Equipment

- ✕ Pasta roller (optional)
- ✕ Perogy Zipper (optional)

Ingredients

- ✕ 3 pounds potatoes, pre-cooked and mashed
- ✕ 1 ½ pounds shredded cheddar cheese
- ✕ 1 teaspoon salt
- ✕ ½ teaspoon pepper
- ✕ 1 large onion
- ✕ 6 strips bacon

8. Optionally, add peirogi to now-empty greased pan. Fry until all wonderful pockets of heaven are cooked and slightly brown.

9. Serve with sour cream or your choice of cream sauce and sprinkle bacon and onions overtop.

✕ *Susan requires me to serve these pierogi with dill sauce. But I'm not complaining.*

Grandma's Cabbage Rolls

SERVES: **6** | *METHOD:* **BOIL & BAKE** | *APPROX. TIME:* **3 HOURS** | *DIFFICULTY:* **EASY-ISH**

Instead of tomato sauce, you may use 1 can of condensed tomato soup and an equal portion of water. It's mellower and a little sweeter, and the creamy taste is wonderful. Try it both ways and see what you prefer, just like that phase you went through in college.

Shell

- 1 large green cabbage (core removed)

Filling Ingredients

- 1 lb. ground pork
- 1 lb. ground beef
- ½ lb. bacon, cooked and crumbled (optional)
- 3 cups cooked rice
- 2 medium onions, \minced finely
- 1 head roasted garlic, mashed
- 2 teaspoons salt
- 1 teaspoon ground pepper

Sauce Ingredients

- 2 cups tomato sauce
- OR
  1 can condensed tomato soup + 1 can water
- ¼ cup brown sugar
- 3 tablespoons lemon juice

Directions

1. Fill large pot ⅔ and bring to boil on stove.

2. In large bowl, add all filling ingredients. Mix well to incorporate, then set aside.

3. Place cabbage had in water to boil. Remove leaves one-by-one as they peel away. Place cabbage leaves on towel to dry.

4. Cut tough center stem from each cabbage leaf. Cut larger leaves to size as you desire.

5. Place ¼ cup meat and rice mix on cabbage leaf and roll up like burrito, tucking over ends to seal roll in pouch shape. Place each roll in baking dish, seam side down. Repeat until you run out of ingredients.

6. Freeze rolls for later, or bake immediately. Very accommodating things, aren't they?

7. If baking, mix all sauce ingredients and pour over cabbage rolls, distributing evenly. Seal baking dish with foil and place in preheated oven at 350°.

8. Bake 1 hour, then turn down temperature to 250° and bake for 2 hours longer. The longer you bake, the more tender cabbage gets.

9. Serve hot, preferably with pierogi, and topped with sour cream.

Spaetzle

SERVES: 4 | *METHOD: BOIL* | *APPROX. TIME: 30 MINUTES* | *DIFFICULTY: EASY*

I normally make a triple batch of this and freeze in bags, 1 lb. per bag, for later. Excellent when fried up and served as a side dish, in lieu of rice or potatoes. To do this, mince 8 slices of bacon and add to large non-stick frying pan. Fry bacon until just done, than add minced onions (½ bunch of green or ½ medium white onion) and cook until onion is translucent. Add crushed garlic and cook for 1 minute longer, then add spaetzle and fry until spaetzle is browned, stirring constantly. Finish with sprinkle of fresh ground pepper. Thank me later with cash or other valuable honourarium.

Kelsey would do almost anything (short of cleaning her bedroom) to have me cook this for dinner. In fact, she'd be a happy camper if I made this and nothing else. Dough. Bacon. Bacon fat, garlic and onions all fried to a golden brown—it's nirvana on a plate. If you took this to a battlefield and served it to the combatants, all fighting would cease immediately. Well, maybe not in, or near, Israel. But any land of pork-eaters will enter a new age of peace.

Special Equipment

- Spaetzle press
  OR
  Potato ricer

Ingredients

- 4 cups flour
- 4 eggs
- 1½—2 cups water or milk
- 1 teaspoon salt
- 1 teaspoon white pepper
- 1 teaspoon baking powder
- 1 teaspoon garlic powder (optional)
- Pinch of fresh nutmeg

Directions

1 Fill large, heavy-bottom pot with water, leaving a few inches for expansion of the spaetzle. Bring water to a boil.

2 Blend flour, eggs, water, salt and nutmeg in mixing bowl. Mixture should be thick enough to stick together, but thin enough to push through holes in spaetzle maker. Add water incrementally while mixing until you get the right consistency.

3 Using spaetzle maker (or potato ricer), force mixture through into boiling water. Press small batches at a time. Let spaetzle boil for 3 minutes, then transfer with slotted spoon to colander.

4 Rinse cooked spaetzle under running cold water to keep from becoming a sticky mass you can't work with. Let cold spaetzle drain, then toss with 1 teaspoon of oil to ensure they stay separated.

5 Repeat process until you run out of mix.

Spinach & Sausage Lasagna

SERVES: *8* | METHOD: *SAUTÉ & BAKE* | APPROX. TIME: *1 HOUR* | DIFFICULTY: *MEDIUM*

Noodles

- ½ lb. lasagna noodles, cooked to a barely cooked but pliable state
- 1 lb. mozzarella cheese, shredded
- ¼ cup fresh grated parmesan cheese

Meat Sauce

- 1 lb. spicy Italian sausage
- 2 tablespoons olive oil
- 1 onion chopped
- 2 sweet red peppers, diced
- 1 can (28 oz.) plum tomatoes, pureed
- 1 teaspoon salt
- ¼ teaspoon pepper

Béchamel Sauce

- ¼ cup butter
- ¼ cup all-purpose flour
- 4 cups milk
- 1 teaspoon salt
- ½ teaspoon pepper
- ¼ teaspoon nutmeg
- 300g spinach (1 commercial package), cooked, squeezed dry and chopped
- 1 lb. shredded mozzarella cheese

Directions

1 Remove sausage from casing. Break up into 1-inch chunks. In Dutch oven, heat oil over medium heat. Cook onion for 3—4 minutes or until tender. Add sausage and cook for 5—8 minutes or until browned.

2 Add red peppers and cook for 5 minutes. Add tomatoes, salt and pepper. Simmer for 20—25 minutes or until thickened.

3 In saucepan, melt butter over medium heat. Whisk in flour and sauté, stirring constantly for 2 minutes. Do not brown! Whisk in milk and bring to boil. Reduce heat to medium-low and cook while stirring 5 minutes, or until thickened.

4 Stir in salt, pepper, nutmeg, spinach and mozzarella. Taste and adjust seasoning.

5 Meanwhile, cook noodles. Once pliable but not fully cooked, remove and rinse under cold running water. Drain and set aside.

6 Spread ¼ béchamel sauce over bottom of 9" × 13" baking pan (an average-size pan). Blanket layer of noodles over sauce, then another ¼ of meat sauce, then another layer of noodles, ½ your sauce, then ½ the spinach.

7 Repeat using remaining sauce and spinach, then top with remaining meat sauce. Cover with mozzarella and sprinkle with Parmesan.

8 Bake in 375° oven for 40—45 minutes or until bubbling. Let stand for 10 minutes before serving.

Taco Seasoned Beef in Pasta Shells

SERVES: 4 | *METHOD: SAUTÉ & BAKE* | *APPROX. TIME: 1 HOUR* | *DIFFICULTY: MEDIUM*

Directions

1   Preheat oven to 400°. In large frying pan over medium-high heat, brown ground beef. Drain and discard excess fat.

2   Return pan to medium-high heat and add onion and garlic. Cook for 5 minutes, stirring constantly. Add taco seasoning and 1 cup water, stir well, then add spinach. Turn down heat to medium and simmer, stirring regularly, until all liquid has evaporated.

3   Remove pan from heat, add cream cheese and mix until fully incorporated with meat and spinach. Season with salt and pepper to taste. Set aside to cool.

4   Cook pasta shells according to directions on package, but not fully! Cook only until shells are pliable, as they will continue cooking in oven. Move pasta to colander, rinse fully under cold water and drain well.

5   Drink some red wine. May I suggest a glass of Red Velvet by Cupcake Vineyards? An excellent, modest-priced red blend.

6   Pour 1 cup of salsa on bottom of 9" × 13" baking dish. Stuff each shell with meat mixture, but don't overstuff—just add enough to fill.

7   Place shells in pan, open side up. Cover shells with remaining taco sauce and both cheeses. Cover with foil and bake for 30 minutes.

Ingredients

- 1 lb. ground beef
- 1 medium onion, minced finely
- 2 cloves garlic, minced finely or pressed
- 8 oz. fresh baby spinach, washed and drained
- 3 tablespoons taco seasoning mix
- 1 package cream cheese (8 oz.)
- 30 jumbo pasta shells
- 2 cups salsa of your choice
- 1 cup cheddar cheese (8 oz.)
  OR
  1 cup fresh cheese curd (preferred)
- 1 cup mozzarella cheese (8 oz.)
- Salt and pepper to taste

8   After 30 minutes, remove foil and cook for an additional 10 minutes. If cheese hasn't developed brown crust, turn on broiler and broil for 2 minutes or until cheese develops crispy exterior.

9   Serve hot with additional salsa, hot sauce, and sour cream even. Be ready for compliments and adoring stares from those you've delighted. Your ego will grow along with your gut.

Seasonings, Sauces, Dips &
Pastes to Make Things Gooder

-or-

From the Cradle to the Gravy

I'm a sauce evangelist. Almost everything goes better with a sauce or gravy. Gravy is essential to roasted chicken or turkey, poutine, or pork roast, or any other item that seems barren and listless and in need of improvement (no, not my life, I use rum for that). Good gravy can stoke the spirits of any meat or potato or rice or pasta or shingle. In short, good gravy is at the center of the meaning of life.

I can say, though without much regret, that I've spread my sauce addiction to my family, and we all now suffer the same. Fortunately for them, they haven't taken on the same midsection measurements I have, so they enjoy their gravy relatively guilt-free, unlike Susan and I. For now. Time will catch up to them, oh yes.

It's worth the time to learn to a few sauces and gravies for your cooking repertoire, as the right sauce can save a mediocre meal or elevate a good one to transcendence. I've supplied a couple of sauce recipes we favour here, but the basics for all white sauces is the same: the roux. You'll have to master that before you become a saucier.

For a good gravy, you'll need roux and also a good-quality stock. This can be from your frozen homemade supply, or store-bought, or the drippings of the roast you've just made. With so many options, there's no good reason to be without gravy.

But what if your cut of meat doesn't offer enough browned drippings or fat? That's where broth and stock come in. If the stock is flavourful and the flour is properly browned, your gravy will turn out just fine.

Generally speaking, stock is made from bones and meat, and broth is made from meat or vegetable and seasonings, no bones about it or in it. But the world seems to disagree with me and has given us a trend called "bone broth," making my definitions obsolete. The process for cooking is the same, at least.

In addition, you should have some cheaters hiding in the spice cupboard (better there than in your bedroom closet). If your drippings are unseasoned or your stock is a little flavourless, that's where cheaters come in. Kitchen Bouquet is a fine choice to darken the gravy, as are onion and garlic powder. My favourite cheater base is a brand called Better Than Bouillon. It's widely available in beef, chicken, vegetable, seafood and more.

Unfortunately they aren't sodium-free (quite the opposite, in fact) but if used properly, they can be excellent. I've used them for a long time and have received many compliments about the results. So here you have it, my soul is bare and my secrets exposed.

In general, cheaters exist to make the sauce more savoury, so look for cheaters that will deliver umami (a Japanese word for the savoriness of cooked meats). It's a flavour imparted by MSG, yeast, miso paste and soy sauce, for example. But keep in mind that flavour bases and seasonings shouldn't be a powder. Ever! Bases are a paste that contains real meat and condensed stock. Powdered stock is not. It's laden with salt and MSG, with artificial components and minimal natural flavouring. It should be avoided. As you might have noted by now, cheaters can be very high in salt. Even if you're not health-conscious, a too-salty gravy can't be easily fixed. Buy sodium-reduced bases (Better Than Bouillion offers a few) wherever you can, if only because it gives you more control over the recipe's outcome.

Think of salt and cheaters as modifiers to the recipe, not base components. Add them at the end, and only a little at a time. Stir well after each small addition and taste to ensure it's doing what you want.

And don't worry about authenticity. Even professional kitchens use bases, since many recipes don't produce enough drippings at the start. Cheating like this is okay. Really, it's okay. Trust me.

Gravy (For Any Kind of Meat)

METHOD: **SAUTÉ** | *APPROX. TIME:* **20 MINUTES** | *DIFFICULTY:* **VARIES**

Although this recipe makes use of dried herbs, minced onion and pressed garlic are ideal at the roux stage if I feel there aren't enough aromatics in the initial drippings. Start with a tablespoon of butter, and sauté 4 cloves garlic and ¼ minced onion before adding roux ingredients to pan.

Directions

1   To make roux, turn burner heat to medium, add flour and fat to roasting pan and whisk well. Scrape all drippings stuck to the pan into the roux mixture. For red meat, cook roux until medium-to-dark brown. For poultry, brown roux to a blonde or light brown.

2   Once roux is cooked to desired colour, remove pan from heat and slowly but steadily add stock, whisking all the time to dissolve all lumps. Then return pan to heat for 5 minutes, stirring constantly to prevent sticking or burning. Gravy will thicken as it cooks, but if it thickens too much, add more stock to balance.

3   If using dried herbs, add them now and simmer on low for another 5 minutes.

4   Pour finished gravy into saucepan and keep covered over warm burner. Gravy will thicken further as it rests, so add more stock and lightly simmer before serving to maintain agreeable consistency.

Roux

✕ ¼ cup roast drippings
OR
¼ cup butter

✕ ¼ cup all purpose flour

Gravy

✕ 4 cups beef stock

✕ Salt and pepper to taste

✕ 1 teaspoon granulated garlic (optional)

✕ 1 teaspoon onion powder (optional)

5   Season gravy with salt and pepper to taste before serving. Voila!

Basic Alfredo Sauce

SERVES: 4 | *METHOD: SAUTÉ* | *APPROX. TIME: 30 MINUTES* | *DIFFICULTY: EASY*

I know, I know, I know, I'm a blasphemer. Alfredo is not made with a roux tradi-tionally. But I like this recipe and so do my kids, and that's what's important to me. And it gets me likes on Facebook, which is even more important to me.

Ingredients

- 2 cups half-and-half cream
- ½ cup dry white wine
- 4 cloves garlic pressed
- ½ cup Parmesan cheese, freshly grated
- 4 tablespoons butter (clarified is best)
- 4 tablespoons flour
- ½ teaspoon white pepper
- Pinch salt
- Pinch ground nutmeg
- 1 large can baby clams, drained
  OR
  1 lb. shrimp
  OR
  1 lb. scallops
  OR
  1 lb. chicken pieces, pre-cooked

Directions

1 Melt butter in deep-sided heavy pan over medium heat. Once melted, add garlic and cook for 2 minutes. Add flour to butter-garlic mixture. Stirring constantly, cook flour into roux until nutty smell starts to rise (like butter cookies… garlicky butter cookies).

2 Once roux has cooked (again, don't brown!) whisk cream slowly in. Once cream is incorporated add wine, salt, pepper, nutmeg and parmesan. Simmer over very low heat for 10 minutes. Stir continuously to prevent scorching, and do not boil!

3 Add protein of your choice as suggested above. If using raw seafood, let sauce raise to simmer once more to ensure it's cooked. If sauce becomes too thick, add additional cream.

4 When sauce simmers again, it's done. Serve hot over good-quality pasta.

Bart's Barbeque Rub

METHOD: BLEND | *APPROX. TIME: 5 MINUTES* | *DIFFICULTY: EASY*

I borrowed this recipe from a book somewhere, and after a while I decided to call it mine since I was the only one I knew who used it. It's terrific and begs to be used on pork ribs, steak, chicken or any other grillable foods.

This spice rub can have other uses, such as flavouring when parboiling pork ribs, or as a general flavouring for red meat stews. Leftover spice rub can be stored in a sealed container and will keep fresh for about a month. Maybe more—we've never had it last that long before using it all up!

Ingredients

- 3 tablespoons sweet paprika
- 1 tablespoon hot Hungarian paprika
- 2 tablespoons sugar
- 1 tablespoon kosher salt
- 1 tablespoon garlic powder
- 1 tablespoon dry mustard powder
- 1 tablespoon onion powder
- 1 tablespoon ground cumin
- 1 tablespoon cayenne pepper
- 1 tablespoon ground cinnamon
- 1 tablespoon dried thyme
- 1 tablespoon dried oregano
- 1 tablespoon chili powder
- 1 tablespoon ground black pepper
- 1 tablespoon ground white pepper

Directions

1   Mix all ingredients well. If you're using coarse or dried leaves, blend all ingredients in blender until it's a uniformly fine, powdery texture.

2   Rub onto meat and let sit for ½ hour before grilling.

¡Loco por la Comida!

I love Mexico. My wife loves Mexico. My kids love Mexico. My parents are fucking *obsessed* with Mexico. I've been there numerous times with the family. We took Kaitlyn and Kelsey to Mazatlan, which was enjoyable for them. We took a much-younger Kristine and Jordan to Tijuana as a side excursion from a trip to San Diego, but for some reason the kids didn't care for it. The dirty streets. The hookers. The panhandlers. The flies. The perpetual reek of nastiness and degradation.

"You'll love it when you're older," I assured them.

Mexico City and Guadalajara are my favourite places in the country. Mexico City is perhaps in the top three cities in the world for me. What a place! The people are awesome, the city chaotic, the traffic insane, the sheer size mind-boggling, and the food.

The food! While it lacks the cultural enlightenment of a Tijuana donkey show, Mexico City has pyramids, museums, music and churros and much more. And the food! Did I mention the food?

Years ago we stayed on the Paseo de la Reforma close to the Zona Rosa, a famous restaurant and entertainment area. Did we ever entertain ourselves, not to mention gorge on great food of all kinds and nationalities (Asian food is very popular there). Fresh produce is abundant there most of the year, along with fresh corn tortillas. And I love a fresh-made tortilla.

Even here, on the frozen tundra in Edmonton, we can get fresh tortillas from Mexico Lindo or Don Antonio. I even have a tortilla press and masa in the pantry to make my own, if I'm feeling ambitious.

Pre-Columbian Aztec feast. Enjoy it while it lasts, folks.

Simple Taco Meat Seasoning

METHOD: BLEND | *APPROX. TIME: 5 MINUTES* | *DIFFICULTY: LOL*

Directions

1   Mix all ingredients together in spice grinder or blender.

2   Once blended, store in well-sealed, appropriately-sized glass jar.

3   That's it! Told you it was simple.

✗   *This spice will keep for a month or so. Longer if in the freezer.*

Ingredients

✗ *3 tablespoons chili powder*

✗ *3 tablespoons paprika*

✗ *3 tablespoons ground cumin*

✗ *1 tablespoon onion powder*

✗ *2 teaspoons garlic powder*

✗ *2 teaspoons cayenne pepper*

✗ *1 teaspoon ground oregano*

✗ *2 teaspoons sugar*

✗ *1 teaspoon ground black pepper*

Simple Tomato Salsa

METHOD: BOIL | *APPROX. TIME: 30 MINUTES* | *DIFFICULTY: EASY*

Ingredients

✗ *1 can crushed tomatoes or tomato sauce (28 oz.)*

✗ *½ medium onion, chopped*

✗ *4 cloves garlic, minced or pressed*

✗ *15 jalapeno rings, canned*

✗ *¼ cup fresh cilantro, minced*

✗ *3 stalks green onions, minced*

Directions

1   Add everything except cilantro and green onion to a blender and pulse until desired consistency is reached. Pour blended mixture into saucepan, place over medium heat and bring to boil. Now reduce heat to simmer for 10 minutes.

2   Add green onions and cilantro and mix well, then remove from heat immediately and let stand for 20 minutes.

3   When cool, place in glass container and refrigerate or simply serve with salsa delivery device of your choice (tortilla, pita bread, barnyard feeder tube).

Pico de Gallo

SERVES: 6 | *METHOD: BLEND* | *APPROX. TIME: 20 MINUTES* | *DIFFICULTY: SIESTA*

Tomatoes ripened on the vine at peak season are ideal. Winter tomatoes from local greenhouses offer a weaker but still tasty substitute, but the colour won't be as appealing.

Directions

1 Place jalapeno peppers and garlic into processor and pulse to your desired consistency. Remove and place into 3-quart glass or non-reactive (stainless steel) metal bowl.

2 Remove cores from tomatoes. Cut tomatoes into 6 pieces each, place small batches in processor and pulse to desired consistency. Pour into bowl with peppers. Cut onion into 6 pieces and repeat the process.

3 Juice limes for about ¼ cup juice. Remove stems from cilantro and discard. Add cilantro leaves and 2 tablespoons lime juice to processor and pulse finely, then add to bowl with previous ingredients.

4 Add salt and pepper into ingredients so far. Stir well to incorporate, then taste. Add more if desired (1 teaspoon salt is a good amount), along with more lime juice if you like.

5 Serve with chips, crackers or just pour it down your gluttonous gullet. It's your life.

Ingredients

✕ 12 large tomatoes
(Roma or beefsteak preferred)

✕ 6 large cloves garlic, pressed or minced
(use whole head if you're not a coward)

✕ 1 large Spanish onion

✕ 3 large jalapeno peppers

✕ 1 large bunch cilantro, washed and drained

✕ 2 limes for juicing

✕ 1 teaspoon kosher salt

✕ ½ teaspoon fresh ground pepper

Pico de Gallo

(CONTINUED)

Notes

To accompany a tortilla, you'll need pico de gallo. Pico de gallo is a tomato and garlic accompaniment similar to salsa, but served fresh and raw instead of cooked.

Every restaurant chef and family cook in Mexico has their own pico de gallo recipe, all claiming to be the original and authentic one. I'm Switzerland here—I like all variations equally, but especially mine.

I love onions and garlic, but not in big raw chunks. In pico de gallo I like them minced very finely, nearly pureed. To mince with the knife is the traditional rustic method, if you have the patience, but when a big batch is required, I'll use a blender to pulse the ingredients to a medium-fine consistency, like a relish. This allows me to enjoy an onion without gagging on a big chunk of it.

Of course, opinionated foodies will tell you that using a blender is wrong, and to them I say, as I always say, piss off. I had a great finely-minced pico de gallo at a taqueria in Mexico City, and it was almost a duplicate of mine, so I suppose my version is as authentic as any. I assure you that a tortilla or pita chip doesn't care whether pico de gallo is made with a blender, a mortar and pestle, a knife, or a chimpanzee slamming two big rocks together. Your taste buds won't care either.

Pico de gallo is best served at room temperature, so I like to remove it from the fridge an hour before serving. This also gives me an opportunity to snarf a bunch down without waiting. It's so good you may not even need a tortilla.

I use leftover pico de gallo as a flavouring for marinade. Add some cumin and orange juice for a chicken marinade, or red wine and cumin for beef. You can also add it to soups, chilis, pasta sauces or anything else that needs a hard veggie-based kick.

Steve and Larry Corn, the inventors of corn.

Roasted Tomato, Corn & Ancho Chili Salsa

SERVES: 4 | *METHOD: GRILL* | *APPROX. TIME: 45 MINUTES* | *DIFFICULTY: WATCH OUT!*

Directions

1 Place dried chilis in a bowl and covering with boiling water. Let sit in water for 30 minutes, then drain and cool fully. Remove stems and discard, then open to remove seeds. Discard seeds or save for different recipe.

2 Preheat grill on hight. Use kitchen scissors to cut tips of corn husks (the part with gross dried corn silk). Set corn aside with husks still on.

3 Now place whole corn, tomatoes, bell pepper, onions and Anaheim peppers on grill. Roast vegetables on high, turning occasionally to ensure all sides char equally. Remove tomatoes first, as they fall apart if roasted too long. When peppers have dark, char-streaked skins and a light pall of smoke, all veggies are done.

4 Remove from grill and place and place peppers in sealed plastic bag to cool. This makes skins easy to remove. After 20 minutes, remove skins, seeds and stems from peppers and discard.

5 Remove husks from corn and cut corn kernels off cobs. Set corn aside in bowl and discard cobs. Next, cut up (but don't skin) charred whole tomatoes to fit in blender. Pulse to fine lumpy-sauce consistency. Pour into large bowl (to include more ingredients later) and set aside.

6 Place onions in blender and pulse to fine or medium mince, then add to tomato bowl. Repeat process with ancho chilis, but pulse to a paste this time. Add bell peppers and Anaheim peppers, pulse finely with chili paste, then add to bowl with tomatoes.

Ingredients

- 8—9 medium tomatoes (Roma or beefsteak preferred)
- 2 fresh Anaheim peppers
- 2 medium onions (Sweet Vidalia or Walla Walla preferred)
- 2 ears fresh corn, husks left on
- 1 bell pepper, red or orange
- 4—5 dried ancho chili peppers
- 4 cloves garlic, pressed
- 1 fresh lime, squeezed for 3 tablespoons juice
- 1 tablespoon kosher salt
- 1 teaspoon fresh-ground pepper

7 Add corn to bowl (without blending it, to be clear) and stir well. Next add lime juice, pressed garlic and salt and pepper. Stir bowl well.

8 Let salsa sit at room temperature 30 minutes to let flavours to get to know each other.

9 Serve with tacos, tortillas chips, or just stand at the bowl with a spoon and eat it like a ravenous wolf at roadside carrion.

- *This salsa has a sweet smoky flavour and isn't spicy at all (that's why we removed the seeds), so it's perfect for spice-sensitive friends. Great to share and goes deliciously with a Corona.*

Guacamole

SERVES: 4 | *METHOD: BOIL* | *APPROX. TIME: 30 MINUTES* | *DIFFICULTY: EASY*

Our friend Maurie would travel vast distances, and has on one occasion crossed provincial boundaries, just for a taste of this guacamole. If Susan and I hadn't seen Maurie and Doug in awhile and began to miss them, I'd simply whip up a batch, and like magic, Maurie and her family would manifest at the door. I could only sit back and watch the piranha-like feeding frenzy. Yes, Maurie loves her guacamole. We love her too, but not as much.

Ingredients

- 3 large avocados
- 3 cloves garlic, chopped fine or pressed
- 1 medium tomato, chopped
- ½—1 teaspoon salt
- ½ teaspoon pepper (I prefer ground white)
- ½ teaspoon paprika
- 1 medium lime

Directions

1 Squeeze lime until it confesses to being on the grassy knoll. Set aside juice for later.

2 Cut avocado lengthwise. Remove pits and set aside for later (yes, really). Scoop out avocado meat and place in glass bowl.

3 Mash avocado to desired consistency, then add chopped tomato, garlic, lime juice, pepper, salt and paprika. Mix well. Taste and add more salt, pepper, lime juice etc. as you like.

4 Place avocado pits on the top of mixture (keeps guacamole from browning) and cover with lid or plastic wrap. Refrigerate 1 hour to allow new flavour friends to mingle and mellow.

5 This assembly of flavours goes well with just about anything: tacos, enchiladas, hamburgers, sandwiches, even eggs benedict if you're really tempting cardiovascular fate.

Seven-Layer Dip

SERVES: **6** | *METHOD:* **LAYERING** | *APPROX. TIME:* **10 MINUTES** | *DIFFICULTY:* **SIMPLE**

I mention Maurie in the guacamole recipe that you'll use in this one. Maurie will testify that this dip goes very well with that guacamole. I can't make either of these when there's an westward wind, for fear the aroma will carry past her home and torment her needlessly. Actually, that's a lie. I love to torment her and her family. The secret ingredient to guacamole is schadenfreude!

Ingredients

- 1 can (14 oz.) refried beans
- 2 cups fresh guacamole
- 2 cups sour cream
- 2 cups homemade salsa
  OR
  2 cups store-bought salsa
  (Herdez is a great choice)
- 2 cup fresh grated cheddar
  (or firm cheese of your choice)
- 1 cup fresh chopped green
  onions (about 2 bunches)
- ¼ cup crumbled bacon
- 1 cup sliced black olives (optional)

Directions

1   In 3-quart glass baking dish, spread refried beans evenly. In order, layer guacamole, sour cream and salsa, taking care to spread gently to keep layers separate.

2   Once salsa is spread, sprinkle grated cheese, then green onions and last but not least, bacon. Once bacon is sprinkled over the top, you can add the olives if you choose, but then it would be an Eight Layer Dip and that's not the name of the recipe.

  You could omit the bacon instead, but what kind of madman would do that? Anyway, feel free to add the olives or not. Do what you want with them, as long as I don't have to watch.

3   When all ingredients are stacked, refrigerate and then serve within 2 hours. Otherwise the ingredients will start to water like Susan's eyes during a Hallmark commercial and begin the separation process (the dip, not Susan).

4   When chilled to your desired temperature, serve with tortilla chips, crackers, baked pita or other dip delivery mechanism. Or, hell, just eat it with a spoon. It's your life, and shame is just a fake idea.

Boston Pizza-Style Potato Chip Dip

SERVES: 6 | *METHOD: MIXING* | *APPROX. TIME: 10 MINUTES* | *DIFFICULTY: BOSTONIAN*

Ingredients

- ¾ cup sour cream
- ½ cup store-bought creamy garlic caesar dressing (I use Kraft)
- ¼ cup green onions
- 1 fresh jalapeno pepper
- ½ teaspoon pepper
- ¼ cup Parmesan cheese, grated
- ½ lemon
- 2 teaspoons Creole spice
- 1 tablespoon hot sauce (I prefer Frank's)

Directions

1 Mince green onions, regular onions and jalapeno peppers very finely. Juice lemon into bowl.

2 Mix all ingredients together in a big bowl and refrigerate a few hours. Simple! This dip is so Boston that it will scream racial slurs at you from the fridge.

3 Goes great as a veggie dip, though the best is with warm homemade potato chips.

Hollandaise Sauce

SERVES: **6** | *METHOD:* **BLEND** | *APPROX. TIME:* **10 MINUTES** | *DIFFICULTY:* **TRICKY**

This is the easiest way I've found to make Hollandaise sauce, cooking the yolks entirely inside the blender using only the ambient heat of boiling water. Perfect for Eggs Benedict, of course, but also incredible on chicken fingers, fish sticks or anything deep-fried.

Preparation

1   Prepare by taking eggs and lemon juice from fridge and setting on counter until they warm up to room temperature. This is important.

Directions

2   Separate egg whites from yolks. You only need yolks here, so save whites for another recipe.

3   This next part is time-critical. Set butter to heat in saucepan or in Pyrex measuring cup in microwave. Use medium setting and watch to ensure nothing is burning!

4   Set small saucepan of water to boil. Keep tablespoon handy.

Always preheat the blender jar when making this recipe! Adding hot liquids to cold glass could result in a very nasty explosion. See my Exploding Chicken recipe for more on this topic.

5   Run blender jar under hottest tapwater until jar is hot to touch. Once jar is hot, empty it and get to work immediately.

Special Equipment

✗ *Blender*

Ingredients

✗ *4 eggs*

✗ *½ cup butter*

✗ *1 tablespoon lemon juice, warmed up*

✗ *4 tablespoons water*

6   Turn blender to medium speed and add egg yolks. Slowly add boiling water from saucepan, 1 tablespoon at a time, until 4 tablespoons have been incorporated. Slowly drizzle bubbling melted butter into yolk mixture.

7   Add lemon juice and blend for 30 seconds, or until sauce is thick. Test by dipping spoon into blender (make sure it's not still on, dummy). Sauce should coat the back of the spoon.

8   Serve over Eggs Benedict, roasted asparagus, or anything else you want to make unhealthier.

Creamy Tomato Vodka Sauce

SERVES: 8 | *METHOD: SIMMER* | *APPROX. TIME: 1—4 HOURS* | *DIFFICULTY: EASY*

The first time I made this was for a celebration dinner for Susan. I served it atop home-made lobster ravioli, which in turn was made with homemade pasta. To say it was enjoyable is to short-change the depraved culinary orgy that ensued. Try it if you're not swingers but you still want to know what your friends' O-faces look like.

Ingredients

- 1 can crushed tomatoes (28 oz.)
- 2 tablespoons olive oil
- 8 cloves garlic, pressed
- ¼—½ teaspoon red pepper flakes
- ¾ cup vodka, any brand (but not the expensive brands)
- ¾ cup whipping cream
  OR
  ¾ cup half-and-half cream
- 3 tablespoons fresh basil, minced
  OR
  2 tablespoons dried basil, crushed
- 2 tablespoons fresh parsley, minced
  OR
  1 tablespoons dried basil, crushed
- ¾ teaspoon salt
- ½ teaspoon ground pepper

Directions

1   Heat olive oil in large skillet over medium heat. Add garlic and sauté until garlic starts to brown, about 2—3 minutes.

2   Add crushed tomatoes, vodka, red pepper flakes, salt, pepper, basil and parsley. Simmer over medium-low heat ½ hour, stirring occasionally, then add cream and simmer over low heat for ½ hour more.

3   Remove from heat and let cool in pot. Refrigerate 4 hours for improved, smoother taste.

4   10 minutes prior to serving, place pot back on medium heat, stirring sauce continuously until hot and ready to accompany pasta of your choice.

Creole Seasoning

METHOD: *BLEND* | APPROX. TIME: *10 MINUTES* | DIFFICULTY: *EASY*

This is one of my own recipes, arrived at after much trial and error. I don't know that it's authentic, or particularly original, but it's perfect for my needs: roasts, barbeque rubs, pasta sauce, étouffée, omelettes, and cuisines of the Tex-Mex, Creole, Cajun, Mexican and even Italian varieties. Experiment with it! Use it everywhere you need some heat or a deep bold set of complementary flavours. There's no wrong way to use it, except in the bedroom.

Special Equipment

✕ Blender
OR
Spice grinder

Ingredients

✕ ½ cup paprika

✕ ¼ cup onion powder

✕ ¼ cup garlic powder

✕ ¼ cup dried oregano

✕ ¼ cup dried sweet basil

✕ 2 tablespoons dried thyme

✕ 2 tablespoons black pepper

✕ 2 tablespoons white pepper

✕ 2 tablespoons cayenne pepper

✕ 2 tablespoons celery salt

✕ 2 tablespoons mustard powder

Directions

1   Mix all ingredients together in spice grinder or blender until you achieve fine, powdery consistency.

2   Store in airtight glass jar. Keeps for a month or so if you don't use it all.

Creole Sauce

SERVES: 4 | *METHOD: SIMMER* | *APPROX. TIME: 30 MINUTES* | *DIFFICULTY: EASY*

Ingredients

- 2 tablespoons vegetable oil
- ½ large onion, diced finely
- 2 stalks celery, diced finely
- ½ red bell pepper, diced finely
- 4 cloves garlic, pressed
- 2 cans tomato sauce (14 oz. each, or big 28 oz. can)
- 2 tablespoons Creole seasoning
- 1 tablespoon sugar
- ½ lemon (juice it, you know the drill by now)
- 1 bay leaf
- Salt to taste
- Cayenne pepper to taste
- Ground black pepper to taste

Directions

1 Place heavy-bottom pan over medium heat. Sauté onion, celery, red pepper, and garlic for 3—4 minutes. Add tomato sauce, bay leaf, sugar, Creole seasoning and lemon juice. Bring mixture to boil, then turn down to simmer for 20 minutes.

2 Remove from heat, remove bay leaf, and season mixture with pinch of salt, a dash of cayenne pepper and fresh ground pepper.

The Creole seasoning already includes pepper and spices, but you may want more or less. Play with proportions if you want it mild, warm or suicide-pill hot.

3 I like to serve this with shrimp. If you wish to follow my lead, and you should, toss in 1 lb. of peeled and deveined raw shrimp at the end and cook for 3—4 minutes right before serving.

4 Serve with rice, noodles, potatoes or what have you. I also like to pour over hot broiled or grilled chicken.

White Curry Sauce for Fish

METHOD: *VARIED* | APPROX. TIME: *30 MINUTES* | DIFFICULTY: *DON'T FUCK IT UP*

I'm not sure where this recipe came from, but the court bouillon part is from Alton Brown. I just doubled it for the amount of fish used, which in my family is a lot. If you're not feeling so ambitious, you can still poach with water and some lemon juice. You can substitute fish for scallops, large shrimp or any other seafood. Heck, serve it with linguine, rice noodles or any noodles, really. Eat it naked over the sink at 2 in the morning if you like. I know I do.

Fish

- 8 sea bass fillets
  (snapper, cod or halibut also work)

Sauce Ingredients

- 1 tablespoon vegetable oil
- 1 medium onion, minced finely
- 4 garlic cloves, pressed
- 2 tablespoons ginger paste
- 1 stalk lemon grass, cut into 1" pieces
- 1 green chili, seeds removed and minced finely
- 1 can coconut milk (400ml)
- 1 cup chicken stock
- 1 lime, hand-squeezed for juice
- 2 tablespoons fish sauce
- ½ teaspoon turmeric
- 4 green onions, chopped finely

Court Bouillion Ingredients

- 3 cups water
- 1 cup white wine
- 2 lemons, juiced
- 2 medium onions, chopped
- 1 celery stalk, chopped
- 2 garlic cloves, chopped finely
- 2 teaspoons black peppercorns
- 8—10 sprigs fresh thyme
  OR
  2 teaspoons dried thyme
- 2 bay leaves
- ¼ cup garlic powder
- ¼ cup dried oregano
- ¼ cup dried sweet basil
- 2 tablespoons dried thyme
- 2 tablespoons black pepper
- 2 tablespoons white pepper
- 2 tablespoons cayenne pepper
- 2 tablespoons celery salt
- 2 tablespoons mustard powder

White Curry Sauce for Fish
(CONTINUED)

Directions

1 Add court bouillon ingredients to wide-bottomed pot. Raise to medium boil, then reduce heat to simmer for 10 minutes to extract herb flavour.

2 Heat oil in skillet over medium heat. Add onion, garlic, ginger, chili and lemon-grass to skillet. Sauté mixture until onions are translucent, about 2 minutes.

3 Add coconut milk, turmeric, fish sauce, lime juice and chicken stock. Bring mixture to boil. Reduce heat to low and simmer until liquid is reduced by about ⅓. Remove sauce from heat and keep warm.

4 Use slotted spoon to remove solid ingredients from court bouillon. Reduce heat to very low and use slotted spoon to add fish fillets. Simmer 2 minutes, then turn off heat and wait for ambient heat to do its thing for 3—5 minutes.

✕ *By now you should know the texture of properly-cooked fish. Don't overcook!*

5 Remove cooked fish from water, drain, and plate with steamed jasmine rice along with your favourite vegetable (okra and asparagus are excellent choices).

6 Ladle sauce over meal and sprinkle with green onion.

Look at that smile. He's daring you to cook him right. Do not fail.

Mock Mornay Sauce

SERVES: *4* | METHOD: *SIMMER* | APPROX. TIME: *15 MINUTES* | DIFFICULTY: *EASY*

Ingredients

- 2 tablespoons butter
- 2 tablespoons flour
- 4 tablespoons grated parmesan cheese
- ½ cup milk
  OR
  ½ cup half-and-half cream
- ¾ cup chicken stock
- ¼ teaspoon white pepper
- Salt to taste
- Grated nutmeg to taste (optional)

Directions

1 Melt butter in a saucier (fancy word for small sauce pot) over medium heat. Add flour and stir until roux is cooked but not browned. It will smell like a fresh-baked butter cookie when ready.

2 Add chicken stock and milk, whisking thoroughly. When mixture is hot and close to bubbling, add cheese, pepper, nutmeg and salt to taste.

3 If necessary, add more stock or milk to achieve desired consistency of sauce. Remove from heat and serve immediately.

Note that when making flour-thickened sauces, sauce will continue to thicken as it rests. If it thickens too much, return to heat and add water, milk or stock as you like.

Panang Curry Paste

METHOD: BLEND | *APPROX. TIME: 20 MINUTES* | *DIFFICULTY: MEDIUM*

With the seafood paste and other nonsense, the final result of this recipe might smell rather horrid to you. At least it does to me. But as a base for a Thai curry recipe (like the ones in this book) it's divine, so don't be put off by the smell. Trust me! And if you don't trust me, trust Kaitlyn, who agrees with me. Oh, you don't trust her either? Well, I don't blame you, we're both rather sketchy.

You can store curry paste in an airtight container in the fridge about 1 month, or in the freezer for up to 3. Just fill up a few ice cube trays with paste, freeze solid, then remove and crack the cubes into an airtight freezer bag for longer storage. There you go! Instant curry paste whenever you need it.

Ingredients

- ¾ cup (3 oz.) dried red chili peppers
- 1½ tablespoons whole coriander seeds
- 2 teaspoons whole cumin seeds
- 2 tablespoons shrimp paste
  OR
  2 tablespoons anchovy paste
- 2 tablespoons roasted peanuts
- 2 small limes for zest
  OR
  2 fresh kaffir limes for zest
- ½ fresh lime for juice
  OR
  8—10 kaffir lime leaves
- 3 tablespoons cilantro, chopped
- 1 large stalk lemongrass
- 2 tablespoons ginger, minced finely
  OR
  2 tablespoons galangal, minced finely
- 1 large head of garlic
- ½ medium red onion, chopped

Directions

1   Split and clean chili peppers and discard seeds. Place cleaned chilis in bowl, submerge in hot water and let soak for 30 minutes, then drain and set aside.

2   Toast coriander and cumin in small skillet over medium heat until aromatic, about 3 minutes. Shake pan frequently to prevent seeds from burning.

3   Place toasted seeds in small bowl to cool. When seeds are cool, place in coffee grinder or mortar and pestle and grind to powder.

4   Add chilis, lime zest, lime juice, cilantro, lemongrass, peanuts, garlic, onion, ginger, shrimp paste, coriander and cumin to blender. Blend 3 minutes into fine uniform paste. Scrape blender jar's sides occasionally so all ingredients mix evenly (do not do this while blender is on, obviously).

5   A malleable paste should result. All done!

✗ *If mixture is too thick, drizzle vegetable oil into running blender with paste, 1 teaspoon at a time.*

Vietnamese Peanut Sauce

SERVES: *4* | METHOD: **SIMMER** | APPROX. TIME: *15 MINUTES* | DIFFICULTY: *BE CAREFUL*

This sauce is the only accepted accompaniment to Vietnamese salad rolls in our house. In fact, we make salad rolls solely to act as peanut sauce delivery mechanisms.

Normally I double or triple this recipe to satisfy any starving guests or vagrants that wander by. Particularly my darling Kristine who, if left unattended, will attack this dish with a force that would give Mr. Peanut flashbacks to the war. Kristine has allowed me to state that, in her expert opinion, my peanut sauce recipe is world-class. I pity the poor souls whose anaphylactic shock prevents them from sharing in this opulence.

Regarding the ingredients, they're not as hard to find as they sound. Sambal oelek, sesame oil, hoisin sauce and fish sauce are staples of any Asian market or super-market section. If all else fails, make the trek to a T&T. You'll be glad you did.

Ingredients

- ½ cup peanut butter (crunchy or smooth, your choice)
- 1 tablespoon toasted sesame oil (real, not sesame-flavoured oil)
- 4 garlic cloves, pressed
- 1–2 tablespoons sambal oelek (Indonesian chili-garlic paste)
- 2 tablespoons ketchup
- 1 cup chicken broth
- 1 teaspoon sugar
- ¼ cup hoisin sauce
- 1 tablespoon nuoc mam (Vietnamese fish sauce)

Directions

1. Heat oil in small saucepan over medium heat. When oil is hot, add garlic and sauté for 2 minutes, but don't burn. Add chili paste, ketchup, chicken broth, sugar, peanut butter, fish sauce and hoisin sauce. Whisk well to dissolve peanut butter. Raise to boil, then reduce to low heat and simmer 5 minutes.

Word of caution: When you simmer this thick gloopy sauce, it will bubble and splatter, and if a splatter lands on you, it will hurt, so cover the pot with a sieve or mesh strainer. Or keep a bag of ice for the burns and a double mojito to assuage the pain centres of your brain.

If sauce is too thick, add more chicken broth heat to bubbling while stirring often.

2. Serve warm, not hot, as accompaniment to Vietnamese salad rolls or anything else.

Grandmas Boos's Barbeque Sauce

SERVES: **6** | *METHOD:* **SAUTÉ & SIMMER** | *APPROX. TIME:* **2 HOURS** | *DIFFICULTY:* **TRICKY**

Ingredients

- 1 tablespoon oil
- 1 medium onion, minced
- 6 cloves garlic, pressed
- 1½ cups ketchup or tomato sauce
- ¼ cup chili sauce
- 3 tablespoons brown sugar
- 3 tablespoons molasses
- 1 tablespoon mustard powder
- 2 tablespoons white vinegar
- 1 tablespoon Worcestershire sauce
- 1 tablespoon hickory liquid smoke (optional)
- 1 tablespoon Creole seasoning
- Salt to taste

Directions

1   Add oil, onion and garlic to saucepan and sauté for 3 minutes, or until onions are translucent.

2   Add all other ingredients and simmer for 1 hour. As sauce reduces over time, add water to maintain consistency and avoid burning (which is quite possible with the amount of sugar here).

3   Remove from heat and let cool to room temperature, about 1 hour. Then pour cooled sauce into blender and whiz at high speed until smooth consistency is achieved.

4   Use on your favourite cuts of meat.

- *Will keep for 1 week in fridge, but I suggest adding leftover sauce to a slow-cooker with pork shoulder.*

Red Enchilada Sauce

SERVES: **6** | *METHOD:* **SAUTÉ & SIMMER** | *APPROX. TIME:* **30 HOURS** | *DIFFICULTY:* **EASY**

Ingredients

- 2 teaspoons olive oil
- 2 medium onions
- 1 tablespoon garlic, minced
- 2 tablespoons chopped jalapenos
- 1 tablespoon chili powder
- 2 teaspoons ground cumin
- 1 teaspoon dried oregano
- 1 can crushed tomatoes (28 oz.)
  OR
  1 can tomato sauce (28 oz.)
- 1 cup chicken broth
- 1 tablespoon brown sugar
- ½ teaspoon salt
- ¼ teaspoon fresh-ground black pepper

Directions

1 Heat olive oil over medium heat in large saucepan. Add onions and garlic and sauté 2—3 minutes until onions are translucent.

2 Stir in all remaining ingredients. Raise sauce to boil, then reduce heat to low. Cover and simmer for 15 minutes. Remove from heat and let cool to room temperature.

Always let ingredients cool to room temperature before adding to a blender, or risk a dangerous explosion. Glassware is a temperamental mistress, and not in the good way. See my Exploding Chicken recipe for a cautionary tale.

3 When sauce is cool, blend with hand blender until smooth, or pour into jar blender for the same purpose.

4 Serve over enchiladas, or use as a salsa-type dip for chips.

Teriyaki Marinade for Beef, Chicken or Pork

SERVES: 4—6 | *METHOD: MARINATE* | *APPROX. TIME: 24 HOURS* | *DIFFICULTY: EASY*

Directions

1. In plastic or stainless steel bowl, mix all ingredients together. Submerge meat, stir until fully distributed, and refrigerate for at least 8 hours. Overnight, or up to 24 hours, is best.

2. Remove from fridge when desired, allow to warm to room temperature, then remove meat from marinade and cook according to directions for the type of meat.

Ingredients

- 2—3 lbs. chicken, pork or beef strips
- 3 cups dry white wine
- 2 cups regular soy sauce
- 10 cloves crushed garlic
- 2 tablespoons fresh grated ginger
  OR
  1 tablespoon ginger powder
- 3 tablespoons brown sugar
- 2 tablespoons Sriracha sauce

Vietnamese Spring Roll Dipping Sauce

METHOD: BOIL | *APPROX. TIME: 1 HOUR* | *DIFFICULTY: EASY*

Ingredients

- ½ cup boiling water
- ½ cup sugar
- ½ cup rice vinegar
  OR
  ½ cup lemon juice
  OR
  ½ cup of both combined (¼ each)
- ½ cup nuoc mam (Vietnamese fish sauce)
- ¼ cup sambal oelek
  (Indonesian chili-garlic paste)

Directions

1. In a 1-quart bowl, add boiling water and sugar and stir until dissolved. Add remaining ingredients and chill for 1 hour.

- *Use this sauce to dip spring rolls or any similar fried stuff, but it's also a great marinade for pork, shrimp or chicken before grilling. If sambal oelek isn't available, you can substitute sriracha, gochujang or other thick, preferably garlicky hot sauce for a similar experience.*

Side Dishes, Starches & Other Temptations

Most rices, grains, and other starches take well to punishment. Cook 'em heavy or light, dry or moist, tender or firm—they'll survive if not excel. Most importantly, they also serve as vehicles for gravy, sauces and seasonings. Oh yes, seasonings.

You need an adequately-stocked spice cabinet if you hope to tackle this section. Get yourself down the Silk Road (or at least to your local Bulk Barn) immediately.

Quinoa

We became fans of quinoa in the last five years or so. Why we didn't glom onto it earlier? Well, quinoa is some hippie shit, and I tend to avoid hippie shit. However, the hippies were right about this one thing. Quinoa is delicious and versatile, and I'm now a convert for life. There are already millions of quinoa recipes in the world, and in my hubris I'm going to give you even more.

When my family moved to St. Albert, we made friends with a couple on our street named Chris and Melinda. As it happened, they were from Mackenzie, a town just up the dirt road from Prince George, so we had a little in common already. Perhaps strange that fate would join us as neighbours in St. Albert, or perhaps it was just (their) bad luck.

We shared interests including good food, good wine, and select rum. Chris and Melinda are the fantastic cooks and hosts every neighbourhood needs. Like us, they're adventurous when it comes to food, prone to sharing novelties and experiments with their friends. Lucky us!

One evening, one of Melinda's side dishes really woke my taste buds: quinoa and beet salad with goat cheese. I know what you're thinking. "What the ever-loving fuck?" But trust me, it was fantastic, especially as I'm not a fan of goat cheese.

Later, when attempting to make my own version, I called Melinda for her recipe. Her reply was simply a list of ingredients: quinoa, beets, olive oil, goat cheese, ground pepper—that's it. We briefly discussed adding cilantro and mint, which she agreed would probably taste great, but I never got any other directions.

I pressed on that night, tweaking her ingredients a bit to complete my experiment. Paired with grilled pork chops, it turned out a winner! I hoped Melinda would be proud of me, although like the selfish ingrates we are, we didn't save her even a morsel to try for herself.

Anyway, Chris and Melinda remain great friends whom we love very much. They've enriched our lives with their friendship, their time, their cooking, and the occasional splitting hangover. When it comes to good friends, you've gotta take the good with the bad, and put the 'fun' in 'functional alcoholic.'

Quinoa & Beet Salad

SERVES: **6** | *METHOD:* **SIMMER & BAKE** | *APPROX. TIME:* **2+ HOURS** | *DIFFICULTY:* **EASY**

Quinoa is covered with a natural substance called saponin, which protects the grain from insects and birds. It tastes unpleasant, but you can get rid of it by rinsing before cooking. Commercial quinoa may be pre-rinsed, so read instructions on your package first.

Directions

1. Rinse quinoa in fine mesh strainer under cold water, stirring 1 minute. Drain well and transfer to medium saucepan.

2. Add chicken stock to quinoa over medium-high heat and bring to boil, then reduce heat to low. Cover and simmer 10—12 minutes, or until it's al dente.

3. Remove from heat and set aside, keeping covered for 10 minutes to complete the cooking and soak up remaining water. Move cooked quinoa to bowl, fluff with fork, then refrigerate 1 hour.

4. Scrub beets well, but don't skin yet. Rub clean beets with olive oil to coat completely.

5. Preheat oven to 400°. Place sheet of foil over baking sheet or flat oven dish. Place coated beets on foil, then fold up, sealing the edges.

6. Roast beets at 400° until tender. This can take up to 2 hours; fresh beets cook faster. Start checking tenderness at 30-minute mark by poking with fork. If ready, fork will pierce beet with a little pressure.

7. Remove beets from oven when tender. Let them sit, sealed in foil wrap, until cool enough to handle. When cool, remove from foil and rub skins off, then dice beets into ¼" cubes and refrigerate 1 hour.

Ingredients

- 1 cup quinoa (see note below)
- 2 cups low-sodium or salt-free chicken stock
- 2 medium beets
- ½ cup soft cheese, diced to ¼" (Edam or Gouda, or goat if you're hardcore)
- 3 tablespoons extra virgin olive oil for salad
- 2 tablespoons olive oil for coating beets
- ½ teaspoon freshly ground pepper
- 2 tablespoons fresh cilantro, minced finely (optional)
- 1 tablespoon fresh mint, minced finely (optional)
- Salt to taste

8. Combine cooled quinoa with cubed beets and toss gently. Add 3 tablespoons olive oil, crumbled cheese, cilantro, mint and pepper in a large bowl and toss to combine. Taste and season with additional salt if desired.

✕ *Sorry to Melinda for butchering her recipe! But then again, not sorry. This shit is delicious. I hope she tries it my way one day and tells me if it meets her approval, like we talked about.*

Barley Casserole

SERVES: **4** | *METHOD:* **SAUTÉ & SIMMER** | *APPROX. TIME:* **1 HOUR** | *DIFFICULTY:* **EASY**

Directions

I   Preheat oven to 350°. Melt butter in pan, and sauté onion and dried barley together until onion is translucent and barley grain starts to brown. Remove from heat and pour mixture into casserole dish. Add rest of ingredients.

✗   *You want 3 cups of stock to 1 cup of barley, because unlike rice, which cooks to just over 100% of its dry size, barley expands about 300% when cooking.*

2   Stir well, cover dish, and bake 1 hour or until barley is tender. Serve hot.

Ingredients

- 1 cup dried pearl barley
- 1 small onion, chopped
- 3 tablespoons butter
- 3 cups chicken or beef broth
- 1 cup salsa
- 1 can corn
- Salt and pepper to taste

Szechuan Spicy Green Beans

SERVES: **4** | *METHOD:* **SAUTÉ** | *APPROX. TIME:* **10 MINUTES** | *DIFFICULTY:* **EASY**

Ingredients

- 1 lb. fresh green beans (long beans preferred)
- 4 cloves garlic, pressed
- 1 tablespoon sesame oil
- 1 tablespoon corn starch and water slurry
- 1 tablespoon chili garlic paste
- ⅓ cup water
- 2 tablespoons hoisin sauce

Directions

I   Wash and prepare green beans by removing the stem end and the stringy bits at the opposite end. Cut beans into bite size pieces.

2   Heat sesame oil in non-stick wok or large frying pan over medium heat. Sauté garlic for 2 minutes until lightly browned. Add chili sauce, green beans, water and hoisin sauce.

3   Add starch slurry if required to thicken remaining liquid. Stir-fry until green beans are cooked but still crisp (about 3 minutes). Serve hot.

Bart's Cauliflower au Gratin

SERVES: 6 | *METHOD: SAUTÉ & SIMMER* | *APPROX. TIME: 1 HOUR* | *DIFFICULTY: EASY*

I tossed this dish together one night to avoid the same old steamed cauliflower. I love a good mayonnaise, and I love Parmesan, so I thought, why not put them together? And after a few attempts this recipe was born. This goes especially well with a roast beef dinner.

I once served this to Darren and Lisa's kids and they went nuts for it, just like mine did. It's not as oily as you'd think; most of the oil melts to the bottom to cara- melize the cauliflower, and stays there when the cauliflower is removed.

Ingredients

- 1 large cauliflower, rinsed, trimmed and cut into small florets
- ¼ cup virgin olive oil
- ¼ cup low fat mayonnaise
- ¼ + ¼ cup Parmesan cheese
- ½ teaspoon salt
- ½ teaspoon white pepper
- ½ teaspoon Creole seasoning, optional (see recipe)
- 1 cup fine panko crumbs

Directions

1. Preheat oven to 375°. Grease 9" × 13" casserole dish with thin coat of cooking oil or Pam.

2. To large bowl add olive oil, mayonnaise, ¼ cup parmesan cheese, Creole seasoning, and salt and pepper. Whisk well to blend. Add cauliflower and toss to coat evenly.

3. Spread coated cauliflower in casserole dish. Scrape all bowl contents overtop. Mix panko crumbs with another ¼ cup Parmesan cheese and cover cauliflower.

4. Bake until golden brown and cauliflower is fork-tender, about 35 minutes.

5. Finish for 3 minutes under broiler to darken the topping. Careful not to burn!

Spicy Indian Cauliflower

SERVES: 4 | *METHOD: SAUTÉ & SIMMER* | *APPROX. TIME: 1 HOUR* | *DIFFICULTY: EASY*

Ingredients

- 2 tablespoons oil
- 1 teaspoon ground cumin seed
- 2 tablespoons ginger paste
- 2 teaspoons minced ginger
- 3 cloves of garlic, pressed
- 2 green chilies, minced finely
- 1 onion, sliced thinly
- ½ teaspoon ground turmeric
- 1 tablespoon ground coriander
- 1 tablespoon curry leaves (whole)
  OR
  2 bay leaves
- 1 teaspoon chili powder
- 1 teaspoon paprika
- ½ cup water
- 1 medium cauliflower, cut into florets
- ½ teaspoon salt
- Pepper to taste

Directions

1. Heat oil in pan over medium heat and add cumin, ginger, garlic, onion and chilies. Stir-fry until onion is soft and translucent.

2. Add coriander, turmeric, paprika and chili powder and curry or bay leaves and stir for a minute. Add water, then cauliflower. Stir-fry for 2 minutes to coat cauliflower.

3. Cover pan and cook for 15 minutes over low heat or until cauliflower is soft. Stir occasionally.

Broccoli & Cheese Rice

SERVES: 4 | *METHOD: **SAUTÉ & SIMMER*** | *APPROX. TIME: **30 MINUTES*** | *DIFFICULTY: **EASY***

Ingredients

✕ *1½ cups rice (Uncle Ben's works best)*

✕ *2 lbs. broccoli*

✕ *1 small onion minced finely*

✕ *1 clove garlic pressed*

✕ *2 tablespoons oil*

✕ *1 ½ cups light cream (half-and-half)*

✕ *4 cups chicken stock*

✕ *2 cups grated cheddar cheese, firmly packed*

✕ *¼ cup parmesan cheese*

✕ *¼ teaspoon cayenne pepper*

Directions

1   Cut broccoli florets into small pieces. Peel stems and cut into ½" cubes.

2   In 3-quart pot over medium heat, sauté onion and garlic for 5 minutes or until onion is translucent. Add rice and stir over medium heat for 3—5 minutes. Add chicken stock and reduce to simmer for 15 minutes.

3   Add cream, cayenne and broccoli. Simmer for 10—12 minutes until rice is tender. Stir often but gently, so you don't turn to rice to gruel.

4   Remove from heat, add cheese, and stir gently until cheese melts into smooth creamy sauce. Cover with tight-fitting lid for 5 minutes to make sure heat distributes properly.

5   Serve piping hot and enjoy! This is a terrific side dish and puts that package stuff to shame.

✕   *Maintain sauce consistency adding a little chicken stock or water as needed. If it splats on a plate as a congealed mass, it's too thick, like something served at a truck stop in Moosejaw. But you don't want it as a soup either, so mind your moisture levels to get the balance right.*

Cuban Black Beans

SERVES: **4** | *METHOD:* **SAUTÉ & SIMMER** | *APPROX. TIME:* **3 HOURS** | *DIFFICULTY:* **EASY**

These beans are absolutely fantastic and the musical serenade will last for hours afterward for the enjoyment of friends, family and irate neighbours. You may even be overtaken by a sudden feeling that Castro wasn't such a bad guy after all.

Ingredients

- 2 cups dried black beans
- ¼ cup light olive oil
- ½—1 lb. bacon or pork belly, chopped
- 4 cloves garlic, pressed
- 1 red pepper, chopped finely
- 1 large onion, chopped finely
- ½ cup white wine
- 1 teaspoon black pepper
- 2 tablespoons cumin
- 1 teaspoon oregano
- 1 teaspoon salt
- 1 tablespoon vinegar
- 3 tablespoons sugar
- 3 bay leaves

Directions

1   Wash beans, then soak overnight in 6 cups water. When ready, add beans (with soaking water) to large pot and cook over medium heat for 1 hour, or until beans are tender. Then remove from heat—but don't drain.

2   In skillet, place olive oil, bacon, onions, red pepper and garlic. Sauté on medium-low heat until onions are translucent and pork is cooked, but don't brown! Now empty skillet into bean pot along with remaining ingredients.

3   Cook over low heat on stovetop, or in the oven at 300° (if your pot is oven-safe) for 2—3 hours until mixture is fully cooked and liquid has reduced to desired consistency.

4   Serve with rice or whatever suits your fancy.

Grandma Boos's Baked Beans

SERVES: 4 | *METHOD: BOIL & BAKE* | *APPROX. TIME: 5 HOURS* | *DIFFICULTY: EASY*

This recipe is similar to Boston baked beans. My Grandma used it for many years, and I in turn. It's a wonderful meal in itself, and makes a great side dish for baked ham, roast beef, grilled hot dogs and burgers.

Like any mature adult, I love the musical feast that are baked beans. For at least a day afterward, I can entertain myself the way I know best. I'm still working on my rendition of Beethoven's 6th. The brass section comes easy, but that clarinet cadenza is a bitch.

I have a very old bean pot that I use to make these. I suppose if you're a Luddite, you could use Corelle or similar baking dish, but I'd truly recommend heading to the flea market for a true-blue ceramic bean pot. It's worth the effort and modest expense.

Ingredients

- 3 cups navy beans, washed
- 1 tablespoon baking soda
- 1 lb. sliced bacon (as lean as possible, or substitute ham)
- 1 onion, minced
- ¼ cup molasses
- 1 tablespoon brown sugar
- 1 tablespoon vinegar
- 1 teaspoon dry mustard
- 1 teaspoon ground ginger powder
- ½ teaspoon salt
- ½ teaspoon pepper
- ¾ cup ketchup
- ¾ cup water

Directions

1 Add beans to large pot with 4 quarts of water and 1 tablespoon baking soda. Bring to boil, boil for 2 minutes, then remove from heat.

2 Let beans sit for 1—2 hours until fully cooled to room temperature. Drain and rinse beans well to remove any trace of baking soda.

3 Place beans in bean pot or crock pot, then add all other ingredients to pot. Stir gently until beans are fully covered with mixture.

4 Place lid on pot, then place pot in preheated oven at 400°. Cook for ½ hour, then give beans a gentle stir. If liquid is required to ensure beans are covered, add more water.

5 Then turn down oven to 275° and bake for 3 more hours. Stir every hour or so, checking liquid levels to keep the beans moist and covered. Add more water as required.

6 When beans are soft, remove from oven, cool and serve.

Classic Risotto

SERVES: 4 | *METHOD: SAUTÉ & SIMMER* | *APPROX. TIME: 45 MINUTES* | *DIFFICULTY: EASY*

Ingredients

- 5 cups chicken broth
- 1 tablespoon olive oil
- 1 medium onion, minced finely
- 1½ cups Arborio rice
- 3 tablespoons butter
- 2 cloves garlic, pressed
- ⅔ cup Parmesan cheese, grated
- Salt and pepper to taste
- Pinch of nutmeg (be careful, just a pinch!)

Directions

1   In small saucepan, bring stock to boil and then reduce heat to a simmer.

2   In medium saucepan, sauté onion and garlic over medium heat, stirring until onion is translucent but not brown. Add rice and stir. Turn heat to medium-high and stir in ½ cup broth. Bring stock to simmer in saucepan, stirring well.

3   Turn down heat to medium, add ½ cup of stock, keeping mixture simmering, and stir continuously. As broth is absorbed, continue to add broth ½ cup at a time. Continue stirring until all broth has been added and absorbed by the rice.

4   Cook 20 minutes or until rice is tender.

5   Finally, stir in butter and cheese. Serve immediately.

Saffron Rice

SERVES: **6** | *METHOD:* **SAUTÉ & SIMMER** | *APPROX. TIME:* **30 MINUTES** | *DIFFICULTY:* **EASY**

Ingredients

- 2 cups rice
- 4 cups no-sodium chicken stock
- 2 shallots, diced finely
- 1 celery stick, diced finely
- ¼ red pepper, diced finely
- 1 lemon (for zest and juice)
- 1 tablespoon olive oil
- ½ teaspoon saffron (American is fine)
- Dash of white pepper
- Salt to taste

Directions

1. Juice lemon, zest entire surface, and set both aside. Place saffron in bowl, submerge in small amount of hot water and set aside. Wash rice until water runs clear, then drain well.

2. Add red pepper, celery, shallots and lemon zest to pan with olive oil. Sauté until shallots and celery are translucent.

3. Using with only 1 tablespoon lemon juice (keep the rest for another recipe or make a whiskey sour), add all ingredients to rice cooker and cook as normal.

4. When rice is cooked, fluff with fork and serve immediately.

Scalloped Potatoes

SERVES: **6** | *METHOD:* **BOIL & BAKE** | *APPROX. TIME:* **2 HOURS** | *DIFFICULTY:* **EASY**

Special Equipment

✕ *Mandoline (the slicer, not the guitar)*

✕ *Cooking spray*
OR
Olive oil sprayer

Ingredients

✕ *6 medium-large potatoes*

✕ *1 cup sour cream*

✕ *1 can condensed, low-sodium cream of chicken soup*

✕ *½ cup milk*

✕ *3 cups cheddar cheese, shredded*

✕ *1 medium onion, minced finely*

✕ *4—6 cloves garlic, pressed (I love garlic, so be daring too)*

✕ *1 tablespoon butter*

✕ *¼ teaspoon ground pepper*

✕ *1 tablespoon truffle oil*

Directions

1. Slice potatoes evenly into coins ⅛" thick (this is easiest with a mandoline). Submerge in pot of ice-cold water to keep from oxidizing and turning gross colours.

2. In small frying pan, melt butter, then add minced onions and cook until slightly browned. Add garlic and sauté for 3 more minutes. Remove from heat and set aside.

3. To medium bowl, add sour cream, cream of chicken soup, milk and pepper. Whisk until fully incorporated, then add cooked onions and truffle oil to mix.

4. Drain potatoes well, then get ready to create some goodness. Prepare deep casserole dish by coating with thin layer of vegetable oil or cooking spray, then layer ½ your potatoes flat in the dish.

5. Cover potatoes with ½ your cream mix and ½ your cheese. Layer remainder of potatoes flat the same way, then cover with remaining cream sauce and cheese overtop that.

6. Place dish in 375° preheated oven and bake uncovered for 60—70 minutes, until cheese crust is nicely browned. Remove from oven and allow to cool and harden up 10 minutes before dinner. Serves 6.

Scalloped Potatoes
(CONTINUED)

Notes

These potatoes are so good, you'll want to serve them to strangers on a streetcorner like a mad preacher. I've made scalloped potatoes countless times, but this recipe is fairly new to me and is by far my favourite version.

Historically I've had trouble with this dish due to the onion chunks in most recipes, which I dislike. But after years of Susan nagging me (okay, she doesn't nag, she just asks really hard), I relented and worked with a recipe she found online. I changed it quite a bit to suit my taste buds, and this was the delicious result.

Don't pooh-pooh the use of canned soup. While I seldom use canned soup in a recipe, it's very useful in this one. If you insist in being snobbish, there's a mock Mornay sauce recipe in this book to busy yourself and your pointy nose.

I used to make scalloped potatoes with cream of mushroom soup, which you may also use instead of chicken.

Everyone in the family loved that except Jordan, who hated mushrooms (and still does). While the rest of us finished our meals, he would sit for hours picking out every single piece of mushroom, deep into the night. At least it kept him out of trouble.

Pity the early potato connoisseurs. They didn't have this recipe.

Morel Mushroom Risotto

SERVES: **6** | *METHOD:* **SAUTÉ & SIMMER** | *APPROX. TIME:* **1 HOUR** | *DIFFICULTY:* **EASY**

Ingredients

- 2 shallots, chopped finely
- 1 clove garlic, chopped finely
- 12 morel mushrooms (fresh or dried)
- 2 cups Arborio rice, dry
- 4—5 cups vegetable or chicken stock (canned is fine)
- 4 tablespoons butter
- 1 tablespoon olive oil
- 2 tablespoons lemon juice
  OR
  1 whole fresh-squeezed lemon
- 1 tablespoon fresh basil, chopped
- ¼ cup Parmesan cheese, grated
- ¼ cup heavy cream (optional)
- Salt and pepper to taste

Directions

1   If morel mushrooms are dried, as is common, soak in warm hot about 20 minutes until rehydrated. If using soup base of the paste kind, mix with mushroom water to create liquid stock for later.

2   Remove morel stems, if any, and discard. Dice mushrooms medium-small.

3   Juice 1 lemon into bowl. About 2 tablespoons of juice should result. Save this.

4   Sauté shallots and garlic in oil and 2 tablespoons butter, then stir in dry rice. Sauté until rice is translucent and smells nicely roasted. Now add lemon juice, and allow rice to absorb it completely.

5   After a minute or two, add 1 ladle of stock to rice. Allow liquid to reduce while stirring constantly. Add another ladle and repeat. Stir in mushrooms. Continue adding stock 1 ladle at a time, until rice is cooked al dente.

6   Turn off heat and stir in remaining butter (2 tablespoons), parmesan, basil and optional cream.

7   Season to taste and fluff with fork. Serve immediately.

Southern India Coconut Rice

SERVES: 6 | *METHOD: SIMMER* | *APPROX. TIME: 20 MINUTES* | *DIFFICULTY: EASY*

Special Equipment

✗ *Rice cooker (optional)*

Ingredients

✗ *1½ cups basmati rice*

✗ *1½ cups coconut milk*

✗ *1 cup cold water*

✗ *2 tablespoons butter*

✗ *1 teaspoon cardamom, ground*

✗ *1 pinch saffron*

✗ *1 pinch salt*

Directions

1 Rinse rice in cold water, drain, and repeat until cloudy water runs clear.

2 Add rice to rice cooker with coconut milk, butter, salt, cardamom and water. Stir well, close lid and turn cooker on.

3 If cooking on stovetop, bring to boil, cover with a tight-fitting lid, reduce heat and cook about 15 minutes or until rice is done.

✗ *Easy! A simple, delicious, one-pot side dish.*

Spanish Rice

SERVES: *6* | METHOD: *SIMMER* | APPROX. TIME: *20 MINUTES* | DIFFICULTY: *EASY*

The recipe is called Spanish Rice, but the addition of salsa makes it more of a Mexican-type thing. I dunno. Just call it Hernán Cortés Was an Asshole Rice.

Ingredients

- 2 tablespoons grapeseed oil
- 1 small onion, minced finely
- 2 cloves garlic, pressed
- 1½ cups uncooked white rice (basmati is best)
- 3 cups chicken broth
- 1 teaspoon cumin
- 1 cup salsa

Preparation

1. For best results, blend salsa into puree before using.

Directions

2. Add rice to skillet, stirring often. Once rice begins to brown, stir in chicken broth, cumin and salsa.

3. Reduce heat, cover and simmer 15 minutes, until liquid has been absorbed. Remove from heat and let sit covered for 5 minutes.

4. Fluff with fork before serving hot..

Wild Rice & Sausage Stuffing

SERVES: 4 | *METHOD: SIMMER* | *APPROX. TIME: 1 HOUR* | *DIFFICULTY: MEDIUM*

....

At the end of the assembly process, before placing the mixture into the fridge, you can add cranberries, pine nuts, walnuts or whatever lights your candle. I really like pine nuts. Cranberries can go to hell.

Ingredients

- 1 cup wild rice
- 3 cups chicken stock
- 2 tablespoons olive oil
- ½ lb. button mushrooms, sliced
- 2 large onions, chopped finely
- 6 cloves garlic, pressed
- 3 celery sticks, chopped finely
- 2 large carrots, grated
- ½ lb. breakfast sausage, cooked and crumbled
- ¼ cup fine bread crumbs (optional)
  OR
  ¼ cup panko crumbs (optional)
- 2 tablespoons fresh parsley, chopped
- 2 tablespoons poultry seasoning
- ½ teaspoon salt
- 1 teaspoon ground black pepper

Directions

1. Add wild rice to chicken stock and bring to boil. Cover with tight-fitting lid, then turn down heat to simmer for 45 minutes.

2. When cooked, wild rice should look like it's just starting to split. Remove from heat and add all pot contents to large mixing bowl.

3. Add olive oil to sauté pan with mushrooms, onion, garlic and celery. Cook for 4 minutes, stirring constantly. When sautéed, add pan contents to mixing bowl with cooked rice. Mix together.

4. Fry crumbled sausage meat until well-done. Drain excess fat from pan, then add parsley, grated carrots, salt and black pepper. Sauté for 5 minutes. Remove from heat and add to mixing bowl with other ingredients.

5. Add bread crumbs and poultry seasoning to mixing bowl. Stir well until all ingredients are well blended. Add chicken stock to ensure mixture is moist, but not soggy! Add salt and pepper to taste.

6. Let stuffing cool to room temperature, then place into refrigerator to chill for 4 hours or overnight.

Never stuff bird with hot or warm stuffing!

7. Once stuffing is cold, stuff into buzzard and cook until internal temperature is 170°.

Dinner Ain't Finished 'Til the Insulin Shots

-or-
Unjust Desserts

I love to cook, as you may or may not know by now. Some people tell me I do pretty good at cooking for a guy with an advanced case of brain-worms, and that's fine by me, as I like to keep expectations low. I'm pretty versatile, too. I like the stovetop and the gas grill and the oven all about the same.

Baking is another thing entirely. I don't normally use the oven to bake things, except for my world-famous tourtier (granted, it's a smallish world), killer cream puffs, éclairs and a mean, nasty and calorically devastating Black Forest Cake. The rest of the baking I leave up to Susan, since she does it so well. Some desserts are best made using the stovetop. Among my favourites are French crêpes and chocolate-dipped strawberries.

Although my fat ass suggests that I eat a lot of desserts, I don't. This is actually water weight, like a camel, for emergency purposes. I'm not even a big dessert fan. Sure, if you wanted to test my mettle, put some whipped cream and dark chocolate on a strawberry and perhaps I wouldn't turn it down.

Susan makes a mean (in the sense of "very good," not her usual sense of mean) pie that sometimes I'm forced to ingest. Once in a while there'll be Saskatoon berry pie, or cherry pie, or blueberry pie, or even a classic, perfectly-constructed apple pie, served piping hot, with a crispy sugar-dusted crust and just the right dollop of vanilla ice cream melting overtop. But like I said, I'm not a big dessert fan.

It's conceivable that if I were extremely hungry, I might be tempted by a tray of pecan-cinnamon sticky buns lovingly made for me by my mother-in-law Doreen, or by Susan using her sainted mother's recipe. You might even cajole me into eating one of Doreen's beloved scruffies, a delectable variation on the rugelach. Maybe. Just maybe. Honestly, I'm not a big fan of desserts.

I've also grudgingly choked down a variety of chocolate cream pies, pumpkin pies, pumpkin or chocolate trifles made by good friends with expert skills. I may or may not have moaned like a herd of cattle lowing in a verdant field. Probably not. I don't normally like desserts. I really don't.

Okay, fine, maybe I do, just a little.

As I've mentioned, my all-time favourite cookbook *The Joy of Cooking*. I have 2 different editions and both are dogeared, soiled and battered. Among the recipes I've lifted from that great book is French crêpes, along with the technique necessary to make them. This allows me to fulfil my darkest cravings: fresh-fried crêpes with warm Asian pear filling, covered with icing sugar, whipped cream and dark chocolate, perhaps with a side of with chocolate-dipped strawberries... uh... I'll be right back.

Where was I? Oh, right. When fresh strawberries are available in season, I'll infuse them in Grande Marnier marinade for a luxurious filling. For variety, I messed

Blackbird pie recipe not included. The guests to that party, like the birds, never came back.

around with some Asian pears one evening (no, not like that, or at least not *that* night) and invented the now-favourite filling I share it with you in this book. I do this for free! Or at least for a bargain price!

In addition to your own copy of *The Joy of Cooking*, you'll need a crêpe pan. In fact, if you master the art of crêpe making, your neighbours will forgive almost anything, even that absinthe-fueled Sunday afternoon romp in the church parking lot with the gimp suit.

So you have your copy of the *Joy Of Cooking* (not to be confused with *The Joy of Sex*, a book whose crêpe recipes I do not recommend). Next, I'll save you time by recommending the 10" non-stick crêpe pan by Starfrit. It's only 20 bucks or so, and it's by far the

best one I've used. It heats well and uniformly, it's perfectly-sized, and it's light, which is important when trying to move batter around. More about that later.

> *I purchased an induction stove since I originally wrote this piece, and my beloved Starfrit crêpe pan didn't work on it since aluminum isn't a magnetic material. So I went shopping. I now own a wonderful 10" nonstick crêpe pan from Cuisinart, and it delivers great results.*

If you're ready, take off the gimp suit and prepare to explore a whole different kind of decadence.

French Crêpes

SERVES: *8* | METHOD: *SAUTÉ* | APPROX. TIME: *1+ HOURS* | DIFFICULTY: *TRICKY*

I've been making these for so long they have become a signature dessert in my home. They look and taste like they take forever to make, but it's not so. All you need is practice and a good crêpe pan.

Say what? You want the pear recipe for the filling too? What the hell more do you want from me? Blood?

Ingredients

- ¾ cup flour
- ½ teaspoon salt
- 1 teaspoon double-acting baking powder
- 2 tablespoons powdered sugar
- 2 large eggs
- ⅔ cup milk
- ⅓ cup water
- ½ teaspoon vanilla
  (up to 2 teaspoons vanilla preferred)
  OR
  ½ teaspoon grated lemon rind

Topping Suggestions

- Whipped cream
- Chocolate sauce
- Chocolate shavings
- Blueberries
- Strawberries
- Gooseberries (my favourite!)

Directions

1   Sift dry ingredients into glass mixing bow to ensure complete mixing. In different bowl, mix milk, water, eggs and vanilla together.

2   Dig a well in middle of sifted ingredients. Pour liquid ingredients into dry ingredients. Combine with whisk. Ignore lumps for now; they'll take care of themselves. Rest batter in refrigerator for at least 1 hour. 3—6 hours is best.

3   Heat crêpe pan over medium heat and grease lightly with oil. (I use Pam, or rub pan with paper towel dipped in a little canola oil).

4   Add small quantity of batter to heated pan. Tip skillet and spread batter over pan bottom by tilting pan by the handle. If using 10" pan, ⅓—½ cup will spread over entire surface, depending on thickness of batter. Work batter to outside edge of pan and keep moving until bottom is covered completely. In a kitchen you typically want your bottom covered.

- *The consistency of the batter is determined by the size of the eggs and the moisture content and weight of the flour. The more settled (heavier) the flour you use, the thicker the batter will be. Be prepared to add a little water or milk to thin the batter enough to flow across the pan.*

French Crêpes
(CONTINUED)

5   Cook crêpe over moderate heat. As it cooks, bubbles will form and burst, leaving dimples on the surface. Keep pan over heat until crêpe surface looks dry, and begins to shrink and pull away from pan sides.

6   Crêpe should be lightly brown underneath by now. Flip over and very lightly brown other side. Set crêpe on plate once done. Repeat process until batter is gone.

7   Serve with filling and toppings.

Cinnamon & Frangelico Asian Pear Crêpe Filling

SERVES: *8* | METHOD: *SAUTÉ & SIMMER* | APPROX. TIME: *20 MINUTES* | DIFFICULTY: *EASY*

This filling is my invention. It did not appear on the Internet. It sprung forth from the mangled furrows of my mind. Countless years of toil and agony and sleepless nights have led to this one triumphant moment. You're fucking welcome.

With a dollop of cool whipped cream, this warm apple pear filling wrapped seductively in the light and tasty crêpe is a joy to behold. As you feed this creation to your guests, sit back and watch their faces contort in orgasmic rapture. Take pictures—you can use them for blackmail later.

Makes 8 servings, so go out and find 7 friends, or 7 strangers whom you want as your cult acolytes.

Ingredients

✕ 5 Asian pears, peeled and diced to ½" cubes

✕ 1 tablespoon unsalted butter

✕ 2 tablespoons brown sugar

✕ 1 teaspoon ground cinnamon (or more!)

✕ ¼ cup Frangelico hazelnut liqueur

Directions

1   Melt butter in a heavy pot over medium heat. Add diced pears. Sauté for 3—4 minutes, then add brown sugar and cinnamon.

2   Once sugar has melted, add Frangelico. Bring to a boil, turn down to low simmer, and cook over very low heat for 20 minutes until liquids reduce by over half and sauce thickens. Stir occasionally.

3   Remove from heat and let mixture cool slightly before adding to crêpe.

Kaitlyn's Cheesecake

SERVES: **6** | *METHOD:* **BAKE** | *APPROX. TIME:* **2 HOURS** | *DIFFICULTY:* **MEDIUM**

Special Equipment

✕ *9" springform pan*

Ingredients

✕ *¼ cup graham crackers (crumbled)*

✕ *1 container 2% cottage cheese (560ml)*

✕ *2 packages regular cream cheese (250g each)*

✕ *1 cup of white sugar*

✕ *2 tablespoons corn starch*

✕ *1 teaspoon vanilla*

✕ *1 egg*

✕ *2 egg whites*

Directions

1 Preheat oven to 450°.

2 Sprinkle graham crumbs evenly over bottom of pringform pan. Set aside for now.

3 Place cottage cheese into strainer and let sit for ½ hour until fully drained. Move cottage cheese to stand mixer. Using wire whisk attachment, blend until fully creamed.

4 Add cream cheese to mixer and whisk until smooth. Gradually add sugar, then corn starch and vanilla. Blend until well incorporated. Add egg and egg whites slowly, with mixer on low, until fully incorporated.

5 Pour mix into pan. Bake in 450° oven for 10 minutes, then reduce heat to 250° and bake an additional 35—40 minutes. Top of cheesecake will begin to crack and turn matte when fully cooked.

6 Remove from oven and let cool in pan. Once cool, move cheesecake from pan to serving plate.

7 Serve with topping of your choice, or use the raspberry one following this recipe.

Raspberry Cheesecake Topping

SERVES: 8 | *METHOD: SIMMER* | *APPROX. TIME: 20 MINUTES* | *DIFFICULTY: EASY*

This recipe comes from Grandma Doreen and is a favourite in our home. When Doreen visits, she knows that Kaitlyn will shanghai her into service making this very cheesecake. Kaitlyn is the beneficiary of this septugenarian slavery, and the rest of us simply stand back.

I'm actually not a big fan of raspberry cheesecake. Besides, Kaitlyn scares me when she gets in her cheesecake protection zone. I'm assured that this recipe is the one to die for—as anyone who's gotten in Kaitlyn's way has discovered.

Special Equipment

✕ *Sieve or cheesecloth*

Ingredients

✕ *2 cups raspberries*

✕ *2 tablespoons water*

✕ *½ cup sugar*

✕ *1 tablespoon corn starch*

✕ *1 pinch salt*

Directions

1   Place raspberries and water in heavy-bottom pot over medium heat. Cook, stirring constantly until mixture has boiled down, seeds are released and liquid has thickened a bit, about 5 minutes. Remove mixture from heat and let cool.

2   Strain out seeds and solids by passing mixture through sieve or cheesecloth.

3   Place raspberry liquid into pot once again. Add sugar, corn starch and vanilla, and stir well to blend. Simmer on stovetop over medium-low heat, stirring constantly until thickened, about 5 more minutes.

Cream Puffs

SERVES: **6** | *METHOD:* **BAKE** | *APPROX. TIME:* **1 HOUR** | *DIFFICULTY:* **HARD**

This recipe came from The Joy of Cooking and is one of my all-time favourite desserts.

Special Equipment

- Mixer
- Pastry bag

Ingredients

- 1 cup all-purpose flour
- ¼ teaspoon salt
- 1 tablespoon sugar
- 1 cup milk
- ⅓ cup butter

Preparation

1   Preheat oven to 400°.

2   Bring 5 eggs up to room temperature (use warm water bath).

3   Sift flour, salt and sugar together in bowl.

4   Have melted chocolate on hand for drizzle (optional) and whipped cream on hand for filling (not optional). Look up recipes if necessary.

Directions

5   Add milk and butter to steep-sided pan and bring to boil. Add flour mixture in one fell swoop, stir quickly with wooden spoon, and remove from heat. It looks rough at first, but suddenly becomes smooth, at which point, stir faster.

6   When paste becomes dry and no longer clings to anything (and when pressed spoon leaves a smooth imprint), it's ready for the mixer.

7   On mixer at low speed, add room-temperature eggs one at a time. Not the shells, obviously. Continue to mix slowly until dough no longer looks slippery and last egg is fully incorporated.

Cream Puffs

(CONTINUED)

✕ *If dough stands up when scooped with a spoon, it's the right consistency for baking.*

8 Use spoon (or better yet, pastry bag) to form cream puffs. It's best to use all dough at once. First, fill pastry bag and press until it's airless.

9 To form puffs, hold pastry bag nozzle close to your greased baking sheet. Don't move it. Simply squeeze bag and let paste bubble up around nozzle until desired cream puff size is reached.

✕ *Cream puffs will expand as they bake, so space evenly on pan and allow room to grow.*

10 To form longer éclairs, draw tube along baking sheet for about 3—4 inches while pressing bag consistently. Always finish with a lifting reverse motion.

11 To form small pastry cups, make 1-inch globules. The little point left when you lift the bag can be pressed down with a moistened finger.

12 Just before baking, sprinkle a few drops of water over each puff. Do this lightly.

13 Now bake pastry shells in preheated 400° oven for 10 minutes. After this, reduce heat to 350° and bake about 25 minutes longer without opening oven door.

✕ *After 25 minutes, you may open oven, but don't remove cream puffs until they're very firm to touch, almost stale-hard.*

14 When pastry hardness is reached, remove from oven. Cool pan on counter, away from any draft, until room temperature is reached.

15 To fill, cut puffs horizontally with sharp carving knife (never a serrated knife!) and open up. There should be plentiful gaps inside. If you see damp dough filaments inside, remove them.

16 Fill empty pastry shells with whipped cream. Dip tops in melted chocolate for an even more delightful treat.

Grandma Doreen's Pie Pastry

SERVES: **8** | *METHOD:* **KNEAD** | *APPROX. TIME:* **30 MINUTES** | *DIFFICULTY:* **EASY**

Ingredients

- 1 lb. Tenderflake lard
  (Canadian brand, not sure about elsewhere!)
- 5 cups flour
- 1 tablespoon salt
- 1 egg
- 1 tablespoon vinegar

Directions

1 Add flour, salt and lard to bowl and cut together into small crumbly bits. Set aside.

2 In 1-cup measuring cup, mix egg and vinegar well. Fill up rest of cup with cold water, making 1 cup of liquid.

3 Pour liquid into flour-lard mixture and knead until smooth. This will take awhile.

4 Divide dough into 4 balls of equal size, then refrigerate to chill before rolling. You may also freeze dough for later, then thaw in fridge until needed.

Mémère

I'm a very fortunate guy when it comes to grand-parents. For most of us, our grandparents mean the world to us, but unfortunately, many people don't get to know theirs. Distance, family squabbles, old age with its related results and other obstacles affect a lot of grandchildren.

I was fortunate that I got to know all four of my grandparents. In regards to my grandmothers, I had their love and companionship well into adulthood, and I had my paternal grandmother in my life into my forties. Sadly they're all gone now, and I've missed them every day since they were taken away.

Violetta

In a previous story I wrote about Grandma Eveline and some of her colourful life—and her baked beans. Oh, those baked beans! I now want to introduce you to my maternal grandmother, Violetta Frigon (nee Roch), a very strong-willed woman, devout Catholic, and legendary cookie-maker. In proper French she was our Grand-Mère, but we all called her Mémère, pronounced *may-may* by us Anglo-tongued children.

Mémère was a great cook (you may be detecting a family theme here). Among her offerings, cookies were my favourite. She was and still is in my mind, the best cookie cooker there ever was, is or shall be. She refined her abilities for decades, supplying mouthwatering memories to legions of people for nearly 100 years.

More than she loved baking cookies, more than anything in life—possibly even more than us—she loved the Montreal Canadiens. The Habs weren't just a hockey team for her, they were a religion equal to Mother Church. To blaspheme against them would spark the fury of a true zealot. Of course, back then, the Canadiens were actually pretty good.

When I grew up and began to travel for work, I often had the opportunity to visit with Mémère. Often I'd bring her a rose or even a bouquet, depending on my cash flow. One time I called to tell her I was coming by, and she informed me she was going to be leaving later the next day, so she suggested I not bring her any roses. Not possible.

When I arrived, I presented her a gold-plated rose broach and attached it to her jacket. She thanked me with a huge hug and a kiss and of course, a bag of cookies. From that day, she wore that rose on her coat often. Years later, I received it back after she died. It's now worn by Susan from time to time, and it means a lot to me when I see it.

Pépère

Mémère, as you probably gathered by now, was French by way of French-Canadian, the best kind of French to be. Her husband Pierre, whom we called Pépère (or *pay-pay* in Anglo-tongue), was a tall, distinguished man who sported a mane of thick white hair. He spoke with a slight French accent and, like his wife, smoked like a chimney. In those days almost everyone smoked, and they smoked everywhere: cars, planes, doctors' offices, hospitals, gas stations, dynamite factories. I'm a man of nostalgia, but I'm glad some things aren't making a comeback.

Pépère was a carpenter by trade. He could make anything out of wood, a skill he passed to most of his sons. He also told stories (of questionable veracity) about his hero Chief Sitting Bull, claiming he had Indian blood running through his veins and that his forefathers had fought General Custer.

He also admonished the kids that we should never, ever eat the hole in a doughnut, because if we did, we'd get a hole in our stomach and everything would fall out. I'm not sure if this was related to Chief Sitting Bull or not. Anyway, for many years, whenever I ate a doughnut, I would leave a careful ring of dough around the doughnut hole, essentially making a smaller doughnut. Pépère was a great storyteller, and a very convincing one.

Mémère and Pépère were married on February 14, 1922, and together produced eighteen children. Yup, eighteen—nine boys and nine girls. That's two whole baseball teams! Pépère must have had a good toe-hold, or lousy rhythm, or... hell, I already mentioned they were Catholic. And they were at it for a long time. The age difference between the oldest child (Romeo) and the youngest (Peter) was about 24 years.

In-Laws & Outlaws

I didn't know all of my aunts and uncles, as a few passed away before I was born, or when I was quite young. Some had moved away from the city due to work, military service or love, and I only ran into them at weddings, funerals and the Golden Wedding Anniversary celebration in 1972.

There were a few rivalries in the family, usually involving spouses of the Frigon children, which unfortunately prevented larger reunions unless there was a casket involved. I'm sure you can think of similar examples in your own family. Pobody's nerfect! Everyone's fysdunctional!

Of eighteen children, seventeen lived to adulthood, and many of them had children of their own. Now, without an organizational chart I can't name them all, or even get an accurate count, but I think it was around 52. I don't know many of them well, due to situations mentioned above, which is a sad commentary on something or other. Some of them passed away far too young.

After we moved away when I was eight years old, this extended family seldom got together. But whenever we did, it was glorious. Regardless of distance or time, Mémère and Pépère and the aunties and uncles all showered us with affection, as if we'd never been apart.

We all have our favourite relatives; be they aunts, uncles, cousins, in-laws, outlaws or weird Cousin Itts. In my world the aunties were, and are still, goddesses to me. Not that the uncles weren't loved, but I would have killed for Auntie Trudy, Terry, Lorrie, Margo, Rosann, Little Flo, Gloria, Jeanne (my Godmother), Big Flo, and Janette. Thankfully they never asked me to.

Then there's the one and only, incomparable, incredibly talented and beautiful Gypsy Rose Lee, my auntie on my mother's, sister's, second cousin's, brother's, mother-in-law's, adopted sister's, half-brother's barber's dog's side. She's a doll and I love her more than life itself. I would do time for her. Not too much time, and definitely not hard time, but time nonetheless.

My love for these women is, in no small part, due to the fact they reminded me of Mémère. They all shared traits that Mémère exemplified, and so does my mom. Kindness, affection, generosity with love and laughter, cooking and baking skills unmatched anywhere, and a love for card games unrivaled in the western world since the heyday of riverboat gambling.

However, I'm saddened to say that none of them knew how to make Mémère's cookies, a fact that's left a void in my being, and my stomach, since 1982. A few relatives have tried, and they came close, right down to the maraschino cherry on the oatmeal cookie. But close is only good enough in horseshoes or hand grenades, not Mémère's cookies!

At Auntie Margo's

Aunty Margo was the oldest daughter, who took on matriarchal duties when Mémère wasn't at hand. Some of my best-loved and remembered family gatherings took place in the wonderful home Margo shared with Uncle Art and their three sons Brian, Greg and Tom.

Mémère was often present at these gatherings, and so were her cookies. They were the stars of the show, above any meal any of us could make, or any beer and brandy that went with it. While exulting in the magic of Mémère's cookies, we played rousing games of 31, or a particularly cutthroat kind of cribbage, or even bingo. My oh my, did we play bingo. Being a Catholic family, genetic disposition compelled us to do so. I'll bet the Pope plays bingo too, or at least calls games at the Vatican now and again.

At our gatherings, bingo was a great distraction for us dozens of rugrats, who played our games in English while the adults conversed with each other in French. Eating those cookies while we played, there was no way to lose a game.

An old family story has me eating a cookie prepared by a relative and complaining to someone (perhaps my mom, whom I complained to often) that, though my cookie resembled those Mémère made, it just wasn't the same.

When told that it was the same cookie, using the exact same recipe, I told the baker it wasn't so. Close, maybe, but not exact! When pressed by the baker to tell her what the difference was, I told her, "Love! Mémère makes her cookies with love!"

Now, when cookies are made in a home, they're all made with love, or arsenic if the baker is trying to hurry up the reading of a will. So the secret to Mémère's cookies couldn't be love... *could it?*

I theorize that maybe a Mémère's love is unlike any other kind of love, a kind of quantum field, maybe, with effects on cookies that cannot be harnessed by mere mortals or non-Mémères. What other explanation could there be?

Pépère passed away in 1972, a few months after their Golden Wedding celebration, and Mémère passed in 1982. Not a day goes by I don't think of her. Of the many memories I'd choose to relive again, celebrating life with Mémère at Auntie Margo and Uncle Art's home with the rest of our family would be at the top of my list.

Or perhaps a family gathering at Mémère and Pépère's home in Edmonton, the living room and dining room tables laden with delicious homemade food. It goes without saying that Mémère, and her incomparable cookies, would be the stars of the show.

The whole fam-damily. Is food an excuse for family gatherings, or is it vice versa?

221

Mémère's Oatmeal Cookies

SERVES: **8** | *METHOD:* **BAKE** | *APPROX. TIME:* **30 MINUTES** | *DIFFICULTY:* **MEDIUM**

Ingredients

- ½ lb. unsalted butter
- 3 eggs
- 1 cup brown sugar, firmly packed
- 1 cup white sugar
- 1 tablespoon vanilla
  (optional, not in her original recipe)
- 3 cups all-purpose flour
- 1 teaspoon baking powder
- 1 teaspoon baking soda
- 1 teaspoon salt
- 2 cups rolled quick oats
- 1 cup chopped walnuts
  (optional, not in her original recipe)
- 1 cup roasted unsalted sunflower seeds
  (optional, not in her original recipe)

Directions

1. Preheat oven to 350°. In mixing bowl, cream together butter, both sugars and vanilla. Blend on medium speed for 2—3 minutes until uniformly blended. Set aside.

2. In separate bowl, whisk together flour, salt, baking powder and baking soda.

3. Add flour mix to mixing bowl with creamed butter. Mix on medium speed for 2 minutes, or until well incorporated. Now add oats and mix until fully blended. If you're using nuts, add them too.

- *Dough is ready at semi-solid, malleable consistency.*

4. Using mini ice-cream scoop (if you have one), drop spoonfuls of cookie dough onto baking sheet, evenly spaced.

5. Bake in preheated oven for 11—12 minutes or until slightly brown around the edges.

- *Stopping here for a moment, when the cookies are done, identify a few of them that you want to kick up a notch. Press in centre with your thumb to dent each cookie. Once done, place a little dollop of jam into the dent, then place on cooling rack with the others. This was a signature move for Mémère.*

6. Serve with milk, tea, coffee or other beverage of choice. Try to eat one without smiling! It can't be done.

Puffed Wheat Squares

SERVES: *8* | METHOD: *SAUTÉ* | APPROX. TIME: *1+ HOURS* | DIFFICULTY: *TRICKY*

These little parcels of sticky goodness were my all-time favourite snack as a kid. My mom had them down to a fine art. Many neighbourhood friends shared in the bounty when mom made her super-size batches. I still love them to this day, and only my mom's will do.

Ingredients

- ⅓ cup butter
- ½ cup white corn syrup (Karo is great)
- 1 cup brown sugar
- 2 teaspoons Fry's cocoa
- 1 teaspoon vanilla
- 8 cups puffed wheat

Directions

1 In large saucepan, combine all ingredients except puffed wheat. Cook until sugar has dissolved to syrup and is no longer gritty.

This is the whole secret!

2 Now add puffed wheat and mix until well-coated.

3 Pour mix onto large baking pan and spread thickly and evenly. Let sit for 15 minutes to harden, then cut and wrap into individual squares to keep moist.

Rice Pudding

SERVES: **5** | *METHOD:* **SIMMER** | *APPROX. TIME:* **20 MINUTES** | *DIFFICULTY:* **EASY**

Ingredients

- 1½ cups cooked white rice
- 1½ cups milk
- ½ cup half and half cream
- ¼ cup white sugar
- ¼ teaspoon salt
- 1 egg
- ⅓ cup walnuts or pecans, toasted
- 1 teaspoon vanilla extract

Directions

1. In saucepan, combine cooked rice, 1 cup milk, cream, sugar and salt. Cook over medium-low heat about 10 minutes, stirring constantly.

2. Beat egg and remaining ½ cup milk, then add to pudding mixture. Cook 2 minutes more, stirring constantly.

3. Remove from heat and stir in vanilla.

4. Line bottoms of 8 ramekins with about 6-8 toasted pecans to cover. Spoon the pudding into ramekins over pecans.

5. Place in fridge to cool, or serve warm (I prefer the latter).

Tiramisu

SERVES: *6* | METHOD: *VARIOUS* | APPROX. TIME: *ALL DAY* | DIFFICULTY: *MEDIUM*

Special Equipment

✕ Double boiler

Ingredients

✕ 24 store-bought ladyfingers (any brand)

✕ 2 cups heavy whipping cream

✕ 3 tablespoons icing sugar

✕ 4 eggs

✕ ½ cup sugar

✕ ¼ cup dark navy rum (any brand)

✕ ½ lb. mascarpone cheese
OR
½ lb. ricotta for a lower-fat variation

✕ 1 package cream cheese (250g)

✕ 1 tablespoon fresh lemon juice

✕ 2 teaspoons vanilla extract

✕ 1 cup strong coffee

✕ ½ cup Tia Maria coffee liqueur
(Kahlua in a pinch, but Tia Maria is better)

✕ 2 tablespoons semi-sweet chocolate, grated

Directions

1 In double boiler, combine eggs with sugar and cook, stirring constantly, until mixture turns pale yellow and coats the back of a spoon like light custard. (Which it is!) Remove from heat and stir in rum. Refrigerate 2 hours to chill.

2 Whip cream and icing sugar together on highest speed of electric mixer, until firm peaks form. Set aside.

3 Combine cream cheese and mascarpone, mixing well. Add lemon juice and vanilla. Mix until thoroughly creamed.

4 Add chilled egg custard and mix at high speed until fully blended and fluffy. Next, gently fold in whipped cream until all elements are blended, light and fluffy.

5 Add coffee and Tia Maria to shallow pan. Roll lady fingers in the coffee mixture to coat and space evenly at bottom of springform pan. Spread ½ your cream mixture over moistened ladyfingers. Sprinkle shaved chocolate or powdered cocoa over cream layer.

6 Repeat with second layer of ladyfingers in the same manner. Slather with remaining cream mixture, then chocolate layer on top.

7 Refrigerate minimum 4 hours before serving.

Chocolate Tiramisu

SERVES: *6* | METHOD: *VARIOUS* | APPROX. TIME: *ALL DAY* | DIFFICULTY: *MEDIUM*

Special Equipment

✕ *Double boiler*

Ingredients

✕ *24—36 ladyfingers*
(any brand, chocolate ones if possible)

✕ *2 cups heavy whipping cream*

✕ *3 tablespoons icing sugar*

✕ *4 egg yolks*

✕ *½ cup sugar*

✕ *⅓ cup dark navy rum (any brand)*

✕ *½ pound cream cheese (see below)*

✕ *½ pound mascarpone cheese*
OR
1 lb. mascarpone and omit cream cheese

✕ *1—2 tablespoons fresh lemon juice*

✕ *2 teaspoons vanilla extract*

✕ *1 cup Gianduia Chocolate Hazelnut Liqueur*

✕ *1 cup Godiva Chocolate Liqueur*

✕ *½ cup chocolate syrup (see note at end)*

✕ *2 ounces dark chocolate, grated or shaved*

Preparation

1   Make chocolate syrup beforehand. Melt 2 ounces dark chocolate in microwave in a glass bowl. Add ½ cup cream and 1 tablespoon butter to melted chocolate, stir well until fully incorporated, and voila, a nice syrup is the end result.

✕ *If it begins to set before it's fully mixed, simply rewarm until you're done. Finished chocolate syrup should not harden further at room temperature.*

Directions

2   In double boiler, combine eggs with sugar and cook, stirring constantly, until mixture turns pale yellow and coats the back of a spoon like light custard. (Which it is, again!) Remove from heat and stir in rum.

3   Refrigerate 2 hours to chill.

4   Whip cream and icing sugar together on highest speed of electric mixer, until firm peaks form. Set aside.

5   Combine cream cheese and mascarpone, mixing well. Add vanilla and 1 tablespoon lemon juice. Mix until thoroughly creamed, then taste and add remainder of lemon juice as you like (or not). Add chilled egg custard and mix at high speed until fully blended and fluffy.

Chocolate Tiramisu

(CONTINUED)

6   Next, gently fold in whipped cream until all elements are blended, light and fluffy.

7   Pour two liqueurs into two different into shallow pans (I use pie plates). Roll ½ your ladyfingers in one of the chocolate liqueurs to coat, then space evenly in the bottom of a springform pan or trifle bowl. Also place liqueur-infused lady fingers along pan sides, standing up like a fence.

8   Roll each ladyfinger in liqueur.

✕   *Be careful! Ladyfingers are delicate and quite the liquor sponges (they remind me of a girlfriend from long ago). Once placed in liqueur, roll each ladyfinger on all 4 sides, keeping immersed only about 1 second per side. Don't soak the ladyfinger, or it'll crumble in your hands in an alcoholic mess, just like that girlfriend from long ago. I digress.*

9   Spread ½ your cream mixture over moistened ladyfingers and smooth flat with the back of a spoon. Sprinkle ½ your shaved chocolate over this layer along with some chocolate syrup.

10   Repeat with other half of ladyfingers rolled in second chocolate liqueur, and stack over first layer the same way, adding cream mixture, chocolate syrup and shredded chocolate in layers to the top.

11   Refrigerate at least 4-6 hours, as it must be well chilled when served.

12   Garnish with fresh strawberries (or, my favourite, gooseberries if in season) just before serving.

Pumpkin Pie

SERVES: 12 | *METHOD: BAKE* | *APPROX. TIME: 2 HOURS* | *DIFFICULTY: EASY*

Special Equipment

✗ 2 pie plates

✗ Mixer (for whipped cream)

Ingredients

✗ 4 large eggs

✗ 3½ cups pumpkin puree

✗ 1½ cups evaporated milk

✗ 1½ cups packed golden brown sugar

✗ 1 teaspoon ground cinnamon

✗ ¼ teaspoon ground nutmeg

✗ ⅛ teaspoon ground cloves

✗ ½ teaspoon salt

⚙ ⅔ lb. pastry dough

Preparation

1   Make sweetened whipped cream beforehand. This is easy enough in a mixer.

2   Preheat oven to 425°.

Directions

3   Roll out pastry to about ¼". Place pastry carefully into pie plates, then pinch (flute) and trim the edges.

4   Beat eggs in large mixing bowl. Whisk in pumpkin puree, evaporated milk, brown sugar and spices until fully blended.

5   Pour pumpkin mixture into the 2 pie shells.

6   Place pies in preheated oven and bake for 15 minutes. After this, reduce oven temperature to 350° and bake another 40 minutes, or until a toothpick placed into the center comes out clean. If the filling begins to crack in the middle as it bakes, it's done!

7   Remove pies and cool on a baking rack to room temperature. Do not leave on windowsill, lest it be stolen by 3 children standing on each other's shoulders.

8   Serve with an insanely large amount of the whipped cream. Whatever you think I mean by "insane amount," imagine that... and then double it. Mmmm.

To My Children

I've puttered away on this cookbook for a very long time. It has been rewritten more times than I can count and I have edited it to death as many times as well. I've added and removed recipes so often I wore out two mice on my computer and drove myself to a frenzy. I have many more recipes that I could have included, but this is long enough as it is, so this is the end of the book.

I hope you kids enjoy this book and use the recipes that I offer in it often. Cook them and share them with your friends and your own families. Spend time together with those you love as you enjoy good food and companionship.

In our home we always strove to have the family dinner held sacred, and to try to meet at the table every day. Most often we did, if only to rush the food down as we raced to other commitments, but we did try to make the time, and I think that is one of the important reasons that all of you children have turned out so well. Okay, Moms, Aunties, Uncles, Grandmas and Grandpas were all essentials to help guide you as well, and we've had a great time being part of your lives, then and now.

My attempt to remain relevant in your lives has taken me down a culinary road to learn and perfect my cooking ability. I had hoped that the better I became at it, the closer we would get as a family, in that, I hope I made the grade. Cooking is a labour of love meant to share with others, but for me it was an entirely a selfish motivation; I sought to instill indelible memories of me into your minds that will remain with you for a long, long time. I also hope the food memories will make faint the not-so-welcome memories you have of me when I was not the father I could or should have been.

I admit my parenting skills were not the best at times, and my money management skills were even less skillful, but through it all, amidst my mistakes and temper tantrums you kids kept putting me back on track and I thank you for that. What we lacked in cash was hopefully made up with laughs and love, with some great food as a backdrop.

I took on the challenge of writing this book to devote it to you kids. I'm a very lucky man having the children I have been blessed with. I'm proud of all the accomplishments you have achieved so far in your lives, and I'm confident you'll all enjoy more of them as the years go on.

I offer you this book to remember the good times we had together. Not only the four of you, but the many other children brought along to our table over the years, some of whom ended up calling me Dad as an honorarium. They've enriched my life as I have watched them grow alongside of the four of you, and they too have grown into wonderful people— Darren, Megan, Hilary, this book is for you too!

Spend time learning to make great meals, and in time when I'm gone (not too soon, I hope!) you can walk through its pages and call me up from time to time. And when you do, I hope that you recall a Super Dad, and not the dad that too often appeared in your life in bad moods and bad examples.

I love you all so very much,

—Dad

Made in the USA
Columbia, SC
26 December 2020